Cultural
Politics in
Revolution

Cultural Politics in Revolution

Teachers, Peasants,
and Schools in Mexico,
1930–1940

Mary Kay Vaughan

The University of Arizona Press
Tucson

The University of Arizona Press
Copyright © 1997
The Arizona Board of Regents
All rights reserved
∞ This book is printed on acid-free, archival-quality paper.
Manufactured in the United States of America

02   01   00   99   6   5   4   3   2

Library of Congress Cataloging-in-Publication Data
Vaughan, Mary Kay, 1942–
Cultural politics in revolution : teachers, peasants, and schools
in Mexico, 1930–1940 / Mary Kay Vaughan.
p.   cm.
Includes bibliographical references and index.
ISBN 0-8165-1675-8 (cloth : acid-free paper). —
ISBN 0-8165-1676-6 (pbk. : acid-free paper)
1. Education and state—Mexico—Puebla (State)—History—20th
century.   2. Education and state—Mexico—Sonora (State)—
History—20th century.   3. Education, Rural—Political aspects—
Mexico—Puebla (State)—History—20th century.   4. Education,
Rural—Political aspects—Mexico—Sonora (State)—History—20th
century.   5. Socialism and education—Mexico—Puebla (State)—
History—20th century.   6. Social and education—Mexico—Sonora
(State)—History—20th century.   7. Teachers—Mexico—Puebla
(State)—Political activity—History—20th century.   8. Teachers—
Mexico—Sonora (State)—Political activity—History—20th century.
9. Mexico—Politics and government—1910–1946.   I. Title.
LC92.M4V38   1997
379.72'48'09043—dc20   96-35639
CIP

British Library Cataloguing-in-Publication Data
A catalogue record for this book is available from the British Library.

Publication of this book is made possible in part by the proceeds of
a permanent endowment created with the assistance of a Challenge
Grant from the National Endowment for the Humanities, a federal
agency.

A la memoria de Mara Velázquez
y al futuro de los otros niños:
Cintia, Alicia, Rubén, Simona, Joseph y Peter

Contents

Maps

Tables

ACKNOWLEDGMENTS

This book took a long time to be written. I began in 1981 after completing a study of educational policy in Mexico from 1880 to 1928. I wanted to understand how that policy got implemented regionally and locally. I chose to look at a later period: the tumultuous 1930s when the policies formulated between 1880 and 1928 reached their most radical statement. Joining in the then current enthusiasm for regional history, I chose to look at policy implementation in two states, Puebla and Sonora. I immediately found that the study of policy implementation had taken me into the uncharted waters of local history: nothing I could generalize about at the national or regional levels helped me to make sense out of what the sources told me at the local level. It took years of reading in comparative social history and peasant studies for me to gain the kind of insight I sought. Fortunately, I benefited from a simultaneous and similarly long and tumultuous shift in Mexican revolutionary studies away from political to social and cultural history. But what made this journey worth the years it took was the opportunity it gave me to learn about Mexico and to make friendships that greatly enriched my life and my understanding. This brief space allows me to recognize only a very significant few of those friends who guided me on my voyage: in Mexico City, Carlos Schaffer, Epifanio López, Sergio de la Peña, Enrique Semo, Elaine Levine, Elsie Rockwell, Susana Quintanilla, Carmen Nava, Fedérico Lazarín Miranda, Gabriela Cano, Victor Mendoza, and my students at the Departamento de Investigaciones Educativas: Candelaria Silva Valdés, Alicia Civero, Salvador Camacho Sandoval, and María de Lourdes Cueva Tazzer. Enrique Florescano, Javier Garciadiego, and Josefina Vázquez helped me to gain access to valuable source materials. In Puebla, Marco Velázquez and Guy Thomson often accompanied me on my trips around the state and in my voyages into history and the world of ideas. To them, Gloria Marroni de Velázquez, Ida García Manzano, Victor Alva, Reyna Manzano, Socorro and Irma Rivera, Conrado Quintero, the late Faustino Hernández, Horacio Caro, his wife Agustina, and a host of schoolteachers cited in this text I am forever indebted. Antonio González Barroso, María Luisa Méndez, and Salvador Vázquez assisted my archival research in Puebla and Zacapoaxtla. In Xochiapulco, Zacapoaxtla, and San Miguel Tzinacapan, long discussions with Donna Rivera, Rafael Alcántara Cárcamo, Ebundio Carreón, Francisco Toral, Filadelfo Vázquez, Miguel Félix Mirón, and Manuel Chávez Rosario taught me things I could never have gleaned from the written sources. In Tecamachalco, Manuel Bravo Bañuelos with his twinkling eyes, leathered face, and biting tongue did the same. In Hermosillo, Cynthia Radding, Maren Von Der Borch, Foncho Mendoza, Juan Manuel Romero Gil, Rocío Guadarrama, Cristina Martínez, Marcelina Saldívar de Murrieta, Xicotencatl Murrieta, Ignacio Almada, and Julio Montañés gave me insights, introduced me to sources and teachers, and shared with me their love for and understanding of Sonora. Gloria Cañez and José Carlos López Romero assisted my research. In Ciudad Obregón, Arturo Saldívar and Manuel del Cid talked to me at length about the Cardenista ejidatarios of the Yaqui Valley. In Vicam, Lorenzo García and his colleagues in Patisi made me aware of the feisty strength of the Yaquis, which friends in Tucson confirmed and fleshed out: Raquel Rubio Goldsmith, Rosamund Spicer, and Francisca Gómez Tadeo.

My research was funded by the Social Science Research Council, a Fulbright research fellowship, and the Humanities Institute, Campus Research Board, and Office of Social Science Research of the University of Illinois at Chicago. I am also indebted to the UIC Latin American Studies Program for having granted me frequent leave time. Jim Dickert heroically facilitated my use of the computer as did Harold Feinberg, and Betsy McEneaney and John Angel Alba processed Mexican census data underpinning the regional and case studies. For assistance with the manuscript, I want to thank Laura López, Josefina Almanza, Linda Montes, and Ricardo Santana. Ray Brod kindly made the maps.

Alan Knight, Cynthia Radding, Maren Von Der Borch, David LaFrance, Guy Thomson, Marco Velázquez, Florencia Mallon, Marion Miller, Steve Lewis, and above all, Heather Fowler-Salamini, read all or parts of this manuscript and gave me excellent feedback, which I could not always operationalize in revisions. Graduate students María Teresa Fernández, Margaret Power, Robert Curley, Anna María Kapelusz-Poppi, Nora Bonnín de Giesso, and Neicy Zeller gave me the confidence to turn out a book, as did the ever encouraging William Beezley and my patient and inspiring husband, Harold Feinberg. My husband and my daughter Alicia did suffer from the research and writing of this book. It took a lot of time away from them. Fortunately, my husband has not left me and my daughter has discovered the richness of her Mexican heritage through channels of her own. These things make it all worthwhile. I hope that through this book, some of the hundreds of Mexican students I teach will become as empowered by their incredible history and culture as I have been.

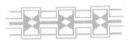

CULTURAL
POLITICS IN
REVOLUTION

1

INTRODUCTION
THE CULTURAL POLITICS OF THE MEXICAN REVOLUTION

The cultural panoply of the Mexican Revolution conjures up a series of images—artist Diego Rivera's swarthy workers hoisting the red flag of the strike, his depiction of the sumptuous marketplace in Moctezuma's capital, Frida Kahlo's Tehuantepec costumes and her incantation of Aztec fertility symbols, gaunt peasants hauling cannon across the stark desert in José Clemente Orozco's murals, and José Vasconcelos's flamboyant crusade for education. These rank among the outstanding achievements in twentieth-century art and social policy. But the cultural record of the Mexican Revolution cannot be measured solely by elite constructions emanating from intellectual circles in Mexico City. Only by expanding the social arena in which culture was constructed and contested can we understand the Mexican Revolution's real achievements. This study examines rural schools where central state policy makers, provincial teachers, and men, women, and children of the countryside came together in the 1930s to forge a national culture.

When in 1994 the Indians of Chiapas rose in armed rebellion, they spoke from the depths of the revolution's cultural legacy. They insisted upon their rights to ethnic identity and traditions while at the same time demanding the tools of modernity: schools, clinics, roads, and factories. They claimed land unjustly taken from them and named their movement after Emiliano Zapata, a non-Indian peasant hero of the 1910 revolution. In calling for democracy, social justice, and national development that would benefit all Mexicans, they appealed to the Constitution of 1917. Although the armed nature of their movement made them outlaws, their discourse resonated through the Mexican nation because they spoke a shared language of values, rights, identities, and expectations. This language is the cultural product of the revolution.

3

How this language was forged can be uncovered only by examining the negotiation between central state, regional, and local actors over definitions of nation and community, culture and modernity, citizenship and history. This was the dynamic three-tiered theater for postrevolutionary cultural formation operative between 1920 and 1940, following the years of armed struggle (1910–1920) and preceding the decades of economic modernization under one-party rule. From the interaction between local, regional, and national actors came the formulation of central state cultural directives. These were in turn disputed, discarded, reworked, and appropriated in unique and varied ways at their points of implementation. Regional and local contestations altered national policies and cultural constructions. In rural communities, contesting and reshaping central state directives became part of the reconstruction of power, knowledge, and everyday life.

Cultural politics refers to the process whereby definitions of culture—in the narrow sense of national identity and citizenship and in the broader sense of social behavior and meaning—were articulated and disputed. Cultural politics were no marginal frill to the revolution. During the years of armed struggle, triumphant Constitutionalist leaders made clear their interest in transforming a so-called feudal society into a secular, modern one by de-alcoholizing, sanitizing, and defanaticizing Mexicans. Created in 1921, the Secretaría de Educación Pública (SEP) set up federal rural schools to discipline and channel the energies of rebellious peasants. The school would nationalize and modernize them. It would transform superstitious, locally oriented pariahs into patriotic, scientifically informed commercial producers. In the 1920s, regional political leaders used SEP teachers and cultural policy—the creation of revolutionary symbols, didactic art, and collective theatrics—to build popular support among peasants and workers. In 1929, with the formation of the Partido Nacional Revolucionario, cultural policy became part of national party-building and state formation.

This study focuses on rural schools as arenas for cultural politics between 1930 and 1940. Scholars such as Eric Hobsbawm, Benedict Anderson, and Eugen Weber stress the importance of schooling to cultural formation and nation-building (Hobsbawm 1983:271, 277, 280–82; Anderson 1991:116–36; Weber 1976:303–38). However, schools and teachers remain inadequately studied. In the Mexican Revolution, they have to be examined because state policy makers and official party-builders invested grandiose hopes in the school. It would alter local behavior and power relations, from the public arena of property and office to the intimate areas of gender, age, and sexual relations.

This study examines schooling in the 1930s. Like other governments in this period of massive market collapse and unprecedented state intervention, the Mexican central government became convinced of its need and capacity to transform culture for purposes of integration, rule, and development. At the time, its fledgling political party, the Partido Nacional Revolucionario (PNR), was a loose association of military and civilian politicians and largely phantom organizations. It lacked a nationally organized popular base of support—a major handicap given heightened levels of social mobilization. This situation privileged the party's left wing, which had accumulated experience in organizing peasants and workers at the regional level. The left wing aimed to build a national party based upon worker, peasant, and middle-class support in opposition to the old landowning elites, foreign property holders, and the Catholic Church. This faction dominated the Secretaría de Educación Pública from 1932 to 1940, wrote the Six-Year Plan that guided the presidency of Lázaro Cárdenas from 1934 to 1940, and had in Cárdenas their foremost leader and representative. Their cultural program, known as socialist education, especially targeted the countryside.[1]

Socialist education supplemented existing policy emphasizing peasant behavioral reform with an intensified attack on superstition, religious practices, and the church. Socialist pedagogy also stressed collective learning and organization for adults and children. Children would learn productive habits through group cultivation of gardens and the formation of cooperatives. Men would form agrarian associations to press for land, producer cooperatives to cultivate it, and sports teams to foster a modern, nationalist, and productivist sociability. Women would join anti-alcohol and sanitation brigades. A new curriculum rewrote Mexican history. It depicted workers and peasants as oppressed social classes, the protagonists of Mexican history, the makers and heirs of the revolution of 1910. The Constitution of 1917—with its clauses calling for land reform, worker rights, and national recuperation of natural resources—became the scripture that underwrote claims to democracy, justice, and the principles and fruits of national development.

The multiethnic elements of popular culture—indigenous, mestizo, folkloric—were celebrated and packaged as national culture, to serve as the point of departure for modernization. The new artistic and ideological curriculum served civic festival as well as the classroom. The emphasis on civic festival was no trifling matter. It had deep historical roots. From pre-Conquest times, ritual involving mass participation in collective, aesthetic performance had served to create knowledge, power, and consensus in Mexico (Gruzinski 1989; Beezley, Martin, and French 1994; Vaughan 1994b). How to stage and compose these rituals was a critical matter for national, regional, and local actors as they redefined themselves and their relations to one another in the course of the 1930s.

In this decade, federal teachers became explicit political actors. They were instructed to organize peasants and workers to press for the implementation of federal agrarian and labor laws that would effect a redistribution of wealth and power. President Cárdenas hailed them as the vanguard in his massive land reform program and looked to them to promote workers in asserting their class rights. Cárdenas called upon teachers to assist in the formation of national peasant and trade union confederations. In 1938, he integrated these as the Confederación Nacional Campesina (CNC) and the Confederación de Trabajadores de México (CTM) into the official party, renamed the Partido de la Revolución Mexicana. Teachers shaped and directed the policy of civic ritual designed to consolidate party and state. In the short run, teachers contributed to the formation of a single state party, which was neither socialist nor left. Rather, the PRM, later named the Partido Revolucionario Institucional (PRI), allowed for the articulation of subaltern interests and claims through the CNC and the CTM within the framework of a capitalist development project.

Opinions abound as to the impact of socialist education. For leftists, it was the quintessential moment of mass mobilization and teacher heroism, diminished only by the fact that its product was a state party rather than subaltern organizational autonomy. For the right, it was anathema—an exotic, foreign (communist) project radically out of tune with Mexican Catholic culture. The proof, conservatives claim, lay in the massive protests that forced the government to curtail its campaign against religion in 1936. A recent, well-informed academic assessment acknowledges that portions of the socialist education project echoed favorably in specific settings, but argues that, overall, it was unsuccessful because it did not alter behavior. After 1940, when the project was abandoned, traditional customs—burning candles for the saints, enjoying liquor, and farming in age-old ways—persisted in rural Mexico.[2]

None of these studies has undertaken an in-depth examination of policy implementation across regions and communities.[3] In this study I compare negotiation around socialist education in two major Mexican states, Puebla in central Mexico and Sonora in the north. I examine the cultural politics of schooling in four rural societies within these states. The four case studies are representative of diverse kinds of campesino societies in revolutionary Mexico. I conclude that the real cultural revolution lay not in the state's project but in the dialogue between state and society that took place around this project. Socialist education occurred at a moment when the state was still weak while social groups were highly mobilized in often frenzied defense of their disparate interests. In the countryside, peasant effervescence reached new heights—campesinos invaded haciendas, formed ejido collectives, even torched schools and de-eared teachers. The school became the arena for intense, often violent negotiations over power, culture, knowledge, and rights. In the process, rural communities carved out space for preserving local identities and cultures, while the central state succeeded in nurturing an inclusive, multiethnic, populist nationalism based upon its stated commitment to social justice and development.

Much of the explanation for the longevity of Mexico's single-party state lies in the fact that the state and its representatives had to—and were able to—make concessions in the area of cultural policy during the 1930s. As local societies accepted, discarded, and altered aspects of the state's project, they appropriated the school and forged new identities and linkages—doing so in a way that created a locally defined and controlled sense of membership and participation in a national mobilization for modernity.[4] If the school functioned to inculcate a state ideology for purposes of rule, it also served communities when they needed to contest state policies. It provided ideological, technical, and organizational tools to do so. It helped to create a national civil society that would eventually render obsolete the single-party state. Teachers facilitated this dual construction. With knowledge of local culture, they could soften and censor distant and alien state directives. By organizing in a national trade union, creating a corporate political identity, and, in many cases, operating in oppositional political parties, they became for several decades a force often disposed to defend local peasant interests against the negative effects of modernization and state and class power.

This outcome of the revolution's cultural politics—a sense of popular, multiethnic inclusion based on the right to protest exclusion and injustice—is unique in Latin America. It accounts in part for the relative political stability Mexico enjoyed from 1940 to 1993. It explains the discourse articulated today in the tumultuous transition from one-party rule to political pluralism. Its strength is evident in the Ejército Zapatista of Chiapas. The Indians involved were never direct participants in or beneficiaries of the revolution of 1910, and yet they speak its language. At the same time, they speak their own very distinct languages. Its strength is evident as well in the Zapatistas' call for a constitutional convention to draw up a new set of principles for rule and protest because the party of the revolution has broken its pact with the people.

NEGOTIATION AS AN ORGANIZING CONCEPT

This study is situated in the small but growing camp of postrevisionist historiography of the Mexican Revolution. In 1968, a new generation of scholars challenged official interpretations of the Mexican Revolution as a consensual process that sought modernity and social justice. From the vantage point of intellectual youth in 1968, the Mexican Revolution seemed to have produced an all-powerful, single-party state that promoted capitalist growth at the expense of social welfare. Their revisionist inquiry into Mexican revolutionary history questioned the popular and democratic nature of the revolution, casting the central state as the revolution's principal actor and as an effective manipulator of the masses in the interest of a bourgeois project. Peasants became victims, who had been mobilized by political bosses to serve the latter's interests rather than their own. Valiant campesinos who had stood up to the aggressive, modernizing state in the name of tradition, community, and Christ became martyrs to a premodern purity corrupted and destroyed by the revolution.[5]

A postrevisionist response to this school of thought has emerged after two decades of energetic mapping of the Mexican Revolution. This new research has questioned the strength of the revolutionary state, the homogeneity of the countryside, and the manipulability of the peasantry. Studies have demonstrated the complexity and variety of revolutionary processes at the regional and local levels. Research on peasant movements has emphasized their diversity. Alan Knight has convincingly argued that the revisionists extrapolated their paradigm of a strong central state from Mexican realities of the 1960s and 1970s and imposed it upon an earlier period of history. The revolution destroyed the state between 1913 and 1915. Reconstructing it across a geographically far-flung, volatile, and fragmented territory was a slow, painstaking process that required accommodation and negotiation as well as coercion. The Mexican state in the 1920s and 1930s was no Leviathan capable of steamrolling society in the interest of its singular project. It was a fledgling institution subject to persistent contention in a context of intense sociopolitical mobilization around conflicting projects (Knight 1985, 1990a, 1990b). Popular mobilization altered the agrarian structure, destroyed the hacienda system, challenged age-old deferential practices, pressed for the formation of labor unions, and derailed the rabidly antireligious campaigns that intermittently obsessed revolutionary governments. The state was formed through contentious interaction with social forces that in moments of heightened politicization articulated their interests in sometimes shrill and sometimes muted voices. Those in command of the state could sustain no single project; it was devised and revised in a dialectical process.

Still, postrevisionist studies are in their infancy. The relative power of state and society in the construction of nation and modernity is not yet fully understood. Historians are now beginning to grapple with the sociocultural processes that intersected with state and nation formation.[6] The current intellectual challenge is to get beyond the narrow political construct of a top-down, clientelist organization sucking a gullible peasantry into the vortex of an unyielding modernity. In relation to rural primary schooling in the revolution, the task is to provide a more nuanced understanding than those that have associated the federal school with benign improvement or repressive domination. As I have examined sources related to the everyday functioning of schools, to policy implementation, and to the cultural, economic, and political processes that created the social ecology of schooling, I have become convinced that we must rely on the concept of negotiation to understand the interaction between state and peasantry. We must examine the negotiating actors to understand their diversity, complexity, and mutual, interactive construction of themselves.

First, the notion of negotiation questions the view of nation-building as top-down social engineering and challenges theories that regard modernization as a process invulnerable to contestation. Benedict Anderson's *Imagined Communities* is concerned with nation-building from the top down. Even though Anderson regards nationality as a cultural artifact and the nation as a shared, imagined community, he examines the creation and dissemination of symbols, myths, songs, literature, and history by elites (Anderson 1991:65–73, 94–101, 124–25). He is less concerned with how this material is provided, appropriated, selected, or reworked by local societies. In his equally influential study, *Peasants into Frenchmen*, Eugen Weber treats modernization as an inexorable process that transforms rural mentalities through the school, commerce, migration, and military service. He alerts us to the externality of the nineteenth-century public rural school. It was an institution designed to shape individuals to a nonrural world, to integrate them into a national framework, a national state, and its market. He acknowledges resistance but is more interested in penetration and transformation. He never contemplates the possibility of the peasantry's reshaping national projects or policies (Weber 1976:303–38).

Neither top-down analyses of nation creation nor modernization theory work for Mexico because of the character of that country's revolution. The revolution of 1910 destroyed the preexisting state, and it took three decades to build a new one. The new one was constructed through dialogue with diverse sociopolitical movements. It emerged from bitter negotiation between actors at national, regional, and local sites where power was disputed and developed. The revolution empowered the peasantry not only because the peasantry mobilized but because the peasantry gained space as a result of statelessness and the dynamic process of state creation. Further, as much as one can argue that there was continuity between the modernizing policies pursued by the pre- and postrevolutionary states, the revolution reshaped modernization processes in Mexico. Broadly, it redistributed wealth and power and refashioned social policy. It did so in large part because of the strength of peasant rebellion. All sectors of the peasantry that mobilized in the revolution had some grievance against the way the prerevolutionary state was carrying out modernization. Many peasants rebelled in order to stop modernization altogether. That is, they wished to return to a premodern autonomy, imagined or real. They did not succeed in restoring their version of premodernity, but neither did the educating state succeed in imposing its model of modernity.

We can locate a central state actor that articulated educational policy, a cadre of social engineers who devised policy, and a general script that established the policy's parameters and logic. The central state actor is the Secretaría de Educación Pública, created in 1921. The SEP had multiple goals, but its first priority was rural schooling. To advance the latter, it absorbed or complemented preexisting municipal and state schools and created new schools. The social engineers were what Benedict Anderson calls the pilgrims of the imagined national community: for the most part, middle-class products of Mexico's public schools and of the civic celebratory culture of the prerevolutionary, modernizing society. They constructed notions of modernity, culture, and nation and translated them into policy within the parameters of a general script they shared with state reformers in many Western and developing countries.

The guidelines for this general script have been laid out by Victoria de Grazia in her work on women under Italian fascism (1992:1–40).[7] She argues that Western states at the turn of the twentieth century faced demographic crisis. By demographic crisis de Grazia means more than the relationship between birth and mortality rates: she is talking about population management. The demographic crisis she describes lay at the intersection between an emerging mass society, brimming with political demands and social ills, and the state's need to control and mobilize that society for national survival and development in an increasingly competitive global order. World War I accentuated the crisis by mobilizing mass societies around a militarized nationalism. It unleashed an unprecedented cacophony of political mobilizations, dislocations, social demands, and experiments, which resonated in a context of mounting international conflict and competition. Each state devised social policies to nationalize its citizens in the interest of order, development, and mobilization. These policies varied from country to country and with shifting political coalitions.

Mexico's demographic crisis was the revolution itself: the spectacle of masses of people, urban and rural, in military rebellion and social movement, marked often by hunger, violence, dislocation, and rapid mobility. From the perspective of the embryonic state that arose from this conflagration, the population had to be brought to order in a progressive manner. The "race," understood to be decadent, diseased, and demobilized by backwardness, oppression, and disruption, had to be vitalized and its energies harnessed for development. Rural educational policy was devised in this broad context. It aimed at the nationalization of the peasantry for participation in a modern global order. It was informed by similar social policies in the United States, Europe, and the Soviet Union and by Mexican participation in international conferences and associations pertaining to children, women, the family, education, eugenics, and health.

De Grazia understands state social policies to be gendered. They are attempts to mold family, sexuality, and gender roles in specific ways. In the case of Mexico, rural educational policy in the 1930s envisioned a modernization of patriarchy. It aimed at destroying regional patriarchal networks of power and provisioning in favor of national, horizontal networks. It sought to remake the family—men, women, and children—in the interests of nation-building and development. As such, it engaged thousands of women as schoolteachers, technicians, and, in rare instances, policy makers.

These were the broad parameters of the script composed by central state educators. Within these parameters, the composition and content of policy shifted with changing political coalitions and in response to a rapid and unrelenting massification of politics between 1921 and 1940. When the Secretaría de Educación Pública was created in 1921, it was led by a handful of intellectuals from elite Mexico City institutions of higher education. In 1923, they made policy for 690 rural "missionaries" and teachers operating in the countryside. For most of these policy makers, the peasant was no more than an imagined construction, and a negative and miserable one at that. By 1936, SEP rural policy was mostly in the hands of self-made, regional intellectuals and pedagogues, radical in their rhetoric and vision and experienced in country life and politics. By then, 16,079 SEP teachers plied the country roads and mountain trails.

The policy makers of 1921 and those of 1936 shared certain goals and methods, but their constructions of culture differed. I decipher these constructions in chapter 2 through reading SEP programs, conferences, directives, teacher training periodicals, manuals, school textbooks, and civic celebratory literature.

At the center of the second tier of negotiation in cultural politics were the federal schoolteachers charged with translating SEP policy at the regional and local levels. More than mere foot soldiers, federal teachers became direct participants in the making of policy through the national teacher training journal, the bimonthly *El Maestro Rural*. To this journal they contributed articles on local art, music, and dance and their own didactic revolutionary theater and songs. These cultural artifacts became the basis for the construction of a multiethnic national culture. Male and female, federal teachers shared a common background in the modest middle class, predominantly rural but sometimes urban. They shared the SEP's enthusiasm for progress, modernity, and patriotism. Most of them had been weaned in the incipient liberal civic culture of the prerevolutionary period. At different points in the 1930s, through their intensive training with SEP inspectors and the often hair-raising hostility they faced in the countryside, they forged a mystical, corporate faith in their revolutionary mission.

Teachers needed this faith because they lacked so much of everything else. They were poorly paid and often went months without receiving wages. Penury left them dependent on villages, state governments, and federal agencies other than the SEP for the very tools and infrastructure they needed to carry out policy. Central state agencies of rural development—agrarian reform officials, agricultural technicians, the ejidal bank, the health authorities—did not always back them up. In fact, they often obstructed SEP work. They also promoted models of behavior at odds with SEP directives.

Federal teachers came to be regionally defined: they reflected distinct teaching traditions forged in the nineteenth-century schools of each region; they experienced the revolution differently at the regional level; and they were dependent upon the regional formation of state power—that is, the state governor, his political alliances, and his relations with the central government. Nothing better demonstrates the formative nature of the Mexican state and its ruling groups than the relationship between federal teachers and state governors.

In this study, I examine that relationship in the states of Puebla and Sonora in the 1930s. At the beginning of the decade, radical governors ruled in both states and called upon federal teachers to assist them in the consolidation of populist political machines. The resources and backup they could provide to teachers differed in each state. Conservative movements destroyed these populist projects between 1933 and 1935. Thus, at the moment when Mexico's most radical president, Lázaro Cárdenas, came to power to enact a bold program of redistributive reforms, both Puebla and Sonora were in the hands of conservative governors who had no use for federal schoolteachers. This situation was not unusual, for Cárdenas in 1935 depended on conservative—as well as progressive—factions in the PNR to unseat Plutarco Elías Calles, the ruling arbiter of Mexican politics. Cárdenas hoped to weaken conservative power at the regional level by forming national class confederations of workers and peasants to be integrated into a reformed official party. He called upon teachers to be his vanguard, but whether he could support them depended upon his own relations with state governors. His policy toward teachers in Sonora contrasted with his policy in Puebla.

The relationships between federal teachers, state governors, and the president influenced teachers in their translation and interpretation of educational policy. It determined the resources at their disposal, the training they received, and the protection they enjoyed. Chapter 3 reconstructs translation of policy by teachers in Sonora and Puebla through a reading of late-nineteenth-century school archives, census materials, teacher biographies and oral testimonies, SEP reports on teacher training institutes, and school inspectors' bimonthly reports. The position teachers occupied in regional politics in the 1930s is gleaned from presidential, state, and local archives, newspapers, agrarian reform records, and secondary sources. Among the latter are studies of regional revolutionary politics undertaken as part of the mapping effort of the last two decades.

The most critical determiner of how teachers translated central state policy was the third actor at the final level of negotiation: the peasants in rural communities. News that an armed band had torched the school and beat up the teacher in one village had a chilling effect on teachers' translation of the SEP's script throughout the surrounding region. Similarly, factions of

villagers who welcomed and allied with teachers pushed SEP policy in specific directions and not in others. Thus, translation of the SEP's notion of
culture depended very much on the script of the other actor, the peasantry.

How does the historian construct this peasant script? One obviously
starts by de-essentializing the Mexican peasantry. One recognizes heterogeneity. The diverse social configurations of rural Mexico make it imperative
to talk not about a single peasant script but about a number of scripts. This
study constructs peasant scripts for four societies in Puebla and Sonora. The
societies were selected for their distinct ethnic composition, gender relations, and schooling practices; their land tenure configurations and market
linkages; their historical relations to state formation; and their participation in the revolution of 1910. The first, in the ex-district of Tecamachalco in
Puebla, is representative of the central Mexican plateau, the core of the Aztec
and Spanish empires. Here, once indigenous, now mestisized agrarian communities mobilized in the revolution to challenge hacienda domination. The
second, in the ex-district of Zacapoaxtla in Puebla's Sierra Norte, is representative of indigenous (Nahua) smallholder communities subject to domination by non-Indian commercial elites. By and large, such communities were
nonparticipants in the revolution of 1910. The third society is that of the
Yaqui Indians of Sonora, occupants in the 1930s of the Yaqui Valley's right
bank. Still tribally cohesive and fresh from decades of war to stop the Mexican state's penetration of their land, they received from Cárdenas the only
territorial tribal land grant in Mexican history. The fourth is a new society of
mestizo peasants, pushed out of their traditional communities and recon-
gregated as workers in modern agribusiness enterprises on the left bank of
Yaqui River in Sonora. Also nonparticipants in the 1910 revolution, they organized in the 1930s and received land from Cárdenas in 1937.[8]

The choice of Puebla and Sonora restricts the range of geographical representation. However, I selected these four societies in part because they are
representative of a broad spectrum of rural social configurations in the revolution. The communities of Tecamachalco and Zacapoaxtla and the Yaqui
Indians articulate aspects of the militant religiosity characteristic of western
Mexico's rural communities. The Sierra Norte Nahua villages have much in
common with indigenous society in Mexico's south. The linkages between
urban labor movements and peasant mobilization typical of the Gulf states
are detectable among the Yaqui Valley agricultural workers and, to a degree,
among the *agraristas* of Tecamachalco and some of the communities on Zacapoaxtla's southern tier. Agrarian mobilizations in Tecamachalco and among
the Yaqui Valley immigrants are representative of two important types of

agrarian movements in the Mexican Revolution: those of villagers and those of workers in agricultural enterprises. Similarly, the Nahuas of the Sierra Norte and the Yaquis of Sonora represent two different kinds of indigenous societies in Mexico: those organized in discrete villages and typical of central Mexico, and those mobilized around a tribal identity as was common in the north.

There are two models for writing scripts for the interaction between rural people and state schools. The first stresses how rural people use the school to empower themselves, in the process altering the state project at least at its point of implementation. The second emphasizes how polarization between the cultural configurations of the state and those of community diminishes the possibility for dialogue. Ben Ekloff's study of rural schools in nineteenth-century Russia represents the first model. He argues that although teachers came to moralize, sanitize, and nationalize peasants, local people selected from the school program the knowledge and skills they wanted. Men wanted to learn how to read and write in order to cope with new landownership and local government following emancipation. They were not interested in absorbing the full curriculum. Teachers complained of children leaving school early, hardly knowing how to spell and still backward in their social behavior. In fact, villagers reshaped the curriculum in order to use schooling for their own purposes and in accord with their own capacity, needs, and changing power relations (Ekloff 1986; 1990:115–30).

Elsie Rockwell and I have used a similar approach to rural community–school relations in the adjacent Mexican states of Tlaxcala and Puebla in the prerevolutionary period.[9] In addition to examining the local shaping of the curriculum, we have noted how control was achieved through village financial support for the school and through institutions of local surveillance and accountability. In places where literacy was a still scarce but increasingly useful commodity and where strong restrictions limited the number of children attending school and the time they spent there, teachers were often in greater demand outside the classroom than in it. They served as scribes, keeping records on internal village matters and conducting oral and written brokering with outsiders. They were responsible for patriotic festival, which in the late nineteenth century took its place alongside religious celebration as a site for confirming community identity and power structures. At the same time, civic festival introduced new notions of nation, citizenship, and community. Teacher and school, then, stood at the intersection between local society and the outside world. They introduced new concepts, ideas, skills, and values, which in turn were subject to community scrutiny, judgment, and reshaping.[10]

The second model was employed by Brian Street (1984:95–128, 183–212) in his work on literacy crusades in Iran and Tanzania and by Marjorie Becker in her 1987 essay on communities in Michoacán, Mexico, in the 1930s (Becker 1987:163–79). They argue that teachers' campaigns are undertaken for the purpose of promoting state control and market penetration. The campaigns are conceptualized and carried out within cultural constructs oblivious to the logic of local practices of productive, reproductive, and ritual labor. They are disruptive of the delicate ecological and social balances that sustain life upon a precarious resource base. The discourse between community and teachers is likely to be antagonistic, characterized by resistance, or absent.[11]

The two models differ in their interpretation of state–community relations as conducted through schooling. The first posits a complex negotiation between state and community—an encounter that alters both. In the second, there is less room for dialogue: the state school, rather than being an empowering institution, is a domineering and corrupting one. Both models are useful to this study. The negotiation model is most appropriate to the two mestizo societies, which received land and experienced a redistribution of power and resources in the revolution. Resistance to the school was more obvious in the short term in the two indigenous societies examined here. Although the Mexican state acknowledged the indigenous foundations of national society and claimed the artistic creativity of the Indian as part of national culture, the state's educational project insisted upon transforming the everyday practices of indigenous societies. To defend their everyday culture and its systems of power and reproduction, most of the Indian communities examined in this study held the school at bay as they sought other channels of negotiation with the state. Simultaneously and over the long term, they pursued their dialogue with teachers and educational authorities in order to bend the school to serve local interests and culture.

My understanding of peasant scripts is grounded in what the two models share in common. Both insist on the need to reconstruct local mentalities, economies and resources, and configurations of knowledge and power in order to understand educational encounters. One must specifically understand a community's gendered socialization practices, including its use of schools. One must understand the role of the teacher prior to the revolution: was he or she a foreign interloper or the articulator of new concepts, ideas, skills, and values that the community members subjected to their own rigorous review and reshaping? Local practices, traditions, and institutions constituted the basis for claims, demands, and denunciations made upon the new federal school as it entered the community.[12] In the case studies, an important prerequisite to constructing the peasant scripts was developing an understanding of socialization customs and of prior schooling practices and teacher behaviors. That understanding has been gleaned from municipal and state archives, census data, anthropological studies, and life histories.

It is equally critical to understand how communities changed through the revolution. Most communities in the revolution were sites where conflict over the redistribution of resources and power unfolded. Useful here is Serge Gruzinski's analysis of the rural community as a conglomeration of power configurations, always in dynamic interaction and vulnerable to jarring by outsiders (Gruzinski 1989:17–18). The revolution was a significant outside interference for each society in this study. Gruzinski's understanding urges the historian to search for the agendas of competing groups at the local level to determine how the school might promote or threaten their interests, or how their conflicts might deter the work of the school. Gruzinski borrows from Foucault (1980) to extend the realm of politics to penetrate everyday life. Gruzinski's notion of power at the community level allows us to probe how the SEP's prescriptions for behavior challenged or meshed with ongoing tensions over familial, gender, and generational power, over the management and execution of ritual labor, and over the creation and practice of local knowledge.[13] To penetrate this realm is difficult, but it is possible through a close reading of teacher reports, school archives, oral testimony, anthropological field notes and published studies, and comparative social history.

When probing disputes within communities, one must examine those communities' potential linkage to outside powerholders. James Scott's *Moral Economy of the Peasantry* eloquently describes how peasant communities subsist in tense, precarious reciprocity with their dominators—for example, landlords and merchants who provide credit, seeds, tools, emergency loans, and employment. (Scott 1976:40–52). The SEP aimed at destroying these vertical relations. Struggles over schools within communities were inevitably linked to competition among outside powerholders for community loyalties. These contests involved—but cannot be reduced to—battles between prerevolutionary dominators and the SEP. The SEP was one among many in an array of local actors associated with the state in formation, including representatives of prerevolutionary elites seeking to shore up their interests in the new order. Local conflicts are difficult for the historian to analyze. They are complex and fluid. Real interests are often masked behind revolutionary or religious rhetoric and associations; real actors frequently operate through surrogates (organizations, politicians, and armed henchmen). I have attempted to uncover these byzantine dramas by examining correspondence in presidential and municipal archives, those of agrarian reform and education, and oral histories.

No peasant script can be deciphered until its modes of expression are identified. First, campesinos wrote and talked in forms accessible to the historian. In a political culture traditionally wed to the written petition, they composed appeals and registered complaints with the president, their governors, and the SEP. They talked with teachers and inspectors, as recorded in SEP reports and documents. They sometimes talked with anthropologists, who recorded their words, or how they heard those words. Campesinos sometimes reconstructed their life histories: writing them down for anthropologists, as in the case of several members of the Yaqui tribes; telling them to friends and children who in turn wrote and published them, as in the case of the Yaqui Valley settlers and ejidatarios; or, in fortunate instances, telling them to me. Testimonials and interviews are, of course, reconstructions of the past. They are selections from memory, made by selected representatives of social groups, and must be balanced with other campesino voices whose expressions are found in other sources.

Peasants' scripts must also be reconstructed from nonverbal actions or from words that mask "hidden transcripts" (Scott 1990:1–14). In two instances recorded here, groups of villagers let their voices be heard against the antireligious aspects of socialist education by withdrawing their children from school. They also used less direct tactics to express their agendas and attain their goals. These "weapons of the weak," as defined by James Scott (1985: 32–36), range from foot-dragging, dissimulation, false compliance, indirect speech, gossip, and avoidance to sabotage and brigandage. They are time-proven ways to negotiate domination. How many school inspectors grew frustrated when, after they met with officials and parents who politely agreed to increase school attendance, attendance hardly improved? How many villagers requested the removal of teachers on grounds of immorality, drunkenness, or dereliction of duty, when in reality such a teacher may have offended sensibilities in entirely different ways? To articulate the real reasons for unhappiness would not convince the authorities. It was expedient to use the authorities' language to achieve the desired result.

For the historian seeking evidence of a deepening national identity at the local level, Scott's concept of a "hidden transcript" suggests caution, for communities or interest groups within them may proclaim fidelity to a certain national symbol or cause in a written document for purely tactical reasons. Such protestation should not be confused with sincere sentiment. Similarly, members of communities may participate in civic rituals under duress or out of calculation without sharing strong loyalties or enthusiasm for the nation. If arguing, as does this study, that notions of national identity and membership were indeed nurtured at the local level by the revolutionary process through the school, one must try to recognize and decipher both tactical expression and real appropriation. One can never be sure, but I have attempted to distinguish between tactical profession and real appropriation by assessing the degree to which national identity and linkage facilitated local interests and by measuring the durability and frequency of expression through time.

In the arena of the school, what were the peasantry's strengths in negotiating claims? For one, in each of the four cases presented here, peasants were feisty, mobilized, and demanding, although their demands differed markedly. At least a portion of their interests had to be accommodated by the state if aspiring bourgeois groups were to pursue their own agendas. Parts of peasant agendas had to be granted. Land reform and an official ideology of agrarianism and social justice were concessions, distasteful to many conservative state governors and local elites. Federal teachers and the central state in the 1930s provided these concessions. But the concessions were not simply in the realm of material redistribution; they were cultural as well. The most obvious cultural concession—but by no means the only one—was the state's suspension of its campaign against Catholicism.

Second, peasant agendas benefited from the state's lack of resources and technical capacity. Elsie Rockwell (1994:195–203) has pointed out that federal teachers were often so dependent on villages for the materials to build and equip their schools and for housing and food that they had no choice but to listen to the villagers and respond to their concerns (Rockwell 1994:195–203). State technical incapacity not only encouraged teacher dependence, it validated the rationality of local customs and knowledge in relation to available resources. The technology for the SEP's projected behavioral transformation was in many cases not available to communities in the 1930s: water, gas, oil, machinery, the mechanical corn-grinding mill, medicines, trucks, roads, sewage systems. Much of this would arrive through the state and the marketplace after 1940. In the 1930s, its absence created an opportunity for local societies to claim space, "authenticity," and effectiveness for local cultural practices. These moral claims proved strongly enduring. To this day, they underwrite a hidden notion of Mexican national culture that finds pride and humor in the greater efficacy of the "traditional" in contrast to the "modern."[14]

Evidence points to an alteration in teacher attitudes toward rural people in the 1930s. Teachers came face to face with their own limitations and with vigorous community defense of cultural practices. At the same time, they had internalized the ideology of social justice and redistribution that characterized Cardenismo—an ideology that had appointed the teachers to a special position in the making of Mexican history. Rather than haughtily writing to the SEP about the difficulties of civilizing local savages, teachers often turned their energies and skills to softening and censoring distant and alien state directives in order to make them more palatable to local people. They took pains to identify and defend community interests not only in relation to old oppressors but to new abusers of power within the emerging state. The degree of this commitment and the shape it took varied regionally. It was facilitated by two factors in addition to SEP policy itself. One was that the teachers themselves came from modest backgrounds just a notch above those of the peasants, so they understood local culture, even if revolutionary idealism and SEP policy had pushed this understanding to the recesses of their minds. The struggles of the 1930s demanded that they recall and cultivate local knowledge and practice. The second factor facilitating teacher identification with communities was their national unionization. The teachers' union institutionalized a corporate political identity at least rhetorically committed to social justice for subaltern groups.

CONSTRUCTING HEGEMONY

Because interactions between localities, regions, and the central state were particular and generated different outcomes, it is risky to draw national conclusions on the basis of a study of two states and four rural societies within them. Nonetheless, I do so in hopes of stimulating debate and in anticipation of future scholarship that will refine, strengthen, or discard my findings. My argument is that the real cultural revolution of the 1930s lay not in the state's project but in the dialogue between state and society that took place around that project. A common language for consent and protest was forged. It was enabled by a simultaneously emerging institutional structure (represented by the official party, popular organizations, state agencies, and the school system); and it was facilitated by a proliferating infrastructural network of communication in the state and private economies (including roads, cheap modes of transport, the print and electronic media, and schools).

Thus I argue that the PRI and the state came to rule not on the basis of an impositional patron–clientelist politics and repression alone, but through the construction of hegemonic consensus. My contention will be anathema to those Mexican scholars who share the revisionist view that the Mexican

state hijacked the revolution. For them, the party was heavy-handed, corrupt, unaccountable, and, at its best, co-optive. However, I agree with Wil
Pansters, who writes in his analysis of Puebla politics in the revolution (1990:
8–16) that the concept of hegemony is a healthy, necessary complement to
studies of political power that focus exclusively on corporate, bureaucratic,
clientelist mechanisms of rule (e.g., Kaufman Purcell 1981).

My argument requires an explanation of my understanding of the Gramscian notion of hegemony as consensual rule.[15] First, the notion does not exclude coercion. Coercion can precede and accompany the construction of
consensus. Coercion in its multiple, violent, and manipulative forms enters
vividly into each case study in this book. Through these stories, one gains insight not only into the opportunities available to subaltern groups in struc-
turing new spaces and identities, but into the restrictions imposed upon
them by the revolutionary process. When I originally chose to examine Puebla
and Sonora, I did so to contrast two major Mexican regions. I did not imagine how thoroughly they would illustrate the complexities of state formation
in the Cárdenas period. A central government espousing principles of social
redistribution faced conservative state governors who were unhesitating in
their deployment of the "weapons of the strong" against these principles and
against those who championed them.[16] The governors in turn had allies at
the local and regional levels who were more interested in consolidation of
power to further personal interests than in redistributive politics that would
benefit the poor. They were often able to take advantage of the contradictions inherent in "progressive policy" (e.g., the attack on religion) to win
broad popular support, but they also resorted to coercive tactics: violence,
harassment, murder, the deposition of legitimately elected officials, and vote
fraud. Cárdenas juggled the demands of these actors and of "progressive
forces" from 1936 to 1938, when he had to acquiesce to those opposed to further redistribution. Fortunately, he was able to temper conservative voices by
institutionalizing national representation for workers and peasants within
the reformed PNR (the PRM) and the state. Because the CTM and the CNC
belonged to the PRM as a corporate entity, they assured worker and peasant
members representation at the local and state levels of government as well.

Just as the concept of hegemony does not exclude the use of coercion, so
consensus as part of hegemony does not necessarily mean the citizenry's acceptance of the state's project, i.e., the project's successful dissemination
through what Louis Althusser called "Ideological State Apparatuses"—elite-
commanded institutions such as schools, clubs, political parties, and the
mass media (Althusser 1975:119–70). Rather, the hegemony achieved for a

time by the Mexican state and ruling party resulted from interactive processes involving multiple social groups and interweaving a multiplicity of
discourses and interests. Hegemony can only be constructed from a variety
of cultural traditions that make up a nation. As the anthropologist Bruce
Kapferer (1988:7–20) has argued, nationalist sentiments hinge on the identification of a deeply personal sense of existence with the continuation of the
nation.

In her work on peasant communities and state formation in nineteenth-
century Mexico and Peru, Florencia Mallon uses the concept of hegemony to
mean

> a set of . . . processes, constant and ongoing through which power relations
> are contested, legitimated and redefined at all levels of society. . . . Hegemony
> is the end point, then, a precarious balance. A contract or agreement is
> reached among contesting forces . . . the leaders of a particular movement or
> coalition achieve hegemony as an end point only when they effectively garner
> for themselves ongoing legitimacy and support. They are successful in doing
> so if they partially incorporate the political aspirations or discourses of the
> movement's supporters. . . . Only then can they rule through a combination
> of coercion and consent. (Mallon 1994b:70–71)

The anthropologist William Roseberry goes further. Hegemony is the con-
flictual construction of a language for expressing both acceptance and discontent: a common framework for living in, discussing, and acting upon social orders characterized by domination. While relations between ruling and
subaltern groups are consistently characterized by contention and struggle,
contention and struggle take place within a "field of force" that connects the
ruling and the subaltern in organic relations (Roseberry 1994:360–64).

In Mexico, the field of force was created in the 1930s. The organic relations
between rulers and ruled were cemented not only through popular, party,
and state organizations but through the making of a shared language. This
notion of a shared language is highly nuanced. Roseberry, Pansters, and Mallon share Chantal Mouffe and Ernesto Laclau's notion of hegemony as a discursive construction based upon the multiple meanings and interpretations
given to an ensemble of symbols, images, concepts, and visions of the past
and future. The orchestration of a hegemonic discourse in the 1930s was successful because it allowed for regional diversity and for multiple discourses
at the local level. Precisely because the postrevolutionary process of state
formation in Mexico engaged local communities so intensely, the very con-

struction of state principles and ideals depended upon how they were understood, reshaped, and discarded at the local level.

To illustrate in advance of the case studies, using somewhat general terms:
Communities rejected outright certain portions of the state's cultural project, such as the abolition of Catholicism. In other instances, concepts promoted by the state as nationally unifying were appropriated at the local level
to serve particular purposes. Broadly accepted was the new notion of "Mexi-
canidad" as multiethnic and inclusive because this notion allowed for the articulation of local distinctiveness and grievances. However, in accepting the
national, some local societies gave far greater weight to the local part of the
equation than to the national. In the case of the two indigenous societies examined here, the "nation" became no more than a puny backdrop for the
articulation—indeed, the preservation—of local culture.

Further, concepts promoted by the state were given particular local meanings that derived from prerevolutionary experiences and specific revolutionary struggles. The Constitution of 1917 was appropriated as a document defining rights to social justice. However, the concept of class rights sanctioned
in the document was understood in local terms that were at once broader
and narrower. That is, the category of "oppressed" was a broader interpretation large enough to embrace agricultural laborers, who saw themselves as
members of the modern working class, and others who defined their rights
as tribal, indigenous, or village-based. Similarly, concepts and processes the
state devised from local struggles and traditions for purposes of rule (e.g.,
the ejido as the land reform unit, Emiliano Zapata as patriot-hero) became,
in local context, meaning, and practice, bones of contention between community and state. That is, they became grounds for repeated local claims,
and stubborn constructors of resistant identities (Martin 1993; Nugent and
Alonso 1994). Further, because popular struggles in the revolution were to
some degree about maintaining and defining culture, the concept of modernity, while accepted rhetorically and in the tangible forms of land, water,
roads, corn-grinding mills, and smallpox vaccine, could be appropriated because local people struggled successfully to legitimize their cultures and assert their right to pace the entry of modernity and determine its content and
meaning. That is, they themselves claimed the right to de-essentialize the
concept and to select from it. At the same time, the external linkages built
through new political identities and affiliations, through state agencies, and
through participation in the expanding market and civil society became vital
to ongoing postrevolutionary community construction.[17]

Ultimately, hegemony is fragile because it consists in a temporal pact between rulers and ruled that can be easily eroded by historical process and agency. In the case of Mexico, the rapid transition from a rural to an urban society between 1940 and 1970 undermined the social basis for PRI hegemony. The anonymous, urban, and highly mobile society demanded a free vote, a secret ballot, and rule by formal law, all of which had been more honored in rhetoric than in practice under the hegemonic pact. At the same time, the rulers themselves broke the pact because they could not adjust their modernization projects to accommodate demands for social justice and inclusion. In the undoing of PRI hegemony, the school played a role. Intended as an arena for articulating state domination, it was also carved out as an arena for contesting that domination. It played that role not simply as a physical and ideological space for articulating subaltern demands, but as a creator of modern Mexican civil society: as the provider of skills, attitudes, linkages, and behaviors that would create citizens who would seek a new pact, a new language, and a new set of political relations.

2

REVOLUTIONARY CULTURAL POLICY
THE SECRETARÍA DE EDUCACIÓN PÚBLICA

This chapter explores federal educational policy. It examines the principles that revolutionary educators shared with each other and with their prerevolutionary predecessors. It then explores the politics that underlay a radicalization of policy between 1929 and 1938 and its subsequent moderation. Finally, it analyzes the educators' evolving definitions of Mexican history, citizenship, and the cultural nation.

The institution through which policy was articulated was the Secretaría de Educación Pública. Between 1921 and 1940, the SEP extended its jurisdiction from the capital to the states and came to control 12,561 rural primary schools enrolling 720,647 students. It absorbed schools from state and municipal systems and set up new ones where none had existed. From the creation of Cultural Missions to train teachers in 1923, mechanisms, institutions, and curriculum materials for preparing teachers proliferated—especially after 1929. The federal rural primary teachers' corps increased from 6,504 in 1930 to 19,134 in 1942. The SEP's share of national primary school enrollment rose from 34 percent in 1928 to 54 percent in 1940. By 1940, 70 percent of Mexican children between the ages of six and ten were enrolled in primary school compared with 30 percent in 1910 (Secretaría de la Economía 1938:99, 1942:342–55).

SHARED PRINCIPLES

For revolutionary educators, history was progressive and linear. Although pre-Hispanic societies had excelled in production, organization, and aesthetics, the European conquest pulled Mexico into civilization. The modern world emanated from Europe. It evolved as a system of technology, communications, trade, and knowledge dominated by competing nation-states. The educators' purpose was to ensure Mexico's successful participation in this system. Every minister of public education cited Mexico's Indian roots as a point of departure along the road to modernity. Although each praised the Indians' artistic creativity, the latter was to be preserved in a modern subject. This subject was a healthy producer and reproducer wired to a national community: one who used bathrooms and telephones and who read newspapers. Many peasants rebelled in 1910 to defend a way of life threatened by modernization. Educators condemned that way of life as backward. They took certain peasant goals—land and sustenance—and reworked them into their own paradigm of improvement.

The assimilative purpose of Mexican education predated the revolution. In 1890, the Porfirian statesman Justo Sierra issued an urgent call for schools to ensure the survival of a country torn apart by decades of civil war, popular revolt, and foreign invasion:

> Our life is linked with iron chains to the industrial and economic life of the world, all that there is of centrifugal force in the heterogeneity of habits, languages, and needs must be transformed into cohesion thanks to the sovereign action of the public school. . . . [The Mexican people need] as a means of their own preservation (a task which becomes more painfully urgent with the gigantic advances of our neighbors) to improve their elements of work to make them more productive; above all, the generating element of the worker himself . . . instruction must transform him. (SEP 1975:265)

With contempt for both the Indian and Spanish legacies, Sierra wagered that the school would defanaticize Mexicans and teach a scientific understanding of the universe. It would nurture habits of work, punctuality, and thrift. It would encourage abstinence from alcohol, gambling, and tobacco. Modernity required the sanitization and domestication of popular space (Vaughan 1982:22–38).

In the revolutionary upheaval, such thinking was reoriented to harness the energies of millions of rebellious workers and peasants. Salvador Alvarado, Constitutionalist governor of Yucatán in 1915, captured the new approach. Like Sierra, he defined Mexico's demographic crisis as the inability of a degenerate people to meet the challenge of nation-building in a competitive environment. "If we, the lucky inhabitants of this privileged land," he wrote, "keep sleeping, if we are not strong, aggressive, and enterprising in the exploitation of our fabulous wealth, take heed—other races more enterprising, aggressive, and tenacious will come and whether we like it or not, they will take what is today ours, our lands, forests, livestock, homes; they will . . . have shown more force in the struggle for survival, and our children will shine their shoes" (Alvarado 1962:202–3). In contrast to Sierra, Alvarado would "liberate" Mexicans from their "feudal" heritage prior to disciplining them for development. He ended debt peonage on haciendas, closed cantinas to "free" the poor from alcohol, excoriated the church as a repressor of human will and knowledge, and sought to free women from domestic cloistering through education, job opportunities, and civic mobilization. "If all sleeping minds enter into action," he exhorted, "the propelling work of evolution will be more intense and effective."[1]

He shared with other middle-class thinkers a critique of Porfirian education as verbalist, authoritarian, and divorced from everyday life. Like them, he embraced the pedagogy of action education, adapted from the European and North American child-centered theories of John Dewey, Adolfo Ferriere, and Maria Montessori. Schools, said Alvarado ([1916] 1962:89–92), should be out of doors, equipped with gardens, workshops, and playing fields. Children would "learn by doing." This "liberating" school would rally energies to a new project mobilized around the Mexican flag. Alvarado introduced the Boy Scouts to promote sports, citizenship, and health. Phlegmatic youngsters would be transformed into agents of regeneration (1962:89–90): "a powerful falange . . . prepared for struggle and resistance." Girls were not to be neglected. They would attend school with boys and learn the same subjects. They were as important as men to national development—as reproductive workers, consumers, and marginal income earners. "Everyone to the factory, shop and home!" Alvarado exhorted, "Let us create the religion of duty!" (Mediz Bolio 1968:67).

Alvarado's notions of action education were shared by many middle-class pedagogues in Mexico. Adopted as official policy by the SEP in 1923, action pedagogy served an integrating, productivist project whose basic parameters did not change. SEP teachers were asked the same questions in 1938 as in 1928. In 1928, SEP inspectors queried teachers on how many children knew how to read, write, and speak Spanish (Sáenz 1970:12–13). What did they know about Mexico, its heroes, its president? Did the school have a flag? Did the children tend a garden, have water, raise chickens, pigs, or bees? Had the teacher undertaken social work outside the school providing medicine or agricultural advice? In 1938, similar questions indicated the SEP's expanded role in community life. What new crops, tools, farming methods, and livestock strains had teachers introduced? Was production cooperatively organized and were profits invested in further production? How many trees had been planted?

How many agricultural and livestock competitions had been sponsored? Did the school have a clinic, a barber shop, baths and bathrooms? Were there sports fields and playgrounds? What human diseases had been tackled? How many home visits had the teacher made to improve household organization and child rearing? Had the teacher introduced potable water or public laundries, organized women into anti-alcohol and hygienic crusades? Had the teacher sponsored the introduction of a post office, telephones and telegraphs, electricity? How many kilometers of roads had been built? Had the public park been "beautified?" Did the school have a library and a theater for the promotion of national culture?[2]

Mexican revolutionary educators rejected social Darwinism. They spurned the theories of biological racism flourishing in Western intellectual circles. The revolution forced them to abandon such ideas. A leveling, democratizing movement, it demanded a democratic response. But the educators' rejection of genetic inferiority was prefaced on an alternative expression of hierarchy. The indigenous and mixed races were decadent and deformed by oppression. They were "easy elements for agitation in the continuous convulsions which have plagued Mexico's independent life."[3] Their saving grace was that they were educable.

"Let us take the campesino under our wing," said José Vasconcelos, the flamboyant founder and first minister of the SEP (1950:12). "Let us teach him to increase his production through the use of better tools and methods." Infantilizing campesinos, educators denied them knowledge, culture, and rationality. The SEP assumed that peasants had no information to contribute to their own transformation. Enlightenment came from abroad and from the cities. What teachers were expected to "know" about a rural society was defined by the need to harness it to the national project: local geography, natural resources, production, disease, diet, clothing, religious beliefs and aesthetics (Vaughan 1982:179–89).

For Moisés Sáenz, SEP undersecretary from 1925 to 1928 and a former student of John Dewey at Columbia Teachers' College, the rural Mexican was an enslaved peon whom the school would convert into a farmer. The Indian was an even greater challenge: "Mute—two million of them do not speak our language—submerged in the childish dream of their illusions, incapable of and unwilling to understand the white man's civilization" (Sáenz 1970:29). "Above all," he wrote, "the school has to teach these creatures how to live" (1928:24). Campesinos were ignorant, rude, inefficient, violent, and beset with vices. They did not properly disinfect or select seeds for planting. They misapplied water. By felling trees, they destroyed the soil. The men drank too much, wasted their time with blood sports and religious celebrations, married too young, and abused their wives. The wives kept animals in the house and let their children go about dirty and undernourished. All carried absurd beliefs in curanderos, witches, priests, and miracles. All customs, beliefs, and ideas that undermined the improvement of "productive capacity" had to be swept aside, wrote Rafael Ramírez, architect of the SEP's Misiones Culturales.[4]

THE POLITICAL UNDERPINNINGS OF RADICALIZING DISCOURSE

In the 1920s, the SEP was in the hands of conservative urban social reformers and pedagogues influenced by U.S. social science. Policy emphasized integrating rural communities into the market economy by introducing new skills and behaviors, product diversification, and cooperatives. Isolation was perceived to be the problem, rather than structures of power that limited peasant access to land, capital, and trade (Vaughan 1982:165–89). Similarly, while committed to nation-building, the SEP was undecided on the nature of national culture and lacked mechanisms for promoting it. In the early 1920s, although the SEP gave lip service to the rich aesthetics of indigenous culture and promoted a rage for serapes, metates, and *huipiles* among Mexico City intellectuals, it distributed the Greek classics to remote hamlets. Musicians and folklorists began to gather up local artistic traditions and publish them through the SEP while mural artists Diego Rivera, José Clemente Orozco, and David Alfaro Siqueiros painted a radically new notion of Mexico as brown, popular, and revolutionary. However, little of this representation was disseminated to rural schools.[5]

A shift took place in educational policy at the end of the 1920s as the SEP became involved in the redistribution of resources, the articulation of a national popular culture, and the processes of party- and state-building. The shift coincided with the formation of the Partido Nacional Revolucionario and with mounting tensions in Mexican society. Formed in the midst of the Great Depression, the PNR was an amalgam of army officers and civilian politicians. Some state governors in the party had organized followings, but the PNR itself had no national popular base. The Confederación Regional Obrera Mexicana (CROM), the national workers' confederation, disintegrated as it lost state backing. Workers began to form new independent organizations as the depression hit mines, industrial centers, and ports. Campesinos were divided. Many were disenchanted, either because of the absence of land reform or out of hostility to the state's antireligious policies. In 1926, the attack on the Catholic Church launched by President Calles had provoked the Cristiada, a major peasant rebellion against the government centered in western Mexico.[6]

In the absence of a popular national base, regional political machines that incorporated workers and peasants through populist programs and rhetoric became models for PNR party-building. These movements relied on teachers not simply as action-oriented pedagogues but as political organizers of peasants and workers. Teachers were also cultural ideologues, crafting unity and legitimacy through the use of song, dance, theater, and oratory, matching new revolutionary heroes and causes to local myth, legend, and artistic expression. The quintessential cultural political machine was that of Tomás Garrido Canabal in Tabasco (Martínez Assad 1979; Tostado Gutiérrez 1991). His Partido Socialista Radical Tabasqueño buried any serious programs of structural reform under a rhetoric of liberation from backwardness and oppression. It lambasted the Catholic Church—conducting ceremonies to burn relics and pillory priests and replacing religious festival with agricultural and livestock fairs. Other populist movements were more committed to land and labor reform: those of Felipe Carrillo Puerto in Yucatán from 1918 to 1922 (Joseph 1982), Francisco Mújica in Michoacán from 1921 to 1923, Adalberto Tejeda in Veracruz from 1920 to 1932, and Emilio Portes Gil in Tamaulipas (Fowler-Salamini 1982, 1990). These movements shared anarchist rhetoric: they would liberate Mexicans from servitude—class, gender, ideological, and corporal. In addition to promoting land reform, worker rights, and cooperatives, they sponsored the organization of women and coeducation; hygiene, sports, and anti-alcohol campaigns to "liberate" the body; and strident anticlericalism to destroy the religiosity that shackled the mind and numbed the will. Their anarchist faith in "rationality" led to a reification of "science."

In 1928, General Lázaro Cárdenas as governor of Michoacán applied the lessons and tactics of these movements to win his compatriots from their allegiance to the Catholic rebellion. He formed the Confederación Revolucionaria Michoacana del Trabajo to mobilize workers and peasants. Teachers were its principal organizers (Raby 1976:202–10, 216; Romero Flores 1948:68–69; Becker 1995:48–60). Governor Cárdenas distributed four hundred thousand hectares of land to twenty-four thousand ejidatarios. Spending 40 percent of his budget on education, he required schools to have sports fields, parcels for cultivation, and theaters for civic festival. He established three centers for technical training for indigenous farmers. Fighting on often hostile *cristero* terrain, teachers fashioned an ideology of liberation from feudal landlords, beguiling priests, and foreign exploiters.

Other regional teachers' corps clamored for a more radical pedagogy linked to land reform. In Coahuila, teachers had been organizing villagers and hacienda workers to press for land in the rich La Laguna region, where conservative state governors protected large landowners (Silva Valdés 1990: 39–68). In Jalisco, teachers were radicalized through bitter experience with the cristero movement. As in Michoacán, many Jalisco teachers saw the Cristiada as a manipulation by the church, ally of the hacendados and other reactionary forces. The SEP had to counter with a pedagogy of radical material reforms—land distribution—and an unmasking of the "counterrevolutionary" force of religion (Yankelevich 1985:33–35).

SEP technical cadres nurtured this thinking. Under the leadership of Rafael Ramírez, the Cultural Missions became mobile teacher training institutes and conduits for the radicalization of policy. Also influential were early SEP missionaries who had risen in the bureaucracy to command SEP offices in the states and rural normal schools. Men such as Elpidio López, Raul Isidro Burgos, Jesús Romero Flores, José Santos Valdés, Rafael Molina Betancourt, and others had been radicalized and had matured through their experiences in the countryside. The conferences they participated in, such as the SEP Asamblea Nacional de Educación in 1930 and the Congreso de Directores de Educación y Jefes de Misiones Culturales in 1932, called for more ambitious policies. Rural education should satisfy economic needs by transforming systems of production and distributing wealth with collectivist ends.[7]

Narciso Bassols, SEP minister from October 1931 to May 1934, nationalized the educational practices of regional populist politicians and operationalized the predilections of SEP technical cadres. He did so by casting policy within an international critique of liberal individualism unleashed by the depression. An engineer and a Marxist, he blamed capitalism for poverty and looked to the state to resolve market irrationalities. The state would redistribute wealth and mobilize the collectivity for modernity through technology applied to production and through science applied to physical and mental health. The government would create a secular, patriotic culture antithetical to the church. Bassols neither minced words nor tolerated ambivalence. He viewed religion as an instrument that was choking the masses. With materialist certainty, he stated: "Modern man has faith in his own power to destroy evil. The other faith is dead." (Bassols:1964:48, 119–311; SEP 1932a:103–5, 217–18).

Under Bassols, action pedagogy became group activity in the form of campaigns for productivist, hygienic, redistributive, and ideological goals within and outside the school. Notions of health and physical education drew from contemporary Western ideas of eugenics, racial fitness, and domestic science that could be used to promote the physical prowess of individuals, collectivities, and the nation. Bassols' promotion of a national civic culture came from Mexico's populist political machines and was implicitly tied to regional and national party-building. His support for land reform as a prerequisite for development and as a complement to the school situated him on the official political left. He had authored the Agrarian Law of 1927 and would help to write the Agrarian Code of 1934, opening land to hacienda resident workers. Entering the cabinet of President Ortiz Rubio (1929–1932), who tried to end land reform, and serving under Abelardo Rodríguez (1932–1934), who accelerated it, Bassols represented the ascendancy of the agrarista left, which led to the choice of Cárdenas as PNR presidential candidate in December 1933.[8]

Bassols expanded mechanisms for teacher preparation and mobilization. To improve competence in agriculture, he merged several Escuelas Rurales Normales with the Escuelas Centrales Agrícolas. Cultural Missions joined these institutions so that teachers could practice their skills in hands-on community development. Instruction in domestic economy, health, and hygiene intensified. More women teachers were recruited. The system of SEP inspectors was expanded and improved. Equipped with normal school degrees, inspectors trained teachers in bimonthly Centros de Cooperación Pedagógica. Most innovative was *El Maestro Rural*, the SEP's bimonthly magazine. To improve technical skills, the journal carried articles by normal school instructors, health professionals, and rural teachers on how to build latrines, organize cooperatives, select seeds, apply fertilizers, and improve children's diets and mothers' cooking. The magazine engaged teachers in the creation of a national civic culture; they contributed articles on music, dance, and theater from their localities. Teachers composed and published morality plays attacking problems like alcoholism and slovenliness and creating a cast of satanic characters upon whose graves the new liberated nation would rise: greedy hacendados, usurous merchants, and domineering priests. *El Maestro Rural* also mobilized teachers for advocacy of land reform, cooperativism, and government assistance for production and marketing.[9] Misiones Culturales, Escuelas Rurales Normales, Escuelas Centrales Agrícolas, and regional federal teachers' corps often spearheaded peasant organization for land (Raby 1976:114; Civera 1993).

Teachers also led the state's penetration of business establishments—haciendas, plantations, mines, and factories. Article 123 of the Constitution of 1917 mandated employer establishment of schools but left enforcement up to the states. In the early 1930s, the SEP took control of existing Article 123 schools and created hundreds more in order to ensure the implementation of the Federal Labor Law of 1931 obliging owners to provide protection and benefits to workers. Teachers became vanguard agents of the state in its efforts to penetrate the space of private capital and secure an arbitrating role between management and labor. At the same time, they were to organize workers into new associations.[10]

As teachers helped to forge campesino and worker associations, the SEP sought to organize them into their own worker organization in order to ensure bureaucratic control over a proliferating, dispersed teacher union movement. Out of the merger between the Unión de Directores e Inspectores Federales de Educación, formed in 1930, and two other teachers' unions came the Confederación Mexicana de Maestros in March 1932. In the heady ambience of the early 1930s, the CMM was immediately challenged by politically ambitious and more radical organizations averse to SEP domination and to Bassols (Raby 1976:70–77). Marxist in thought, Bassols was autocratic in style. In part, his snarls with unions in Mexico City forced his resignation in May 1934 (Britton 1976: vol. 1, 70–97).

So did his attack on religion. In his ministry, religion for the first time became an explicitly defined enemy. Although accords had been signed between the state and the church ending the cristero war in 1929, in 1930 hostilities flared when Pope Pius XI published an encyclical establishing the superiority of Christian education. Bassols moved to control and secularize urban private schools. He inflamed Catholic sensibilities by promoting co-education. He argued it was the natural and progressive way to eliminate artificial, discriminatory barriers between the sexes. He set up a committee to review a proposal from the Mexican Eugenics Society to introduce sex education to schools. The proposal came out of a resolution passed by the Sixth Pan-American Congress of the Child, held in Lima in 1930. The Eugenics Society argued that sex education would ensure the nation's moral and physical health. Freud had determined that children were sexual beings, and the circumstances of modern life made puberty a sexually dangerous, critical stage in the life cycle. Sexuality had to be understood, regulated, and controlled for purposes of individual, family, and societal development (SEP 1934a:14–15; Britton 1976: vol. 1, 97–115; Meneses Morales 1986:629–32.)

Catholics did not see it the same way. They were morally outraged at the pretensions of the state and its "incompetent" agents to teach matters that belonged only to the family and church. They equated the proposal with Soviet despotism and labeled it a virus of moral degeneration and unimaginable perversion. They faced their virtue off against the state's attempt to cre-ate a new secular morality. The issues of secularizing Catholic schools and of promoting coeducation and sex education incurred the wrath of Catholic groups, notably the Unión Nacional de Padres de Familia, which was well organized in Mexican cities. The political right controlled the discourse over family values. Hysteria about impending moral cataclysm spread like wild-fire in 1933. The theaters of Mexico City packed with people shouting alle-giance to Cristo Rey, and in western Mexico, the cristero war threatened to reignite. In May 1934, Bassols was forced to resign as Minister of Education (SEP 1934a:57–58, 1932b:103–4; Britton 1976: vol. 1, 97–114; Meneses Morales 1986:633–45, 620).

The introduction of socialist education as reformed Constitutional Arti-cle 3 reflected the politics of the PNR: a battle between its left and right wings relatively isolated from sentiments in the wider society. In October 1930, the legislature of Tabasco sent a proposal to the National Congress for the adop-tion of the "rational school." In 1932, Veracruz delegates asked Congress to consider an educational reform that would combat capitalism, orient class struggle, and fight religion. In 1933, the Chamber of Deputies appointed Al-berto Bremauntz, a socialist lawyer from Michoacán, to head a commission to draft a reform to Article 3 concerning the role of church and state in edu-cation. Bremauntz had to balance three factions: those who believed educa-tion should be antireligious, those who believed it should be both antireli-gious and redistributive, and those who opposed reform in either direction. The educational platform adopted by the PNR in its Six-Year Plan of Decem-ber 1933 stated that religious teaching would be forbidden in all schools and that scientific rational education based on the postulates of "Mexican social-ism" would be instituted. It was part of a platform of structural reforms af-fecting land, labor, and industry on which PNR candidate Cárdenas ran for the presidency in 1934.[11]

The explicitly antireligious faction gained the upper hand in July 1934 when Jefe Máximo Calles declared cultural war in his Grito de Guadalajara. The revolution, he exclaimed, was not yet over. It had entered the stage of "spiritual" and "psychological conquest." Control had to be secured over the minds of youth. The enemy had to be dislodged from the trenches of educa-tion. "The child belongs to the collectivity." Enacted into law in December 1934, reformed Article 3 established that "education which the State imparts will be socialist and in addition to excluding any religious doctrine, will combat fanaticism and prejudices, for which the school will organize teaching and activities in such a way as to create in youth a rational and exact concept of the Universe and social life."[12]

Out of the SEP under Minister Ignacio García Téllez came the Plan de Acción de la Escuela Socialista. The plan put a Jacobin twist on existing school programs. Although it honored principles of class struggle, suggesting that the curriculum nurture in the child "a sentiment of revulsion against the unjust and ignoble in systems of exploitation," its major thrust was "defanaticization" (SEP 1935:8–11, 24–27). García Téllez enthusiastically supported purges of teachers reluctant to accept the new ideology. He called for the creation of a Social Action Committee in each school. Consisting of teachers, students, parents, authorities, and representatives of worker and campesino organizations, it would carry out defanaticizing campaigns, prepare for land distribution, form cooperatives, and raise class consciousness through conferences, art, and festival. García Téllez issued a school calendar to replace the religious calendar. Fully sixty days were to be dedicated to the heroes and representations of nation and modernity: from Cuauhtemoc, Obregón, and Zapata to the production of fruit, vegetables, metals, and electricity (García Téllez 1935:54, 139–44).

As in an earthquake, Mexican society erupted. Seasoned by years of protest, Catholic groups took to the streets and sparked boycotts in cities and the countryside (e.g., Lerner 1979b:32–57). The explosion helped to destabilize national politics, caught in the throes of a critical battle between the longtime strongman, Calles, and the new president, Cárdenas. Although Cárdenas had promoted antireligious activities while governor of Michoacán from 1928 to 1932, he now found it expedient to retreat from iconoclasm in order to dethrone Calles and rule the country.

In June 1935, Cárdenas demanded the resignation of his Callista cabinet. García Téllez left the SEP. Gonzalo Vázquez Vela, veteran of Adalberto Tejeda's movement in Veracruz, became minister of education. He soft-pedaled the religious question and lent SEP support to Cárdenas in the implementation of extensive land reform, the expansion of trade unionism and worker rights, and the nationalization of key industries.

Socialist education served a project of state integration. It helped Cárdenas to give the ruling party a popular, civilian base. Rather than destroying capitalism, it became part of Cárdenas's effort to eliminate precapitalist obstacles to modernization. It facilitated the formation of national worker, campesino, and teacher organizations (the CTM, the CNC, and the CTM-affiliated Sindicato de Trabajadores de la Enseñanza de la República Mexicana) and their integration into the reformed PNR, the Partido de la Revolución Mexicana.

What was new in rural educational policy under Cárdenas was a cultural and ideological emphasis on popular mobilization and inclusion. Provincial pedagogues experienced in regional radical experiments, such as Gabriel Lucio of Veracruz, and Mexico City Marxist intellectuals, such as Luis Chávez Orozco, left their mark in an outpouring of SEP materials: textbooks, pamphlets, theater, and songs. Gone was Bassols' strident collectivism and didactic moralizing. Instead, anarchist precepts stressed group solidarity and grassroots democracy while Marxist notions elucidated structures of exploitation and the dialectics of struggle. Teachers were to join forces with campesinos to ensure land reform, higher wages, loans, and fair prices. Action education became a vehicle for the politics of oppressed groups. Projects were to aim at increased production and a redistribution of wealth. The teacher was to explain local and national structures of property and power. Arithmetic problems calculated the excess profits of factory owners. Geography teaching explained ownership and use of regional resources and elucidated the impact of imperialist exploitation of Mexico's natural wealth.

After 1938, Cárdenas clipped the SEP's radical wings. Following his expropriation of oil in March 1938, he moderated his policies under pressure from foreign businessmen and governments, national entrepreneurs, and sectors in the PNR and wider society. To defeat Calles, he had allied with conservative—as well as progressive—groups in the PNR. In May 1938, one such conservative ally, General Saturnino Cedillo, rebelled against him. For months, U.S. diplomats had been expecting Cedillo to lead a Fascist coup backed by Catholics and property owners. The government was able to contain the revolt because in March 1938, Cárdenas made major concessions to the country's predominantly conservative governors. He granted them greater control over land and education. Plans for full federalization of primary education were postponed. Governors repressed radical teachers' movements. The SEP Cultural Missions were closed in response to criticism of their agitational character. State governors began to articulate a notion of socialist education as a means of socioeconomic improvement within a setting of class conciliation. Cárdenas's successor, Manuel Avila Camacho, was a moderate, interested in capitalist growth. Abandoning the promotion of "class struggle," rural educational policy returned to an emphasis on improvement through group projects. The potential for implementing policy was enhanced by state consolidation and the proliferation of government institutions promoting production, credit, consumption, and health.

SHIFTING IDENTITIES: NATIONAL HISTORY, CITIZENSHIP, AND CULTURE

Between 1920 and 1940, rural educational policy altered notions of Mexican history, citizenship, and national culture in curriculum, textbooks, and cultural representations for civic ritual. The new notions were constructed out of the interaction between the SEP and rural society within the context of state formation via populist party-building. They were the product of the educators' imaginations, ideologies, and interests. Rural society provided the primary source material, which educators interpreted, packaged, and returned to rural people. The following pages explore the SEP's shifting constructions.

NATIONAL HISTORY

In the 1920s, the SEP published no textbooks to establish an official revolutionary vision of Mexican history. Those texts it recommended were written primarily by pedagogues trained in the Porfiriato. They viewed the revolution as the breakdown of order and the unleashing of barbarism. Porfirio Díaz had brought unity and progress to a miserably divided and backward Mexico. The revolution destroyed his work. "Never had so much blood been spilled! Never had the Mexican family been so divided!" wrote Gregorio Torres Quintero in his *Patria Mexicana* (1923:174, 180). In his reader, *Adelante,* Daniel Delgadillo painted an idyllic picture of the countryside in the Porfiriato. Shepherds and peons went off to the fields, women gracefully balanced water jugs on their heads, and the countryside basked in the "grandeur of God." For Delgadillo, the revolution was not something peasants made, but a terror foisted upon them by invading, raucous armies (1920:22–23, 43–44, 105, 214).[13]

Textbook writers of the 1920s understood the revolution as a movement geared to restoring political liberties. They glossed over the issue of social causation and abhorred social movements. The rebellious insolence of workers and peasants had to be curbed by a strong leader. Historian Rafael Aguirre Cinta (1926:365–66) wrote in praise of President Obregón: "[He] tried to conciliate . . . the interests of owners and workers, who inflamed by the preachings of false redeemers, wasted time and energies in strikes and protests, without understanding that they could only obtain better benefits and comforts by educating themselves, preparing for struggle for life in school, in order to achieve a just compensation for their labor according to their effort, aptitude, and in exact fulfillment of their obligations."

He praised Obregón for repressing "the so-called agrarista leaders, who have only managed to damage our incipient agricultural industries with their disruptive preachings."

Yet the writers could not avoid the social issues raised by the revolution. In his civics text, José María Bonilla had to explain the redistributive clauses of the Constitution: Article 27 on land reform and Article 123 on workers' rights (Bonilla 1918a:10, 13, 202; 1918b:13, 98, 141–42). He said they were intended to secure order by state mediation of conflict. In explaining Article 27, he emphasized that the initiative for land redistribution lay with the government, not communities, and that action had to follow due process. The purpose of Article 123 was to protect workers "without killing the goose that lay the golden eggs, i.e., without depriving capital of the guarantees it needs for conservation and prosperity." He warned against independent workers' actions and socialist theories, which would have negative results "contrary to the principles of justice." The nation could not afford to substitute for the "despotism of money . . . unbridled ignorance and low passions."

In the 1920s, the mural art movement led by Diego Rivera and José Clemente Orozco painted a different revolution. They celebrated violence and gave it a clear logic and purpose. Orozco depicted the naked suffering of the peasantry in revolutionary struggle and the hypocrisy and cruelty of an oppressive ruling class. Diego Rivera's portrayal of the sugar plantation destroyed Daniel Delgadillo's rural idyll. In Rivera's mural, the merciless overseer whipped the backs of workers; sweat streamed from their brawny arms as they strained to squeeze sap from cane. Rivera painted dense collectivities of workers and peasants, dark-skinned, armed, and resolute in their demands for a redress of grievances. The enemy was transparent: the hacendado, the plantation manager, the Rockefellers, the Porfirian elites. The solutions were evident: land reform, worker rights, and technology in the hands of producers. The tactics were spelled out: strikes, class war, and organization. Celebrating the leveling and liberating aspects of the revolution, the members of the Revolutionary Syndicate of Painters created art to deepen class consciousness, awaken struggle, and depict a prominent place for the subaltern classes and indigenous peoples as agents of Mexican history. This art met with a flurry of disgusted reaction in Mexico City. Students defaced the murals and slashed them with knives, Catholic ladies rallied against them, and the majority of Mexico City intellectuals shuddered.[14]

The muralists' art entered the SEP's rural curriculum in the form of illustrations in the 1929 publication of *Fermín*, one of the first readers to focus on rural life. Written by the pedagogue Manuel Velázquez Andrade, *Fermín* told of the son of a peon who lived in a hut on a hacienda owned by a man who lived a life of luxury in the city. Whereas Delgadillo had situated the hacienda manager as a kind parent in his home, Velázquez Andrade's overseer was a scowling man who abused the workers. Fermín's family lived a miserable existence circumscribed by heavy labor, arbitrary treatment, and inflated prices at the company store. In 1911, Fermín's father joined the revolution to fight for land and justice against foreign exploiters, the rich, and the clergy. Revolutionary events were woven fictionally into tales of family life as Fermín and his mother suffered food shortages, the overseer's increasing repression, and forced levies of workers into the army. Although Fermín's father appeared to be a Zapatista, the author was faithful to official interpretations of the revolution. He pictured the father fighting with workers and schoolteachers for the Constitutionalist cause. As a result of the 1915 Constitutionalist decree on land reform, he became a renter on the hacienda with the promise of receiving ejido land. Fermín himself became a delegate to the Constitutional Convention of 1917, where he championed Articles 27 and 123. He went on to become a leader in his village. In 1929, Velázquez Andrade advised him to keep his rifle, for there were enemies lurking, communities to be organized, and a legacy to be vindicated and preserved (Velázquez Andrade [1929] 1986:11–20, 43–70, 102–25).

Fermín marked the beginning of the SEP's construction of the Mexican Revolution as a popular movement. To greater and lesser degrees, texts of the 1930s embraced dialectical materialism and rewrote history as the evolution of productive forces, class formation, and struggle. Porfirio Díaz became a dictator who had favored foreign investors over national development, sponsored hacienda expansion at the expense of campesinos, and permitted the exploitation of a nascent working class (Castro Cancio 1935:238–41). The revolution's causes were social as well as political. Its protagonists were peasants and workers. Zapata, a mere bandit for Rafael Aguirre Cinta, became a revolutionary hero. From the Wars of Independence, writers rescued General José María Morelos as the progenitor of social democracy and agrarianism (Castro Cancio 1935:150).

The Constitution became the implantation of "socialist" principles on a liberal base. The historian Teja Zabre summarized these principles as betterment for the working class; recognition of its right to organize and to intervene "moderately" in the direction of production; land reform, which limited private property in the public interest; state intervention to regulate capital and to promote health, education, and welfare; and the emancipation of women. To these, text writer Jorge Castro Cancio added nationalization of natural resources. Teja Zabre defined the revolution's goals as "equalization," "socialization," and economic development. Both writers interpreted the Cárdenas presidency as the fulfillment of the revolution's "radical" tendencies in a popular front based upon democratic norms (Castro Cancio 1935: 273; Teja Zabre 1935:248–52).

The 1930s textbooks and rural curriculum altered the notion of agency in Mexican history. Concepts of rebellion, struggle, and the right to social justice were etched into the core of the Mexican cultural nation and legitimized as intrinsic to national identity. Historians of the 1920s had consistently looked to paternalistic rulers to civilize society and guide it in a progressive direction—whether these were Aztec kings, colonial viceroys, or Porfirio Díaz. For them, Indians in the colony were little more than "beasts of burden," inhabiting "another world" where they vegetated in "a complete state of ignorance and abandon" (Bonilla 1923:115–16). "Resigned to their religious fiestas," historians explained, "they spent the little they saved and maintained the superstitions and idolatries they had practiced before the Conquest" (Sierra 1922:63). By contrast, historians of the 1930s portrayed the subaltern from pre-Colombian times to the present as energetic workers who created wealth under oppressive conditions and active subjects who sought justice through association and struggle.

In the 1930s, peasant and worker as agents of history were abstracted out of real social conflict. Their outrage was channeled and alleviated by new state institutions. However, as constructions in a new Mexican history, they could be used to legitimate popular claims. While incorporated into a discourse seeking hegemony, they were the kernel for the composition of counterhegemonic discourse, or at least of protest and resistance. Fermín, after all, had been urged to keep his gun.

CITIZENSHIP

Between the 1920s and 1930s, the SEP's textbooks refashioned the Mexican social subject, moving from an almost exclusive focus on the urban middle-class family to target, in the case of rural schools and texts, the campesino family. This refashioning was radically inclusive. It involved a shift from an exclusively urban setting to a rural one; from middle-class to poor families; from the privileging of hierarchy to an affirmation of equality; from a posture of intense discipline and control to one of greater freedom and flexibility; from a highly restricted notion of privatized, individual citizenship to an inclusive notion of public, group citizenship.

In the 1920s, Daniel Delgadillo's reader, *Adelante*, centered on families of the modest urban middle sector. In these patriarchal nests, women were subservient and never left the house. Problems and strife were absent. Children helped and obeyed their parents and studied. References to children from richer and poorer strata encouraged charity toward the poor and acceptance of the rich. Depicting the modest home of a bureaucrat, his wife, and his daughters, Delgadillo noted, "Ah! How certain it is that happiness does not always consist of riches!" Social mobility was possible through conformity, hard work, and education. The family was insulated from all forms of political activity and association: worker unions were portrayed as discouraging individual initiative and talent (Delgadillo 1920:30–31, 24–25, 127).

Children were kept on short leashes at home and in school. They were considered prone to evil—dirtiness, greed, dishonesty, laziness, ingratitude, disobedience, and disrespect. They needed strict discipline. "El hijo obediente y bueno, / Se verá de bienes lleno" (The good and obedient child will be rewarded) rhymed the author. "¡Trabaja y vencerás!" (Work hard and you shall triumph!) He condemned anger, pride, and envy, the seeds of contestatory citizenship. "Quien tiene caridad y una alma pura, De las faltas ajenas no murmurá" (He who has charity and a pure soul will never criticize others). He exalted heroism as sacrifice to God and country. "Da por tu patria la vida" (Give your life for your country), he exhorted (Delgadillo 1920:40–41, 49–52, 65–72, 81–88, 110–12).

Manuel Velázquez Andrade's *Fermín* shattered this portrait. It moved the campesino child and family to center stage. It described the misery of class hierarchy and the struggle of the poor to improve their lives through arms and politics. *Fermín* marked the beginning of a torrent of campesino-focused textbooks and didactic material (pamphlets, theatrical productions, corridos) flowing from the sep in the 1930s. The new rural subject was the ejidatario family, recipient of government land. The construction of family sought a modernization of patriarchy at the familial, communal, and regional levels.

The vertical, precapitalist system of power that shackled the adult male campesino had to be replaced with horizontal, national solidarities and linkages. These would liberate him from his oppressive providers—landlords, merchants, and priests. His production would be commercialized, reorganized in cooperatives, and traded through national marketing mechanisms. The traditional networks were sealed by an alcoholic, religious, and machista sociability that crushed and deformed him. Male sociability would be sanitized and nationalized. A flood of sep skits, plays, poems, and songs condemned the use of alcohol and begged the campesino to turn his back on the priest, superstition, and religious festival. The priest took his hard-earned pesos in fees. Saints' days squandered his energies and capital.[15]

He had to forfeit blood sports and womanizing—both identified with violence and bodily degeneration. When the SEP constructed Zapata as a hero, they sanitized him: he did not drink, womanize, or gamble, nor did he carry the banner of the Virgin of Guadalupe. The snappy horseman from Tlaltizapán, who enjoyed a match of fighting cocks and had fathered many children in his short life, became a didactic articulator of SEP values. As an adult, Fermín too epitomized the SEP's model of virility. After attending school, he became a commercial farmer, introducing new seeds and machinery and practicing soil and water conservation. He emerged as the local authority on agrarian matters, and he organized patriotic festivals. In his spare time, he read newspapers and history books and listened to music on his victrola.[16]

Team sports—basketball and baseball—became the panacea for masculine degeneration. Replacing alcohol, blood sports, and violence, they would promote health, cooperation, and competition. They would stimulate horizontal competitions between communities, between regions, and at the state and national levels, so as to build national identity and citizenship.

The Ten Commandments of the Ejidatario, published in *El Maestro Rural* in 1933, recommended that in ejidal affairs, the campesino should avoid "politics, gossip, and nepotism."[17] The disciplinary prescriptions eased in the Cárdenas period as the principle of class struggle privileged collective action over moralizing. Texts promoted organization for redress of grievances, production, and consumption. They examined the issues involved in running ejido Comisiones de Vigilancia and Consejos de Administración and prescribed how to conduct meetings, organize strikes, keep accounts, introduce new crops and tools, and guard against *caciquismo* (boss rule).Through the SEP's construction, the ejidatario became a cooperative producer, a member of his ejido, and a voting citizen of the Mexican nation. He also became part of a social class. He was no longer just Juan Quevedo from San José Tenopa, bound to sustain a centuries-old blood feud with his neighbors in San Juan Tilapa. Those neighbors, like him, were members of the same social class— and the same class organization, the CNC or CTM.

SEP texts and curriculum also sought to curb what was purported to be Juan Quevedo's excessive and irrational control over his wife and children. The SEP promoted linkages between female schoolteachers and campesina wives, independent of their husbands, to foster healthier conditions of reproduction. Women professionals and SEP technicians designed policies for reproductive reform based upon the latest European "domestic science," in the hope of producing more robust children and preparing women for participation in the modern world as more autonomous social subjects. Early marriages of girls just entering puberty had to be curbed. All marriages had to be registered with the state. The campesina mother would learn more nutritious ways of feeding her family, adopt modern medicines and vaccines, and abjure *curanderas*, witchcraft, and useless herbs. She would regularly bathe her children and wash their clothing. Soap had to be made, latrines built, garbage burned, flies swatted, and water boiled. Pigs, chickens, and dogs were to be banished from family living quarters and a door built to bar their entrance. The smoke from the *tecuile*, the earthen hearth, was to disappear with the construction of a waist-level stove and chimney: these would preserve women's backs, purify the air, and reduce accidents. Windows were to be introduced and paned to let in light. The living space was to be partitioned into kitchen, salon, and sleeping quarters, and urban furniture was to be adopted—beds, full-size chairs, tables, benches—along with knives, forks, and spoons to replace the tortillas with which many ate food.[18]

The installation of mechanical corn-grinding mills, sewing machines, and water sources closer to home would reduce women's work and release them for activities outside the home. SEP officials Eliseo Bandala and Rafael Ramírez calculated that women spent an average of ten to twelve hours a day grinding corn for tortillas, sewing, and laundering. In 1933, these officials vowed to fight the "quijotismo" and male pride that scorned women as income earners, because their remunerative activities were necessary to supplement the meager income of campesino men. From the early 1920s, the SEP hoped to instruct women in small industries, crafts, and food preservation, and in the 1930s it prescribed organizing the marketing of these products through cooperatives.[19]

The SEP did not relegate women to a docile space marginal to civic life and citizenship. Although Mexican women did not vote in national elections until 1958, several states encouraged their voting in municipal and state elections in the 1930s. Simultaneously, the SEP called upon women to take up public roles as guardians of community health and socializers of children. Educators sought to nurture a new feminine sociability linked to civic, secular action. Women would gather not to dress the Virgin but to undertake crusades against alcohol, dirt, and disease. They were to organize school festivals and serve on the PTA.[20]

Children were a privileged part of the SEP's construct. They gained in power, mobility, and space in textbooks and curriculum between 1920 and 1940. Campesino children would be mobilized for national development through the school—a space under state dominion independent of parents and church. Here, boys and girls would learn together through cooperative, scientific gardening and marketing, 4-H clubs, team sports, theatrical performances, and folkloric dance groups. The text *Simiente*, written by SEP undersecretary Gabriel Lucio in 1935, described cooperative learning and democratic process. In one school, a student commission wanted to build an open-air theater. To do so, they had to dig up a row of bananas planted by the school cooperative. A vigorous debate ensued, in an assembly, between students who wished to preserve the bananas to enrich the cooperative and those who argued that the theater would benefit the entire community. When the latter opinion prevailed, the teacher praised the children for preferring a project of benefit to all. The texts indicated appropriate political forms for airing opinions and arriving at consensus. As the children organized to build the theater, they elected a director who later insulted one of the members. In another assembly, the students removed the abusive director.[21]

In contrast to the 1920s texts' insistence on silence and obedience in children, activity, controversy, and dissent were privileged in the texts and programs of the 1930s, especially under the Cárdenas presidency. The stiffness and formality of *Adelante*'s classroom and the moralizing prescriptions of the Bassols period yielded to greater spontaneity and group work. As children from an urban school went off to visit the countryside, they talked, laughed, skipped, and yelled. The teacher acted as a guide, assisting students in cultivating gardens, introducing a new strain of bees, and setting up libraries. The children had "cariño" for the teacher. Rather than punishing a child for his or her lack of punctuality, the teacher asked the student to reflect on the consequences of tardiness for himself and others. In contrast to the days of *Adelante,* the attitudes of teachers to children ceased to be punitive and the children's world expanded beyond the classroom into a larger social and natural order they could participate in, control, and criticize (SEP 1938b:88).

THE CULTURAL NATION

These children were exposed to an increasingly diverse, multiethnic notion of the Mexican cultural nation. Since 1921, when José Vasconcelos as the first minister of education had launched the cultural nationalist movement, the SEP had championed the aesthetics of Mexican culture.[22] The mural movement redefined the Mexican as Indian, brown, mestizo, mulatto. Although Mexico City's Europeanized intellectuals shuddered, this coloring of the Mexican took hold as the state-building phase of the revolution progressed in the 1920s and 1930s. The revolution made the darkening of the prototypical citizen necessary. That the state and party recognized and built upon this was to their credit. It was one of the most significant achievements of the revolution.

The cultural nationalist movement relied as much on the talent of the provincial middle class as it did on Mexico City artists. The elaboration of a repertoire of national music engaged not only Mexico City classical composers such as Manuel Ponce, but provincial musicians, who had begun their careers playing in hometown orchestras. They were part of an emerging civic aesthetic created by and benefiting the incipient middle class in the Porfiriato. Those who shared this aesthetic were national in their cultural orientation. At the same time, they had a unique grasp of local artistic expression. Following a professional path through municipal, state, and military bands in the revolution, musicians like Estanislao Mejía of Tlaxcala and Candelario Huizar García de la Cadena of Jerez, Zacatecas, found themselves teaching at the National Conservatory in the 1920s (Velázquez del Albo 1992). Here, they engaged both in the composition of a Mexican classical music based upon folkloric themes and in the compilation of Mexican popular musical and dance traditions (indigenous, mestizo, mulatto, and creole). They became the collective, often anonymous authors of a new national culture based upon a potpourri of local and regional art. Rubén Campos's compilation *El folklore y la música mexicana,* published by the SEP in 1928, was a work of cultural rescue and creation that became a repertoire to be disseminated through the schools.

Acting as foot soldiers in the cultural nationalist movement were the SEP teachers and staff of the Misiones Culturales and the Escuelas Rurales Normales. They transcribed local dances, many of explicitly religious origin. They recorded indigenous legends, mestizo folktales, and scores of corridos celebrating love, tragedy, and rebellion. They published these works in *El Maestro Rural,* for use elsewhere in civic festival so central to the federal rural school in the 1930s in its effort to outcompete the church and form the official party. They invented revolutionary corridos and plays, which they filled with lessons on sobriety and with rhetoric championing agrarianism and lambasting the church. They turned Zapata into the official civic hero.[23]

In the production of such works, they moved beyond the civic culture of the Porfiriato with its martial airs and European operatic arias to incorporate the often collectively authored art of communities. Simultaneously, they created a national teachers' culture, informed by *El Maestro Rural*'s reproduction of Diego Rivera's swarthy workers, Leopoldo Méndez's woodcuts of popular city life, Fermín Revueltas's allegoric murals depicting "the people enchained," "the Revolution," and "the bourgeoisie," and Fernando Leal's portraits of Latin American liberators.[24]

The result was a nationalization of popular culture as Nahuatl-speaking children in Tlaxcala learned the Yaqui Deer Dance and Tarahumara children learned the criollo *jarabe* of Jalisco. This notion of national, popular culture rested heavily on the achievements of the Indian past and contemporary Indian aesthetics, which were nationalized as symbols, objects, and artifacts. The SEP appropriated them out of their daily context in order to build a common culture. Never abandoned was the notion that although being Mexican rested on strong indigenous cultural foundations, being Mexican meant becoming modern: adopting urban, Western behavior and culture. The educators' notion of modern Mexico appeared to be the antithesis of indigenous society, which was seen as insular, religious, and subsistence-oriented, abjuring the modern market and the Patria.[25]

The seminal moment in the feverish movement to create a national culture was President Cárdenas's nationalization of foreign-owned oil wells in March 1938. Teachers turned this moment into one in which a nation for the first time in its history massively articulated its identity. Teachers mobilized communities, children, and families to support the Mexican nation's assertive stand as a personality on the world stage, recuperating control of her natural resources from foreign usurpers for purposes of national development and social improvement. This mobilization gave shape to a shared, constructed national hope.[26]

～

Revolutionary educators shared a commitment to the incorporation of Mexico into the world of Western nations on a footing more equitable and competitive than had prevailed in the past. Such incorporation required education to transform the behavior, loyalties, and identity of rural Mexicans. Educators differed, however, on the nature of incorporation and on the structure and content of the Mexican nation. Between 1929 and 1938, educational policy was radicalized as a result of the conjunction between the educators' accumulated experience with rural communities and social movements and the massification of official Mexican party-building. Educational policy promoted a redistribution of property and power in favor of workers and campesinos and articulated new, inclusive notions of citizenship and the cultural nation. The next chapter explores how SEP teachers understood and translated this policy in regional contexts.

3

TRANSLATING CULTURAL POLICY
The Mobilization of Federal Teachers in Puebla and Sonora

In the 1930s the Secretaría de Educación Pública had no loyal bureaucracy to ensure uniform policy implementation. Teachers translated policy in regional context. Differences between teacher interpretation in Puebla and Sonora are partially explained by processes and events predating the 1930s: distinct teaching legacies from the Porfiriato and the contrasting paths the revolution took in the two states. In the 1930s, processes of state and party formation in each state shaped teacher interpretation of SEP policy. This chapter discusses these factors and highlights the role of state governors in shaping the conditions within which federal teachers operated in the 1930s. The SEP project was ultimately one between teachers and rural communities, thus the latter are an essential part of the regional space demarcated in this chapter, but their major role and their dialogue with teachers are reserved for subsequent chapters.

During the first half of the 1930s, radical governors in Puebla and Sonora mobilized federal teachers to build statewide PNR organizations based upon an alliance between workers, campesinos, and the progressive middle class. The teachers' real and imagined antireligiosity became grist for conservative movements aimed at destroying these populist projects. Between 1933 and 1937, conservative governors took power in both states at a moment of radical ascendancy in the central government. President Cárdenas directed teachers away from regional party-building to the task of establishing central state hegemony through redistributive policies and the formation of national worker and peasant associations to be integrated into the PNR. As conservative governors sought to control these processes, they obstructed the work of federal teachers or tried to marginalize them.

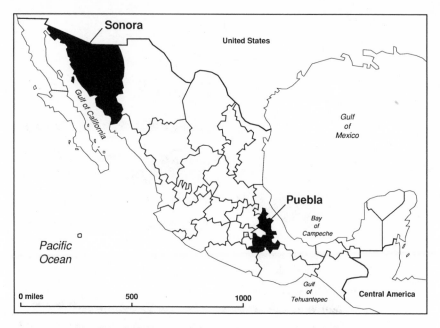

MAP 1   The location of Sonora and Puebla

To a large degree, the margin of maneuver teachers enjoyed depended on Cárdenas's support. The president intervened to protect teachers in Sonora, but not those in Puebla. The difference is explained by the dynamics of national politics. To advance his radical policies, Cárdenas had to defeat Plutarco Elías Calles. As Calles's home state was Sonora, Cárdenas intervened there to establish control over the state. However, to defeat Calles, Cárdenas depended upon conservative allies such as the Avila Camacho family, which took over the Puebla PNR after 1933. Cárdenas did not intervene in Puebla but left the consolidation of popular organizations and party-building up to the Avilacamachistas. The crafting of progressive teacher politics depended on Puebla's SEP leadership and on the teachers themselves.

In both states, teachers faced resistance. Census data show that between 1930 and 1940, despite SEP expansion, youth literacy outside the city of Puebla declined from 41 to 32 percent for boys ages ten to fourteen and from 32 to 30 percent for girls, while in Sonora outside the capital of Hermosillo it fell slightly, from 70 to 65 percent for boys and 72 to 71 percent for girls. Though these statistics must be read with skepticism, they are symptomatic of a difficult decade for schools.[1] Similarly, although the federal portion of school enrollment rose between 1928 and 1940 (from 21 to 52 percent in Puebla and from 12 to 33 percent in Sonora), its growth slowed after 1935. Presidential and SEP hopes for full federalization were disappointed. The SEP came to dominate rural education, but state systems consolidated in cities and county seats. They adopted much of SEP curriculum and method but ultimately avoided its most radical aspects. Nonetheless, the decade can be read as one of intense, often bloody negotiation over the political and cultural dimensions of the SEP project. Through negotiation, federal teachers in both states played a critical role in the creation of institutional, associational, political, and discursive space that linked campesinos to the central state/party in such a way that domination could become hegemonic—that is, inclusive and, to a degree, accommodating of difference and dissent.

PORFIRIAN TEACHING LEGACIES

Porfirian teaching experiences created vocations for teachers, and relations between them and communities, that shaped postrevolutionary practice. In general terms, these experiences can be regionally defined for Puebla and Sonora.

Puebla's Porfirian public schools were strongly marked by the liberal ideology of army officers from the state's Sierra Norte, who defeated the Conservatives in the midcentury civil wars. For their support of Porfirio Díaz in 1876, they were rewarded with the state governorship through the 1880s. These men saw secular schooling and citizenship, republican institutions, and material progress as antidotes to clerical domination, aristocracy, and caste privileges. As governor in 1879, General Juan Crisóstomo Bonilla created Puebla's normal school, the first in Mexico. Its graduates assumed a liberal mission, as did hundreds of teachers who never benefited from its training.[2]

However, Puebla's rural Indian and mestizo communities could only partially (often minimally) appropriate liberal culture. Puebla's was a Catholic society forged on the broad, indigenous base that existed in the sixteenth century. Communities organized themselves around conservative configurations of power: interpenetrating civil and religious authority, communal organization of productive and ritual labor, and familial patriarchy. They lived in precapitalist subordination to haciendas in the center and south of the state and to non-Indian commercial monopolies in the Sierra Norte. Midcentury civil wars, the Liberal victory in 1867, and state consolidation and market expansion under Porfirio Díaz stimulated some secularization. Formally, communal and church lands were privatized, civic rule was separated from religious, and municipal governing institutions, including the school, were reconstructed. However, communities and local powerholders mediated and

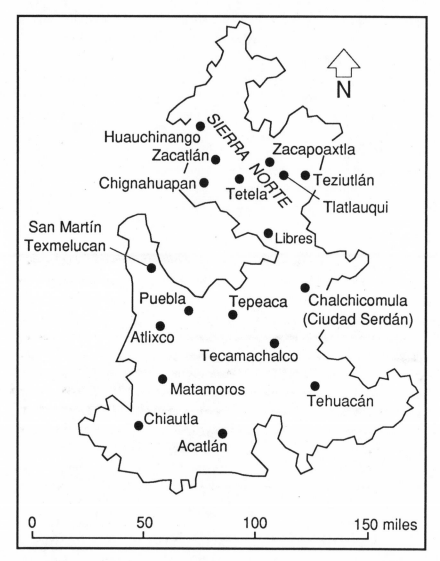

MAP 2   The state of Puebla

tempered secularization in such a way as to restrict the teacher's space and voice.

Schools and teachers were locally controlled. Residents paid for them through taxes, labor, and fines. Local Surveillance Committees (Consejos de Vigilancia) made up of leading citizens were in charge of upkeep and attendance. At annual graduation exercises, a jury of local notables judged the achievements of the teacher on the basis of student oral examinations. Community pressures persuaded teachers to reduce the increasingly elaborate curriculum recommended by state officials to emphasize the teaching of reading, writing, arithmetic, and patriotic history.[3]

Local control of schools and teachers was hierarchical and exclusive. For the most part, the district *jefe político* and officials of the municipal head-towns chose teachers and regulated their behavior. Although pueblos had schools, most haciendas and many smaller population centers known as rancherías or barrios lacked them. Schools for boys were abundant, but schools for girls were few, as were coeducational schools. Poverty, social relations, and cultural mores limited school attendance. In Puebla outside the capital in 1910, literacy for men (over the age of twelve) was only 23 percent; female literacy was 16 percent.[4]

Teachers had to adjust their messages accordingly. One important space that provided a wider audience was civic festival. Under the watchful eye of the jefe político and in conjunction with town councils, teachers organized festival. Civic ritual had special meaning in Puebla because it celebrated the Fifth of May, the day in 1862 when poblano soldiers defeated invading French armies at the city of Puebla. The visceral, local experience of having expulsed the foreign invader rooted the imagined nation. In communities historically defined by collective, symbolic performance, patriotic festival took its place alongside religious celebration in affirming power, cohesion, knowledge, and place. At the same time it articulated new messages about the nation, citizenship, and modernity (Vaughan 1994a).

Representative of poblano teachers was José María Cordero. Son of a hacienda peon, he was a part-time farmer and itinerant teacher of "la buena letra" and "sabe contar" (reading and arithmetic) in towns in western Puebla and Tlaxcala. Although he had no normal school training (he had learned how to read and write from members of a Catholic brotherhood), he was an ardent liberal and believer in "progress." "Our children must evolve," he told his students. "If we have little and suffer, our children must have better things and a better life." His expert violin playing endeared him to communities. He became adept at arranging Cinco de Mayo festivals—preparing the program and speeches and going to Puebla city to buy flags, confetti, fireworks, and pine torches for the parade. For the 1910 centennial celebrations of Mexican independence, Cordero purchased newfangled gas lamps to "iluminar mi tierra" (light up my homeland). He made sure that a portrait of Miguel Hidalgo, the priest who had initiated the independence struggle, got nailed to every door. Thus, they celebrated "el gran libertador . . . de la esclavitud, el lider del movimiento revolucionario de nuestra patria" (the great liberator . . . from slavery, the leader of our country's revolutionary movement).[5]

No doubt, most Sonoran rural teachers shared Cordero's liberal values. They expressed them with less missionary zeal, for in Sonora secular culture was strong—fed by the late-eighteenth-century Spanish settlement of the frontier region, the spectacular growth of its mining economy in the Porfiriato, and the settlers who flocked there to take advantage of it. Survival in the desert had always demanded mobility, and Sonora's rural communities were often more porous and shifting than Puebla's. Porfirian growth accelerated mobility and fostered more open social, class, and gender relations. Although Sonora had its traditional cities, families, and haciendas, by 1900 it was an immigrant society made up of displaced Mexican peasants, Chinese traders, European adventurers, tough miners and cowboys out of the U.S. West, Yankee capitalists, and a multinational force of ladies of the night.[6]

Sonoran society valued literacy as it rapidly became a necessity of life. In 1910, 47 percent of both men and women older than twelve knew how to read and write. Yet, Sonora had no normal school for training teachers. The Colegio de Sonora graduated a handful of students with certificates in pedagogy after 1903, but they served primarily urban schools, as did Normalistas recruited from central Mexico by the governors (Rivera Rodríguez 1975:31–33). Outside the major cities, most teaching remained pragmatic and haphazard. Rural teachers were not necessarily admired or looked up to. Many male teachers were transient, bored, and given to "una vida poco ejemplar" (a less than exemplary life). Schoolteaching was a rite of passage for literate, ambitious young men obliged to pull themselves up by their own bootstraps. Pay was so low that they remained only briefly at the job, or supplemented their income with businesses and public office. Many balked as well at the often arbitrary authority of prefects (Sonora's jefes políticos), municipal presidents, and police commissaries. More admired for their dedication and morality were the women teachers. Handicapped by lack of texts, pens, paper, and maps, by makeshift buildings and sparsely furnished classrooms, they were more likely than men to stick it out fighting the desert dust and heat. They often saw themselves as civilizers of the hard-drinking, hard-gambling, shoot-on-sight frontier.[7]

Although theirs was not as ritualistic a culture as the poblano, Sonoran towns also celebrated patriotic festival. Like that of poblanos, Sonorans' understanding of Mexico was more regional than it was national. The frontier with the United States made them Mexicans. Their connections with the rest of the country were vague. Sonora's railroads were part of the U.S. system,

MAP 3 The state of Sonora

linking it to California, Boston, and New York. Not until after 1909 did Sonoran lines move southward toward Guadalajara (Ruiz 1988:12, 187; McGuire
1986:30).

The other factor that made Sonorans Mexicans was its Indian population.
Most public schoolteachers hardly knew indigenous Sonora; many regarded
assignments to indigenous communities as exile and punishment. Indigenous
communities were not porous but thickly glued by religious, military, political, and familial institutions. They resembled Puebla communities except

that they were tribally organized rather than village-centered. Though there had been a tradition of *mestizaje* (racial mixing) between Indians and Europeans since the seventeenth century, in the last half of the nineteenth century bitter antagonism reigned between the remaining tribes and the settlers who coveted their lands. Sonoran development followed the defeat of the Apaches after 1880. The Mayos surrendered in 1886. Mexican armies waged war against the Yaquis through 1910. Vivid memories of torture and death electrified and defined both sides. Neither Yaquis nor Mayos could accept Mexican schools in the late Porfiriato. Sonoran authorities saw Indian education as punitive. It would "extirpate vices." Schools had to "reconcile them with the white people and kill forever the germs of eternal discord which have produced their incessant rebellion."[8]

TEACHERS IN REVOLUTION

Many teachers in Puebla and Sonora joined the Mexican Revolution. They aimed to further the secular progress being thwarted by backward, arbitrary, and monopolistic power. Organizers for the revolution, many rose through the process to unanticipated political heights (Cockcroft 1967; Morales Jiménez 1986). Onetime Sonoran teachers Alvaro Obregón and Plutarco Elías Calles, for instance, became generals, presidents, and arbiters of national power from 1920 to 1935.[9] What is pertinent to this story is how the course of the revolution in each state shaped the possibilities for SEP teachers and laid the groundwork for their interpretation of SEP policy in the 1930s.

Raised on the principles of nineteenth-century liberalism and fired up by the promise and potential of the revolution, Puebla Normalistas provided strong leadership and talent for the fledgling SEP in their state. Rafael Molina Betancourt, for example, was nurtured in Sierra Norte liberalism and trained at normal schools in Puebla and Mexico City. He was one of the SEP's first missionaries in Puebla in 1923. By the 1930s, he was a major power in the SEP both in Puebla and in Mexico City.

However, the revolution in Puebla created difficult conditions for the realization of the SEP project. As in the midcentury civil wars, Puebla became an arena for confrontation between the revolution's two major factions, the Constitutionalists and the Convention, backed by the forces of Emiliano Zapata and Pancho Villa. This confrontation encouraged a peasant assault on the hacienda system in central and southern Puebla and a militant textile workers' movement in Puebla City, Atlixco, and San Martín Texmelucan. Everywhere, it promoted a reassertion of subregional and local autonomy.

Between 1920 and 1929, Puebla had eighteen governors. Statelessness begat more mobilizations and spatial fragmentation. Teachers hoping to "civilize" the countryside ran into new brambles of political interest and contention growing over the thickets of conservative cultural practice that had stymied them in the Porfiriato.[10]

Sonora too was an arena for struggle between Constitutionalists and Villistas. However, while mine and railroad workers, campesinos, Yaquis, and Mayos joined the revolution there, neither popular movements nor state administration escaped the control of the triumphant Constitutionalist generals. A transfer of rule—bumpy but not explosive—took place from Porfirian modernizers and hacendados to a new, buccaneering entrepreneurial political class led by Generals Obregón and Calles (Aguilar Camín 1977, 1982; Almada 1971; Radding 1985:254–311). The transition was not without ideological militance. As governor in 1916, Calles invited Luis Monzón, a staunch anticleric, to set up a state normal school. The anticlericalism of Monzón and Calles was more fervent than that guiding Puebla teachers (Rivera Rodríguez 1975:37–40). The latter knew from experience that they had to coexist with a powerful church. By contrast, the church was weakly organized on the frontier (Almada Bay 1992:41–44; Valenzuela Duarte 1992:50). Sonora did not have its own bishop until 1888. In 1919, there were nineteen priests in the state, most of them old and sick. Calles's rabid anticlericalism further weakened ecclesiastical presence. His Jacobinism linked modernity and virility to a snuffing out of backward Catholicism. Such feelings had expressed themselves among a portion of the frontier middle class in the spiritist movement at the turn of the century. Progressive in a scientific, political, and social sense, spiritists were anti-Catholic.[11]

Through the normal school, Calles sought to inculcate Jacobinism in Sonoran teachers. He saw to it that they would also be the state's loyal agents. In 1916, to ensure the extirpation of Villismo, he forced all teachers and other state employees to fill out a questionnaire testifying to their political beliefs, activities, and revolutionary affiliations. The questionnaire was part of a purge designed to exact obedience. The rigidity in the emerging administration, combining bureaucratic zeal with ideological dogmatism, contrasted with the relatively democratic, open society in which it operated.[12]

While lessons in bureaucratic discipline were not lost on Sonoran teachers, they were not a homogeneous band of subordinate civil servants. Most rural teachers still lacked normal school training. Many held religious beliefs in what was still a majority Catholic society despite the weakness of the church hierarchy. Others were radicals in their own right. In 1930, a major teachers' strike took place at the Escuela Talamantes in Navojoa in the Mayo Valley. Among the teachers participating was Santos Valdés, who would become one of the SEP's most militant personalities in the Cárdenas period when he would lead teachers and communities in the massive land distribution in the Laguna region of Coahuila. Also leading the Talamantes strike were two Sonoran Normalistas, Leonardo Magaña and Francisco Figueroa. Magaña soon became the director of the Article 123 railroad workers' school at Empalme in southern Sonora. After being fired at Navojoa, Francisco Figueroa went to Hermosillo, where he, shoemaker Jacinto López, and others formed the group El Huarache, the core of Sonoran radicalism in the 1930s. To these men, to the larger corps of teachers, and to the SEP, Governor Rodolfo Elías Calles turned in 1931 to engineer a controlled popular revolution through his construction of the state PNR.[13]

CULTURAL POLITICS IN SONORA AND PUEBLA, 1929–1935: HARNESSING TEACHERS TO PARTY-BUILDING

In 1929 and 1931 respectively, Puebla governor Leonides Almazán and Sonoran governor Rodolfo Elías Calles engaged federal teachers in the construction of mass-based state PNR machines like that of Lázaro Cárdenas in Michoacán. However, the cultural politics of teachers differed in the two states, in part because of the governors' policies. Governor Calles sponsored the radical training of teachers and provided material support to communities. Governor Almazán did not sponsor such uniform training for teachers, nor could he provide communities with the resources necessary to achieve SEP objectives.

Rodolfo Elías Calles, son of the *jefe máximo,* sought to build a political machine that would marginalize the Calles family's rivals, partisans of the late Alvaro Obregón. Young Calles intended to build a party under the aegis of an emerging agro-bourgeoisie. The members of the latter were not necessarily hostile to his alliance with peasants and workers. They were businessmen who depended on state and federal governments to provide them with land, irrigation, highways, technical assistance, and credit. Calles organized them into cooperatives to buy and sell at favorable prices. New agribusinessmen in the southern Yaqui and Mayo Valleys hoped to emerge dominant as Calles directed worker and peasant discontent against foreign entrepreneurs and merchants (principally Chinese and Yankee) and traditional cattle ranchers in northern Sonora. Calles Jr. probably saw himself as channeling popular discontent before it got out of hand. In the depression, the northern mining and cattle industries shut down as U.S. markets dried up. Forced repatriation flooded Sonora with refugees from Arizona. Families fled the north for the southern agricultural camps in the Yaqui and Mayo Valleys. If there were not a managed land reform here, the agro-bourgeoisie could lose, because the migrants were needy, angry, and aspiring.[14]

Calles envisioned a teacher vanguard to form the Federación de Obreros y Campesinos de Sonora, modeled after Cárdenas's CRMDT in Michoacán. In February 1932, the SEP obliged him and sent Elpidio López to head the SEP's Sonoran office. A native of Chiapas and a seasoned militant, his mission was as explicit as it was grandiose: "The Sonoran proletariat awaits the fulfillment of revolutionary laws. It falls to my humble authority to resolve the problem of organizing, orienting, and sustaining the Sonoran proletariat ... and, united with the federal and state governments, to apply the laws to better the lives of those forgotten by the social revolution in this moment of National Reconstruction."[15] The governor turned over the state's rural schools to the SEP while he continued to pay state teachers. The number of federal schools increased apace. They were augmented by new Article 123 schools in mines, haciendas, and agricultural camps. To train teachers in radical pedagogy, López replaced existing federal school inspectors with out-of-state personnel. Two ideological firebrands from Michoacán, Lamberto Moreno and Ocampo Bolaños, arrived as inspectors charged with training teachers and organizing campesinos and workers.[16]

Although the SEP's Escuela Normal Rural at Ures had begun training, most rural teachers in 1931 had no more than a primary school certificate. Many were new. Others long in service qualified as "old-fashioned," verbalist instructors. Many knew little beyond their hometowns, let alone anything about the SEP's lofty ideals. Frequently they were part of the local power structure like Josefa Saijas of Jecora Grande in Alamos, who decorated the school walls with images of Santa Teresita del Niño Jesús rather than of patriotic heroes Hidalgo, Juárez, and Morelos. Her father was the Comisario de Policía and trafficked in the making and sale of *bacanora*, the liquor brewed from the local maguey plant.[17]

The new inspectors systematically trained and watched the teachers. They weeded out the "inactive," "backward," and hopelessly local. In Centros de Cooperación, inspectors taught teachers action pedagogy as it had been recast as collective group learning. Teachers learned how to set up Comunidades Infantiles Escolares and organize children into campaigns for hygiene, health, reading, and arithmetic. They learned how to teach national language, history, geography, and culture through Mexican songs, poetry, and dances. They built chicken pens, orchards, latrines, wells, and sports fields. They were told how to organize Sociedades de Madres and Clubes de Señoritas to tackle problems of health and alcoholism; how to organize men into campesino leagues; how to collect statistics and fill out bureaucratic forms. They studied *El Maestro Rural,* the Labor Code, the agrarian laws, and the Constitution of 1917. The inspectors organized teachers into regional trade unions, consumer cooperatives, and savings societies.[18]

In the summer of 1933, 261 teachers attended a compulsory training institute in Hermosillo. Carefully supervised, they lived in dormitories, formed an eating cooperative, did Swedish tumbling and marching exercises, played basketball and baseball, and invented political skits and dramas. They received instruction in small industries (tanning, embroidery, furniture making) from teachers at the Cruz Gálvez trade school and in the care of pigs, chickens, and seedlings from an agronomist at the Escuela Rural Normal at Ures. Federal health agents lectured them on smallpox. The Michoacán inspectors drilled them in radical Mexican sociology. The inspectors stressed unionization and cooperativism and taught the teachers revolutionary and folk music, theater, and dance. At the institute's conclusion, teachers formed the Federación de Agrupaciones de Maestros Socialistas de Sonora.[19]

Teachers were to organize their communities—workers and campesinos, parents, mothers, youth, and children—in order to replace vertical systems of power, resources, and alcoholized sociability with popular organizations linked to the state, market, and nation. In communities, teachers formed or fortified campesino leagues and mineworkers' unions and brought these together into worker-campesino federations. They pushed for land through ejidal dotación or the Law of Idle Lands, for access to water, for the implementation of labor laws, and for the election of municipal officials from their own groups. They set up newspapers for the federations and drew them into a national movement to affirm worker and peasant rights.[20]

Governor Calles provided plows to campesino unions and seed for planting to the federations. The peasants were to pay for the seed with proceeds from harvests purchased by local price commissions. Made up of representatives of the campesinos, merchants, and the municipal president, the commissions were to assure fair prices and efficient marketing arrangements. The governor's innovative support was of more value to peasant agriculture than the teachers' technical assistance. Despite their hasty training, teachers knew little about farming.[21]

The governor provided funds and supplies to build and equip schools, theaters, and sports fields. He donated first aid equipment, fabric, food, overalls, shoes, and clothing to hungry children. For families suffering from mine shutdowns, the collapse of the cattle trade, or crop failures endemic in this arid land, the governor's gestures counted. With SEP inspector Bolaños and the merchants of Ures, Calles put the unemployed to work building an open-air theater for the new Parque Campesino Revolución. The governor, state deputies, and SEP inspectors gave the schools paper, pencils, texts, libraries, barber's shears, patriotic altars, tree seedlings, and an endless supply of oil lamps for adult evening classes.[22]

The project of community reconstruction amply engaged women. They were the majority among federal teachers. High female literacy rates facili-tated the mobilization of women. Women teachers organized mothers and adolescents into Clubes de Madres and Asociaciones de Señoritas. Women led campaigns to burn the garbage, clean the streets, and tidy homes. They awarded a white flag to the cleanest house. They fought against the making and sale of alcohol. Women locked horns with Comisarios de Policía, who trafficked in local brews and stills. They traveled miles to solicit the support of authorities to close the stills. Bands of women stood guard at the edge of towns to see that no liquor entered. The women's organizations and the Aso-ciaciones de Señoritas received cloth from the governor and turned it into pants and skirts. They got vials of smallpox vaccine from health officials and learned how to inject it. They staged cultural festivals to raise money to buy medicines for the school, to support public dining rooms for the indigent, and to repair the school. They ended the traditional selection of a "queen" for the patriotic festivals and substituted "La Mujer Campesina," selected for her civic engagement and enterprise.[23]

Women schoolteachers were often crucial to comprehensive village mobi-lization, for they could organize both men and women. They participated in campesino leagues and mineworkers' unions and spoke at cultural festi-vals on topics such as "The Worker and Mexico's Future." María Valenzuela's school in La Cebolla, Alamos, boasted a theater, a garden plot, and toilets. She advised the Unión Campesina, the Comité Agrario, the Sociedad de Madres, and the Club de Señoritas and organized a wood-selling cooperative to bypass usurious merchants. In contrast to Puebla, women teachers in Sonora were less engaged in a project to alter the customs of their social in-feriors than they were caught up with community women in a mutual mobi-lization to civilize the frontier society.[24]

As cultural organizers, teachers began to nationalize the regionally insular sonorenses while promoting new notions of class identity and citizenship. Their *veladas culturales* (evening cultural programs) engaged men, women, and children in the enactment of the SEP's three-pronged cultural reper-toire—folkloric, political, and developmentalist. Children learned the *danza tarasca* and the jarabe from Jalisco and sang songs like "Los chaparritos," and "Las palmeras." Parents and children heard eulogies to Zapata and organized celebrations honoring the anarchist "Martyrs of Chicago." They watched and produced theater condemning alcohol and promoting hygiene and sports. Communities raised money for flood and hurricane victims in Tampico, San Luis Potosi, and Veracruz. One school got an oil portrait of the "martyr of national agrarianism," Emiliano Zapata, from the Morelos state congress for a school that would bear his name. Sara Madero donated an oil portrait of her late husband, Francisco, the "Martyr President," to a school that took his name.[25]

Community festivities were political. Assisted by the governor and the state PNR committee, Ocampo Bolaños brought organized campesinos and teachers of Ures to 1933 May Day ceremonies in Hermosillo to hear the chief of the revolution, Plutarco Elías Calles. The celebrations were also social. At the Christmas velada in Magdalena, ejidatario families sang songs and danced, ate *tamales* and drank *atole*. The president of the Comité Agrario arrived at midnight, dressed as Santa Claus, with sweets, fruits, and toys for the children.[26]

In rural Sonora, positive response to the SEP project was facilitated by the governor's support of campesinos in pursuit of a more equitable distribu-tion of resources and power; by prior high literacy rates and positive attitudes toward schooling; and by more open gender and class relations than those prevailing in rural central Mexico. Sonoran rural communities lacked the historically embedded institutional fabric that defined central Mexican com-munities. Often, in Sonora, the new school itself—a whitewashed building with a red roof, bordered by plants and flowers giving life to the desert—be-came the symbol of community. Community openness was strengthened by the fact that Sonora had had no agrarian revolution from below so that the school was not competing with already organized popular movements. Rather, it facilitated them. There was a symbiotic relationship between the prolifera-tion of a politicized, redistributive school project and the traditions of trade union activism radiating out of northern mining centers or the southern railroad depot at Empalme into surrounding agrarian communities.[27]

However, communities limited curriculum by seeking no more than three years of schooling for children. Poverty inhibited schooling. Small, shifting communities and constant migration in search of work were further obsta-cles. The most desolate communities were in the Sierra Madre—in the ex-

districts of Sahuaripa and Moctezuma—where conditions of endemic isolation and dry soils were now aggravated by the collapse of mining. Schools
worked best in places like Magdalena, south of the Arizona border, where
communities were larger, wealthier, and near the newly paved highway.[28]

Ethnicity deterred schooling. The Papagos (Tohono O'odham) of Altar
insisted that their tribal governors had to approve any teacher. Besides, they
wanted one who spoke English, not Spanish. They did not recognize the
U.S.–Mexican border, so symbolically powerful for the SEP. Cordoned off
into camps under the Mexican army, the rebellious Yaquis were not recipi-
ents of federal schools in the early 1930s, so the brunt of the assimilationist
project fell on the Mayos. In the 1930s, they shared the fertile valley south of
the Yaqui with increasing numbers of non-Mayo settlers. The school inspector noted that Mayo children had difficulty with the Spanish language. Their
parents took them out of school through summer to help with plantings in
distant fields. Female attendance in night classes and elementary school fell
far below the state norm. The inspector complained that it was almost
impossible to organize these communities. Instead, teachers focused on the
non-Indian settlers. By doing so, they provoked more antagonism among
the Mayos. In Macoyahui, teachers formed an agrarian committee among
the non-Mayos on one side of the river while the Mayos on the other side
rejected the school and agrarianism. The radical school inspectors had no
sensitivity toward the Indians of Sonora: rather, they shuddered at their
backward customs.[29]

What pushed the Mayos to the breaking point—and alienated other communities as well—was the antireligious campaign. In late 1931, Governor
Calles limited the number of priests who could officiate. Between 1932 and
1934, many of Sonora's churches were turned into army barracks, ware-
houses, and union and party offices. In mid-1933, more than a year before its
approval at the national level, SEP inspectors began to push for the Escuela
Socialista and a reform of Article 3. They understood this school to be antireligious and, in the words of Ocampo Bolaños, "the cleanest, most glorious
standard of collectivist social emancipation, the pure preacher and educator
of Mexican institutional life." In May 1934, Calles expelled all priests. He
asked teachers to form Bloques Juveniles Revolucionarios along the model of
Garrido Canabal in Tabasco to sack the churches and destroy the symbols of
religiosity in homes and towns. He sent a group of teachers to Tabasco to
learn how to implement sex education. Like his father, Calles believed anti-
Catholicism signified modern virility. Religion was something for Indians,
hillbillies, and ignorant women.[30]

But sectors of Sonoran hill folk, women, and Indians were not compliant. In Oputo, in the desolate Sierra district of Moctezuma, where churches were well preserved and used, the inspector asked the governor for authorization to dispose of the bells and pews. Teachers, he said, infused every social meeting with defanaticizing discourse. "There are only a few little schools where the crosses, engravings, and fetishes have yet to be destroyed. The saints disappear—burned, hidden, or buried." In the Sierra districts of Moctezuma and Sahuaripa and in the Mayo Valley and Alamos in the south, as religious images were sacked from homes and chapels and thrown onto bonfires, school attendance dropped dramatically in the fall of 1934. On December 22, 1934, thirty men shouting vivas to Christ the King attacked the police station and federal garrison at Navojoa in the Mayo Valley.[31]

In January 1935, the Michoacán inspector, Lamberto Moreno, became SEP director in Sonora. "The Revolution," he announced, "has reached its stage of spiritual reconstruction." He urged the teachers to "drastic action" in the antireligious campaign "so virilely undertaken by the national government." He applauded the children of Macoyahui who helped the teacher and the ejido officials "liberate" the saintly images from homes and the church. They tossed these "symbols of fanaticism and exploitation" into a bonfire around which they sang and danced. Moreno composed theater and symphonies attacking priests. His "Iconoclastic Hymn" was sung by thirteen hundred public school students at PNR May Day celebrations in Hermosillo in 1935. In June, he used a teacher institute to create a Comité de Depuración to dismiss noncooperating teachers. Firings and resignations followed.[32]

In the "red" summer of 1935, organized teachers, workers, and campesinos supported the Calles gubernatorial candidate, Ramón Ramos. Many among them ran for political office. Their plan was to unite the regional federations into a Confederación de Obreros y Campesinos de Sonora in concert with the Federación de Maestros Federales de Sonora. This would constitute a unity of workers, campesinos, and teachers in line with Cárdenas's ideal of bringing school and community together in pursuit of economic and social betterment. But it was not to be. Claiming antireligious excesses as their rationale, conservatives revolted in October 1935 against the election of Ramos. In the south, Mayo rebels assaulted schools, demanded an end to socialist education and local unions, and barred the teachers from communities. In the north, cattle ranchers and *caciques* took up arms against the Callista agraristas. They blew up a railway bridge near Magdalena and killed the newly elected agrarista municipal president of Santa Ana. In the district of Moctezuma, Luis Ibarra Encina, a veteran of the cristero wars in Jalisco, launched a revolution in the name of Christ the King. He appealed to the religious sentiments of poor, isolated communities around Oputo. Here, in Granados, villagers captured a young teacher and beat him into a coma. The movement was said to be nurtured by Sonoran Bishop Juan Navarette and his fellow priests. Rather than endure exile, Navarette had sought refuge in a ranch near Granados, where he ran a clandestine seminary. Around 250 young cowboys and ranchers joined this movement, in the course of which rebels killed the municipal presidents of Granados and Sahuaripa.[33]

Whether or not Cárdenas had a hand in instigating the revolts, they allowed him to destroy Callismo. The anti-Ramos movement began as Cárdenas expelled Callistas from his cabinet in June 1935. In December, Cárdenas deposed Ramos and five other governors. He charged them with sedition just as the elder Calles returned from his exile in the United States in hopes of regaining power. Cárdenas appointed General Gutiérrez Cázares as Sonoran interim governor. Although the collapse of Callismo in Sonora did not end teacher militance, it ended the antireligious campaign and altered conditions for teacher interpretation of policy as Cárdenas became a key player in Sonoran politics.[34]

⌒

In Puebla between 1929 and 1933, Governor Leonides Almazán tapped federal teachers to help him consolidate the statewide PNR, but they never achieved the militance of their Sonoran counterparts. Formidable obstacles faced Almazán as he tried to forge a progressive alliance between workers, campesinos, and the organized middle classes (Sánchez López 1992). He had to eliminate military caudillos who controlled the state's subregions. He exiled the regional boss of the Sierra Norte, General Gabriel Barrios. He hoped to co-opt the caudillos of central and southern Puebla into a statewide campesino organization, the Confederación Campesina Emiliano Zapata (CCEZ). Wagering that local agrarista groups, wooed by land grants, would sign on, Almazán distributed 218,977 hectares to campesinos, less than they had received between 1915 and 1930, but more than would be distributed by his successors. In the urban areas, he relied on a radicalizing labor movement, centered in the textile factories of Puebla, Atlixco, and San Martín Texmelucan, that had declared its independence from the central government's CROM (Malpica 1980; Ventura Rodríguez 1986).

Unlike Calles in Sonora, Almazán had no buccaneering bourgeoisie on his side and no resources. Class warfare and the depression had flattened the textile industry and Almazán chose to ally with the militant working class.

The revolution had hobbled the rural economy. Private owners in the Cámara Agrícola Nacional de Puebla were adamantly opposed to land reform. To make matters worse, Jefe Máximo Calles mistrusted him because of his friendship with the ambitious radical Veracruz governor, Adalberto Tejeda. Calles withheld from Almazán the support he more readily funneled to his son in Sonora.

Although Almazán wished federal teachers to be his vanguard in party-building, he could give them no resources to penetrate a difficult terrain. Like their Sonoran colleagues, Puebla teachers found poverty and dispersed populations an obstacle to schooling. As in Sonora, they made inroads when prior schooling traditions converged with land and water resources, proximity to cities, and Spanish-language facility. However, the revolution in Puebla had created a density of political struggle that now overlay the density of cultural practice. By 1930, these had been reinforced by almost two decades of autonomy from urban, state directives.

Unlike their Sonoran colleagues, poblano teachers did not receive systematic radical training. In central and southern Puebla, SEP inspectors were homegrown Normalistas whose guiding principles were closer to Porfirian liberalism and the paternalistic crusade of Vasconcelos than to the firebrand radicalism of Michoacán inspectors in Sonora. In Centros de Cooperación, they trained novice teachers in how to teach the three Rs, patriotic history, and geography and how to fill out bureaucratic forms for enrollment, attendance, and grades.[35] Pedagogically, they combined a Porfirian attachment to discipline with Vasconcelos's desire to civilize campesino behavior and Bassols' directive to organize collective campaigns for sanitation, sports, health, and production. Economically, they knew little about agriculture and small industries, although they promoted reforestation and were sometimes assisted by an agronomist. Politically, they had little to say about the revolution as a social movement: they celebrated the nineteenth-century patriot heroes while introducing new folkloric national culture in music and dance. Their attitude toward communities was often blatantly deprecatory. Manuel Quiroz, inspector in Cholula, described his mission in the early 1930s:

> A campaign to combat sadness, melancholy and passivity which characterize the Indian peasant; providing him with family meetings, sports, counseling, and moralizing conferences with the understanding that only by introducing joy, enthusiasm and distraction, can the diseased state of the campesino be transformed, awakening a spirit of progress and sociability. If not, routine, vice, and superstition will continue to fatally influence their destinies and will be an obstacle to the betterment of our country.[36]

As chapter 4 details for the region of Tecamachalco, teachers had difficulty penetrating agrarian politics in central and southern Puebla. They could assist in the redistribution of resources and power by facilitating bureaucratic processes of land reform and the upgrading of community status. However, they could not organize campesinos, who were already mobilized and engaged in contentious dispute with each other, with municipal authorities, and with private landowners. To make matters worse, the teachers had little to offer. The governor could provide nothing for the school effort. Federal agencies provided a trickle of assistance in the form of credit and productive inputs, but they were more competitive with teachers than cooperative.[37]

Whereas the prerevolutionary school had etched itself into a restricted place in daily life, the revolutionary school presumed to overflow customary boundaries in order to transform community life. The presumption was provocative. The most contentious issues concerned gender and age relations and religion. The SEP wanted to school boys and girls together and to organize women for household and community reform. These mandates challenged patriarchal practices—parental control over children's sexuality, the privacy of the hearth, strict delineation of gender spheres. Patriarchal sensibilities had more often than not been reinforced by the revolution, entailing as it did a recuperation of local autonomy, the collapse of the market, the empowerment of armed men, and endemic violence. In comparison with Sonora, there were few mother's clubs or women in adult night schools. The presence of women teachers encouraged female participation, but they were a minority in the early 1930s.[38]

Although poblano teachers were not antireligious iconoclasts, they were suspect and were satanized by the opposition. Puebla's organized Catholic movement was stronger than Sonora's. It had an active press that churned out alarmist leaflets and an ample network of priests and religious brotherhoods (*cofradías*) in the countryside to post and read them. The SEP inspector in Chalchicomula chafed at the festivals priests staged to counteract the work of the school. Worse, municipal officials protected the priests. The inspector bristled at the priests' insistence that children attend doctrinal lessons on Tuesday mornings during school hours. It maddened him that in the midst of drought and freezes, campesinos resorted to prayer, pilgrimages, and "witchcraft." These remedies, he surmised, only further impoverished and obscured them—they were part of the "sickness." The teachers' own threatening gestures stoked the fires. Presumably for reasons of sanitation but clearly in a bid for symbolic power, they reinitiated a movement begun by the Porfirian jefes políticos to move the cemeteries from the churchyards to the outskirts of towns. It was part and parcel of the campaign to appropriate citizens for the state. Along with schooling and the civil register of births, deaths, and marriages, it wrested control over life and death from the rival institution. From the villagers' perspective, the SEP tampered with the souls of the ancestors and the repository of village memory.[39]

Thus, the school met little success in transforming village life and had to be content with mini-mobilizations of handfuls of young schoolchildren. The one significant entrée the communities allowed teachers was patriotic festival, for which the teachers had been traditionally responsible. In the 1930s, teachers seized the opportunity of Cinco de Mayo and Independence Day celebrations to mobilize energies otherwise unavailable for the educational crusade—to build a new school, to repair roads, to clean streets and plant flowers in the town square. But they relied on a prerevolutionary political and artistic repertoire and had only partial success.

Although federal teachers were not leaders of land reform in central and southern Puebla, they were in the Sierra Norte, a region of Nahua, Totonac, and Otomi villages dominated by nonindigenous commercial and administrative *cacicazgos* (fiefdoms). Here, there had been no agrarian movement from below and little subsequent restructuring. As detailed in chapter 5, Governor Almazán exiled the regional strongman, General Barrios, to facilitate party-building. He encouraged teachers to ally with the Confederación Campesina Emiliano Zapata in organizing indigenous communities and displacing traditional elites. Rafael Molina Betancourt, a native of Zacapoaxtla in the central Sierra and now a SEP official in Mexico City, worked with his brother Fausto, SEP inspector in Zacapoaxtla, to create the Escuela Rural Normal in Tlatlauqui to train teachers in radical pedagogy. Teachers left the school to set up agrarian committees and implement labor laws. They promoted Almazanista cadres running for municipal office.

However, in early 1933, Plutarco Elías Calles ended Almazán's populist party-building. He ousted Adalberto Tejeda of Veracruz and Almazán from their governorships. Calles switched his support to a more conservative group in the Puebla PNR, led by the Avila Camacho family (Glockner 1982:20–69; Márquez Carrillo 1983; Pansters 1990:47–75). The group coalesced under the governorship of José Mijares Palencia (1933–1936), and pursued a rapprochement with Puebla's conservative textile owners. They sought to pacify the countryside by ending land redistribution and conflicts between agrarians and municipal officials. They aimed to reorganize the PNR by destroying Almazán's popular base. They marginalized the Confederación Campesina Emiliano Zapata. In the labor movement, they sponsored the revival of the

CROM to weaken the Almazanista Federación Regional de Obreros y Campesinos (FROC) (Malpica 1980).

The conservative ascendance coincided with the introduction of socialist education and gave ammunition to the Avilacamachistas who sought to displace the Almazanistas by linking them to antireligious radicalism. From the city of Puebla in the fall of 1934, with strong support from the middle and upper classes, Catholic organizations unleashed into the countryside a torrent of pamphlets denouncing the satanic reform of Article 3. In 1935, students deserted rural schools. In the center of the Sierra Norte, traditional ruling families ruptured the incipient alliance between federal teachers and indigenous communities: they denounced the teachers as agents of the Devil and painted themselves as defenders of an indigenous cultural autonomy threatened by the foreign bearers of a dangerous, transformative agenda. In November 1935, conservative elites, backed by the Avilacamachistas, trounced Almazanista candidates in municipal elections throughout the Sierra.[40]

Thus by late 1935, as Mexico's most radical president defeated his conservative rival, Calles, progressive regional movements engaging teachers in Puebla and Sonora came to an end. Fueled by popular dissatisfaction with socialist education, conservative mobilizations strove for hegemony in both states.

CULTURAL POLITICS IN SONORA AND PUEBLA, 1935–1940: TEACHERS, CÁRDENAS, AND GOVERNORS

In late 1935, President Cárdenas suspended the antireligious campaign and asked federal teachers to focus on central government directives for redistributive reforms and on the formation of national worker and peasant associations to be linked to the PNR. He asked them to be the builders of a progressive national hegemony. Conservative ascendance in Sonora and Puebla hindered teachers' compliance in those states. Between 1936 and 1938, Cárdenas assisted Sonoran teachers through land and labor policies, resource allocation, and appointment of a strong supporting cast: military officers, the new labor organization, the CTM, and other federal agencies. He was less helpful to poblano teachers.

In Sonora, Cárdenas used the anti-Callista rebellion to gain control over a state that had become the personal fiefdom of two national presidents, Obregón and Calles. Supported by loyal generals in the region, he installed General Gutiérrez Cázares as interim governor and ordered a reorientation of teachers. In November 1935, the SEP replaced director Lamberto Moreno with Fernando Ximello. Ximello arrived to upgrade teachers' pedagogical skills and curb their antireligious zeal. He was not the first SEP official to note the deficiencies of Sonoran teachers, especially the men who preferred politics to teaching children and taught in a verbalist manner despite prescriptions for action pedagogy. Ximello revamped the Centros de Cooperación, which Lamberto Moreno had turned into cells of political indoctrination and ideological cleansing. He replaced some school inspectors. However, he urged that the teachers remain "the intellectual architects and direct organizers of workers and peasants."[41]

The SEP focused on the southern valleys, where the Obregón and Calles families and friends had their wealth. They shared the fertile lands with foreign, mostly U.S. owners. Here, 90 percent of the state's labor force was concentrated in the production of wheat, rice, cotton, beans, and vegetables. In the Mayo Valley, where indigenous wrath over socialist education left the schools in shambles and the teachers ostracized, the only thing for the SEP to do was to push for land, water, and cooperatives. This the teachers did in conjunction with the Callista-inspired Federación de Obreros y Campesinos del Sur de Sonora (FOCSS). Leaders of the teachers and the FOCSS were old buddies from the Talamantes school strike and the Huarache group: Jacinto López, Francisco Figueroa, and Leonardo Magaña. Magaña left the directorship of the flourishing railroad workers' school at Empalme to head a new SEP district in the Yaqui Valley. Here he federalized state-run Article 123 schools in the agricultural camps. Teachers and FOCSS organizers pushed for unions, land, cooperatives, and better living conditions. Magaña also moved onto the Yaqui River's right bank, where the Yaqui Indians lived cordoned off in colonies under army control. Less sensitive among the Yaquis than among the campesinos, Magaña intended to put the Indians on "el sendero de la verdadera civilización" (the path to true civilization) through schooling.[42]

Neither the FOCSS nor the teachers had trouble switching loyalties from Calles Jr. to Cárdenas because both groups had their own radical agendas. They also curbed their antireligiosity. But they objected to Ximello. When he arrived in Sonora, federal and state teachers were at the pinnacle of organizational militance. Many had joined the Communist Party. New inspectors complained that federal teachers abandoned classrooms to politick, changed schools if they did not like their assignments, and seldom turned in their paperwork. Ximello accused Hermenegildo Peña, the Sinaloan-born head of the federal teachers' union, of calling meetings at will, regardless of teachers' work obligations. Executive committees of federal and state teachers were privileged. The federal teachers' union controlled the SEP Promotion Committee, which determined salaries and posts. The SEP paid the wages of two union officers. The state teachers' executive committee members held plum teaching positions. When the acting governor turned the state schools over to Ximello, leaders of the state teachers' union protested and demanded the appointment of a Sonoran. They feared Ximello would check their power. Similarly, leaders among the federal teachers worried that Ximello might replace less credentialed members with normal school graduates. Federal teachers protested against two new inspectors they accused of conniving with conservative municipal authorities and mine and land owners. Both state and federal teachers found support from the Confederación Nacional de Trabajadores de Educación (CNTE). A new radical movement out of Mexico City, the CNTE challenged the Confederación Mexicana de Maestros, a moderate union formed in 1932 and controlled by SEP inspectors. Ximello supported the CMM. Organized campesinos and workers backed the teachers against Ximello.[43]

The federal teachers won the battle when Ximello resigned in late 1936 and their former mentor, Elpidio López, returned as SEP director. Subsequent steps in unionization sealed an alliance between SEP teachers, the FOCSS, and the CTM. In February 1937, the Sonoran Federación de Maestros Socialistas, led by Hermenegildo Peña, joined the Federación Mexicana de Trabajadores de la Enseñanza (FMTE), the result of a SEP-negotiated merger of the CMM and CNTE. A precursor of the Sindicato de Trabajadores de la Enseñanza de la República Méxicana (STERM), formed in 1938, the FMTE joined the Cárdenas-backed CTM. Sonoran teachers and FOCSS militants moved to create a Sonoran affiliate of the CTM, which would include both workers and campesinos.

The worker-campesino-teacher alliance ran up against an implacable foe when Román Yocupicio became governor in January 1937. An anti-Callista out of his long-standing loyalty to General Obregón, a Mayo Indian, and a traditionalist, Yocupicio handily won primary elections as an independent. As a precautionary measure, Cárdenas persuaded him to become the PNR nominee. Once governor, he moved to trounce the radicals. He withdrew state schools from SEP jurisdiction. His new state director fired militant teachers and split state from federal teachers by forming a separate union of state teachers under the director's control. In February, Yocupicio deposed the municipal presidents of Huatabampo and Ciudad Obregón who cooperated with SEP/FOCSS efforts to forge a CTM affiliate. As he wanted to organize his own campesino and worker confederations, he viewed the radicals' initiative as a treasonous act of outside intervention. He denounced them as foreigners and disloyal Sonorans.[44]

Neither the teachers nor FOCSS organizers nor the CTM were daunted. In June 1937, they formed the Federación de Trabajadores del Estado de Sonora (FTES), with its base among valley workers. Inspired by the recent agrarian reform in the Laguna region of Coahuila and amid Yocupicio's arrests of their leaders, they pressed for a division of large estates. In October 1937, Cárdenas responded by distributing 24,905 hectares of irrigated land to 4,257 families in the Mayo Valley and 17,577 hectares of irrigated land to 2,160 families in the Yaqui Valley. He gave 17,000 irrigated hectares and 450,000 hectares of pastureland to the Yaquis on the right bank of the Yaqui River. Yocupicio-allied municipal authorities and estate owners—foreign and national—protested, subverted, and harassed but could not prevent the *reparto*. Federal agrarian officials and armed CTM agraristas carried it out under the protection of Cardenista military officers. While Cárdenas's intervention obeyed his democratic and nationalist principles, it also gave the central government a key role in the politics and economy of one of Mexico's richest states. Land division was complemented by a federal irrigation project, which made surviving entrepreneurs and new ejidatarios dependent upon the central government.[45]

The Yaqui Valley was one of the few regions of Mexico that received not only land but water, technical assistance, credit, and marketing facilities to make the SEP's project of campesino transformation a real possibility. And yet, the negotiation of the educational project by the Yaqui Valley's two populations—the mestizo immigrant *colonos* (smallholders) and field workers on the left bank and the Yaqui Indians on the right bank—was strikingly different. The first group—uprooted, mobile, future-oriented—embraced it wholeheartedly. They shared its assumptions and values. The Yaquis did not. The stories of these two negotiations are told in chapters 6 and 7.

The agrarian reform enraged but did not defeat Yocupicio. Where he could throughout the state, he used his crony municipal presidents to alter the composition of Comités Agrarios and separate them from their teacher advisers. These comités then joined Yocupicio's CNC affiliate. He used state agencies such as the Departamento de Trabajo and the Junta de Conciliación y Arbitraje to split the CTM-affiliated unions. He provided money, gifts, and contracts to woo workers to his own Confederación de Trabajadores de Sonora (CTS).[46]

In spring 1938, when Cárdenas ceded important powers to governors, Yocupicio used them to undermine the alliance between the central state and the local progressives. He dismissed the agrarian reform delegate and Ejidal

Bank director who supported the southern agraristas. He then waged war on the valley ejidatarios. Known as the "colectivistas" for their support of the collective ejido, they were jailed by Yocupicio officials and challenged by a well-supported counterforce of "individualistas" belonging to Yocupicio's CNC affiliate.[47]

Yocupicio fired Elpidio López as SEP director. The governor then named a conservative replacement, who dismissed and isolated radical inspectors and teachers. Many organized campesinos protested. Ejidatarios from the northern town of Casa de Teras wrote to Cárdenas: "All our efforts to escape the oppressive hands of the hacendado would have been nil . . . that we cultivate land on our own account and not under the tyranny of the *amo,* we owe not to Señor Yocupicio, but to the federal teachers whom he persecutes." Yocupicio plunged forward. He had state teachers replace SEP teachers in Alamos on the grounds of dereliction of duty. Encouraged by Yocupicio, the local press rebuked SEP teachers as immoral, incompetent "politiqueros."[48]

In August 1938, a delegation of Sonoran federal teachers went to Mexico City to see Cárdenas. They added their complaints to a stream of denunciations from Sonoran CTM-istas and federal senators and CTM leader Vicente Lombardo Toledano. All accused Yocupicio of sabotaging the president and allying with the renegade General Cedillo and Fascist groups. Cárdenas sent Defense Minister Manuel Avila Camacho to Sonora to investigate. The future presidential candidate failed to submit the report the left wanted. Yocupicio's campaign escalated with arrests, beatings, and murders of teachers and CTM-istas throughout Sonora. In October, Cárdenas met Yocupicio's request to remove the CTM-friendly army zone commander. By January 1939, new army officers joined in the repression of Sonoran radicals.[49]

The CTM-SEP-FTES-Cárdenas alliance reached its lowest ebb in the 1939 gubernatorial elections, when factions within the alliance backed two different candidates and neither of them won (Bantjes 1991:613–47). Yocupicio's candidate, Anselmo Macías Valenzuela, was elected. But Yocupicio did not win the war. Anselmo Macías proved more moderate and conciliatory than Yocupicio and reached a rapprochement with the CTM. Neither the CTM nor the southern valley radicals nor the teachers' union was routed. They far outlived Yocupicio as political actors.

However, 1940 marked the end of the SEP's golden years of populist nation-building in Sonora. SEP teachers had been major players in the redistribution of resources and power, providing new space and voice to peasants, workers, and women. They helped forge a progressive national civic culture in the isolated frontier province. They developed important national, class-based, associational linkages for workers, peasants, and teachers. In the Yaqui

Valley, their legacy endured in what remained a persistent pocket of independent popular radicalism that continued to resonate in local, state and national politics through the 1970s.

～

Between 1935 and 1940, federal teachers in Puebla faced a conservative state political machine, enjoyed little support from Cárdenas or from national worker and peasant confederations, and had a weak popular base. SEP leadership in the state was in the hands of the Molina Betancourt brothers. In 1935, Fausto became SEP director in Puebla while Rafael occupied important posts in the national SEP and the PNR and was the power behind the moderate, official teachers' union, the CMM. These brothers were anticlerical but never *comecuras* ("priest-eaters"). Committed to redistributive policies, they had launched agrarian reform in the central Sierra Norte in 1932. In 1935 they brought to the Sierra's Escuela Rural Normal Raul Isidro Burgos, exemplary founder of the Rural Normal School of Chiapas. With his flowing white hair and beard, clad in huaraches and campesino *cotón* in honor of his native Morelos, Raul Isidro Burgos was the embodiment of SEP ideals—an inspiration to dozens of young teachers.

These men faced a daunting environment. They did not, as in Sonora, live the apex of a popular revolution, but its disarticulation by a strident, heavy-handed bourgeois movement. They did not, as in Sonora, forge strong organic links with new, militant leadership in communities; rather, the struggle against the antireligious dimensions of policy left many communities more alienated from the federal school than they had been in 1933. It was in this hostile milieu that the astute Molina Betancourt brothers applied their negotiating talents to ensure that much of the SEP's cultural repertoire and ideological principles were transmitted to teachers, and from them to communities where the teachers displayed their own negotiating skills. Teachers managed to carve independent space for resistance for themselves and for communities while at the same time participating in the construction of party/state hegemony.

In most parts of Puebla, school attendance plummeted in 1935–36. Clerical opposition festered, often with the support of municipal officials and agraristas—to say nothing of the rancheros and hacendados struggling to hold on to their remaining properties. Between 1934 and 1939, at least seventeen teachers died in the countryside. Teachers complained to Cárdenas that neither Governor Mijares Palencia (1933–1936) nor Governor Maximino Avila Camacho (1937–1942) defended them. They protested that the murders were never seriously investigated. Army officers, friendly to teachers in

Sonora, were hostile in Puebla. They reported that teachers exaggerated the dangers to which they were exposed. Until 1939, the band of Odilón Vega, ex-soldier of exiled boss Gabriel Barrios, marauded through the Sierra Norte, attacking teachers and agraristas in the name of Christ the King. Another gang led by El Tallarín terrorized southern Puebla and western Morelos, assaulting any symbol of state power from tax collectors and mailmen to teachers. On several occasions, teachers had to leave their communities for shelter in district capitals.[50]

Maximino Avila Camacho ran in the PNR primary for governor in 1936 on an antisocialist, pro-Catholic platform. Railing against agitators who would implant "exotic" ideologies foreign to Mexican culture, he targeted the Almazanista gubernatorial candidate, Gilberto Bosques, a federal deputy and Normalista. Bosques had support in the Confederación Campesina Emiliano Zapata and the FROC, affiliated with the CTM. The FROC dominated the urban worker movement and had a base among campesinos in districts near Puebla city. In Puebla's equivalent of Sonora's "red summer," in the spring of 1935 the FROC called a general strike against CROM divisiveness in Atlixco and promoted dozens of campesino invasions of hacienda lands. As military zone commander, Maximino Avila Camacho crushed both movements. Nonetheless, in 1936, to the horror of the Avilacamachistas and the propertied classes, the FROC won the town council of Puebla city and proceeded to campaign vigorously against Maximino Avila Camacho's gubernatorial candidacy. When Maximino was declared the primary winner, the FROC took its case to Mexico City, but neither the CTM nor President Cárdenas responded. Maximino and his brother, Manuel, national minister of defense from November 1936, had supported Cárdenas against Calles. In return, Cárdenas would not directly interfere in Puebla.[51]

Maximino Avila Camacho gained a free hand in consolidating the state PNR and jealously guarded his autonomy from national agents of the CTM and CNC. He revived the CROM to weaken the FROC and divided the latter until he got a CTM affiliate to his liking. His rural strategies, detailed in chapters 4 and 5, were designed to conclude property redistribution, incorporate agraristas into a CNC affiliate he could dominate (the Liga de Comunidades Agrarias), and insure power to those rancheros, hacendados, and merchants who had toughed it out in central and southern Puebla after the big estate owners had fled. Maximino Avila Camacho appropriated Cardenista reforms for his own ends. Automatic *ampliación,* the extension of ejidal lands to satisfy those left out or left short in original land grants, was written into the Agrarian Code of 1934 and reiterated by presidential decree in November 1936. Most of the 193,874 hectares Maximino distributed were in ampliación, and they permitted him to dilute the strength of original agraristas by incorporating new ejidatarios.[52]

In this violent consolidation, federal teachers enjoyed the support of no organized political power. Although implicitly allied with the FROC as part of the Almazanista-Bosques block, in 1935 the federal teachers, led by SEP director Fausto Molina Betancourt, failed to support a FROC-backed strike of state teachers in Puebla city. Thus they separated themselves from the radical urban labor movement. Nor were they directly allied with the campesino movement as it was reorganized. Politically isolated, they had to negotiate with Avilacamachismo. Negotiation was evident in union politics. Fausto Molina Betancourt had control over SEP inspectors, who in turn dominated the teachers. He guided federal teacher unionization so that they formed with state teachers the Sindicato Unificado de Trabajadores de la Enseñanza de Puebla. Although this union joined the STERM-CTM, it was conciliatory toward Maximino Avila Camacho.[53]

The SEP's challenge in Puebla was to introduce socialist educational policy into a highly constrained environment. The experience of harassment and martyrdom coincided with an influx of new cultural materials—the canonization of Zapata, texts depicting the campesino family, corridos of strikes and land reform, the Yaqui Deer Dance and Tarascan melodies, Marxist pamphlets explaining class struggle and history lessons unveiling a populist, democratic version of Mexico's past. Huddled in their Centros de Cooperación, emboldening themselves to face the dangers around them, inspectors and teachers absorbed new principles and identities. The exhilarating hopes of Cardenismo energized young recruits like seventeen-year-old Socorro Rivera. She recalled: "Neither we nor the villagers had the slightest idea what socialist education was all about, but it was a powerful feeling, a spontaneous emotion."[54] And to explain herself, fifty years later, she burst into song:

> *Let us march, Agraristas, to the fields*
> *To sow the seed of progress,*
> *Let us march forever united*
> *Working for the peace of the Nation.*
> *We want no more struggles between brothers,*
> *No more quarrels and malice, compañeros,*
> *We will fill the granaries with wheat,*
> *The longed-for redemption bursts forth*
> *and tells the truth to the señores capitalistas,*
> *It is the song of the poor,*

those of us who work in the fields,
Who cultivate our lands with so much toil and sweat,
Ay, ay, ay! struggling for our dreams,
That God has in heaven.
Don Porfirio and his government of dictators
Never heard the protests and clamors of the people
Ay, ay, ay! struggling for our dreams,
So many brothers died that God has in heaven.

With this, Puebla's educational crusade lost its condescension toward the hungry, the unwashed, and the sick and became a collaborative effort for mutual liberation and national development. It propelled a generation of teachers into confident negotiation with communities. It made them see people differently. It helped them to listen—not only to listen to why mothers cured with a certain herb or men prayed, but to hear discord and injustice and to correct it. That was the Cárdenas legacy. Even stuffy inspectors got the spirit. Salomón Pérez told his teachers in Chalchicomula that they were leaders sowing the ideals of the revolution in the communities where they served. Miguel Villa told disputing agraristas in Texmelucan that they had to work out their differences and pull together because this was a class struggle: it was their revolution to make or lose.[55]

Once the teachers censored themselves, children began to return to school. However, because the classroom remained a puny platform for the propagation of new messages, festival became the teachers' wider stage. On it, the prerevolutionary middle-class civic culture democratized and extended to new popular groups through the imagined media of revolution, nation, class, democracy, and progress. The music changed from Italian arias and military marches to revolutionary corridos and Tarascan love songs. The pantheon of patriotic heroes opened to welcome the peasant Zapata. The pièce de résistance became the basketball tournament. The extent to which communities appropriated new identities, values, behaviors, and linkages varied, as described in subsequent chapters on the mestizo, agrarista region of Tecamachalco and the Nahua communities in the central Sierra Norte.

As much as civic festival may have in the short run embellished the power of the Avilacamachista PNR/PRM, its messages, content, forms, and participants also shaped a repertoire for resistance.[56] This dual role was epitomized by teachers' use of festival in the oil expropriation of 1938. In Puebla, this event, publicized in the press, radio, and official propaganda, drew popular support based on deep sentiments of defensive nationalism nurtured since nineteenth-century struggles against foreign invaders (the United States in

1846 and France and Austria from 1862 to 1867) by their commemoration in official civic festival. It drew as well from the participation of ordinary men, women, and children in the revolutionary cataclysm and subsequent reconstruction. Above all, the campaign in favor of the expropriation and for payment of the debt was the construction of teachers. They organized the fairs, festivals, raffles, and dances. Socorro Rivera recalled the moment:

> It was a magnificent thing, because for everybody, the people, the workers, the campesinos, the children, the merchants, for everybody it was a precious feeling. I cry remembering it. Every Monday morning, the children would come to school to give their centavitos for the oil payment. Everyone cooperated. We organized fiestas and raised a lot of money. In the dances, we sold bouquets of flowers, confetti, serpentina, *chalupas,* tamales. The people of the community did this. The entire product was to pay the oil debt. And the workers—you should have seen with what cariño they came to give their money. It was so moving because these were people so poor they had no money even for their daily needs, but with what cariño they brought the little they had to pay the debt.[57]

The mobilization around the petroleum expropriation helped to cure the wounds suffered in battles around Article 3. It deepened sentiments of national identity. It articulated a vision of modern development. Oil was defined as a natural resource that could transform production and increase wealth if it was exploited in a manner that would benefit Mexican society and individual citizens and if the workers who extracted and processed the oil enjoyed decent wages and benefits, health protection, housing, and education.

～

The revolution permitted teachers in Sonora and Puebla to escape the strictures of local power that had shackled them in the Porfiriato. Their employment by a federal agency, membership in a national trade union, and partnership with local, regional, and national political actors gave them space to alter power relations. But their space was severely circumscribed by the regional constitution of power and by the antireligious aspects of the SEP project. Ironically, the teachers' project strengthened the conservative movements that blocked them as much as their opposition to injustice, exploitation, oppression, and imperialism and their role in the reorganization of political power created space for immediate and ongoing resistance. That space was most intimately constructed through SEP–community interaction at the local level. We now turn to those negotiations.

4

An area of cultivated valleys cut by low, balding mountains on the eastern tier of Mexico's central plateau, the region of Tecamachalco lies midway between the city of Puebla and the Sierra Madre Oriental along the historic route between Veracruz and Mexico City. Part of the indigenous core of the original Spanish empire, Tecamachalco peasants had been mestisized through centuries of interaction with the state and the economy. On the eve of the revolution, they lived in pueblos, rancherías, and barrios scattered across eight municipalities. There they grew corn, maguey, ixtle fiber, chiles, onions, and beans. To survive, most depended on surrounding haciendas for sharecropping, renting, part- or full-time employment, credit, and marketing. In the revolution, villagers rose up to reclaim land, power, space, and dignity from the haciendas. By 1930, 8,533 Tecamachalqueños, one-third of the male population, were ejidatarios, or beneficiaries of land reform.[1]

SEP negotiations with Tecamachalco villagers in the 1930s were contentious. The negotiating parties held different visions of the school and culture. Both lacked the material resources to implement the SEP's project. Both were ensnarled in a vortex of political dispute. The SEP entered Tecamachalco at a moment when campesinos confronted their own differences and a state government ruthless in its reconquest of the countryside. Despite SEP expansion, official statistics show that literacy fell between 1930 and 1940, from 30 to 26 percent for boys between the ages of ten and fourteen and from 25 to 22 percent for girls.[2] While these figures probably exaggerate losses, they speak to difficulties of the educational encounter that are fully evident in more qualitative data. Yet through their interaction, the SEP and communities mutually created the school. In the process, they salvaged portions of an agrarian revolution as it was being dismantled by Avilaca-

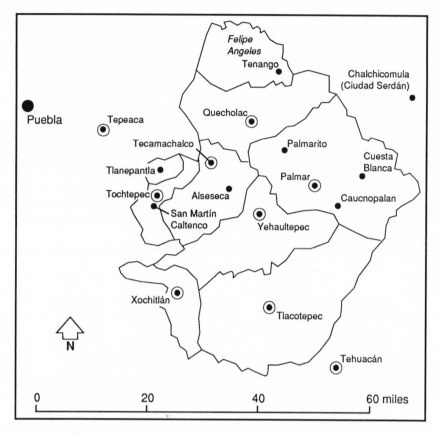

MAP 4 The region of Tecamachalco in Puebla

machismo. Federal teachers altered their behavior toward villagers while communities selected from SEP discourse those elements that would strengthen their voices under conditions of domination and modernization. They appropriated the school as a space for articulating consent and dissent and as an institution conducive to the creation of a national civil society.

PORFIRIAN LEGACIES

Porfirian schools shaped villagers' expectations in the 1930s. They created a precedent by their occupation of space, their curriculum, and their place in community life. Experience with them also nurtured different schooling cultures, which communities carried into the revolution.

Named for the patriot heroes—Benito Juárez, Vicente Guerrero, Porfirio Díaz—Porfirian schools were part of a liberal appropriation of community space for purposes of rule, instruction, and transformation. This space included the central plaza, or zócalo, refurbished with flower gardens, kiosk, gaslights, and statues of national heroes; the new municipal palace with its prominent clock; and the streets, which shed the names of saints to broadcast the events and personalities of the nation's nascent liberal history: Cinco de Mayo, Independencia, Hidalgo. These institutions coexisted with the church on the town square and were intended to reduce its centrality to community life.

Liberal institutions in a socially conservative setting, schools became rooted through mechanisms of local control. The town council had a *regidor* (alderman) in charge of schools and/or a Consejo de Vigilancia, made up of prestigious male citizens charged with school oversight. Local taxes paid the teacher; local labor built and repaired the schoolhouse. Parents, officials, and citizens attended graduation exercises, where a local jury judged teacher competence on the basis of pupil performance. The teacher began the ritual with an apology. If the students failed, it was because they attended irregularly, or as the teacher in Xochitlán said in 1890, because his students were "indígenas ignorantes de español" (Indians ignorant of Spanish). His fifty pupils stood up to recite the alphabet in unison and to demonstrate their knowledge of arithmetic, geography, and patriotic history.[3]

However, schools excluded on the basis of class if class is understood to combine occupation, income, place of residence, and social relations. According to the 1910 census, 24 percent of Tecamachalco men over the age of twelve and 18 percent of women could read and write. Low literacy reflected poverty. Although centrally located and traversed by a major railway, Tecamachalco lacked water. Haciendas could not exploit new water-dependent cash crops like sugar. They stuck with traditional grains and the maguey plant, from which they fermented the beverage pulque. For lack of opportunity, young men left the region and the middle class stayed small. In 1900, 81 percent of the labor force worked in agriculture (Ministerio de Fomento 1902).

Schools dug their deepest roots in county seats or headtowns (*cabeceras*) and larger pueblos, where institutions of local government were stronger and income higher than in the smaller population centers. The schools attracted children of professionals, hacienda administrators, merchants, artisans, and better-off campesinos. Many an agrarista leader of the 1930s had fidgeted on the crude school benches for a period of time in early 1900s. Middle-sector families often took advantage of the full primary school program to send their children to Puebla city to continue their studies at the

Instituto Metodista or the Normal School. By contrast, schools and their enrollments declined in outlying barrios, rancherías, and smaller pueblos, pop-
ulated by agricultural wage-earners and land-poor families. Until 1909, no
hacienda or rancho had a registered school.[4]

As table 1 shows, male literacy varied among Tecamachalco's eight municipalities. Differences between Tochtepec and Quecholac serve to illustrate
this variation and its causes. In 1900, 35 percent of the men in Tochtepec
could read and write. In Quecholac, the percentage was 15. Agriculture occupied 91 percent of the labor force in both counties. Higher literacy in Tochtepec can be explained in part by the relative prevalence of landownership
among small-scale producers. Fifteen percent of Tochtepec's agricultural
population registered as property owners in 1900 compared with 8 percent
in Quecholac.[5] Further, in Tochtepec, concentrated pueblos with strong traditions of self-government nurtured schooling cultures despite the presence
of haciendas. In Quecholac, small, scattered population centers dotted the
plains, dominated by haciendas and ranchos. Dire poverty and physical and
social distances stunted schooling culture. Because the families of rancheros
and hacienda administrators used the schools, peon children were not likely
to attend.

Isolation from modernizing processes also hurt literacy. Tochtepec towns
were close to one another and near the railroad, the important regional market at Tepeaca, and the city of Puebla. Tochtepec marriages were sanctioned
by both church and state. By contrast, in Quecholac most couples married
only in the church. Under conditions of isolation, weak schooling cultures
easily reproduced themselves. Schooling was often perceived as a waste of
time, an invitation to vice and idleness, fit for sissies and the lame who could
not perform field work.[6]

Everywhere, gender was an excluding factor in schooling. In 1902, 42 percent of eligible boys were enrolled in schools but only 24 percent of girls.
Patriarchal values ensured male control over activities in which literacy was
useful—politics, law, religion, field production, and marketing. Women
walked barefoot, always a respectful distance behind their sandaled husbands. Women were expected to spend most of their time secluded at home
bearing children, grinding corn, preparing tortillas, and training their daughters to do the same. Still, in Tecamachalco between 1900 and 1910, women
raised their literacy rate from 10 to 18 percent. The rise resulted from the construction of girls' schools in the larger towns. Female literacy correlated with
nonagricultural occupations. However, female literacy also rose in decidedly
agricultural Tochtepec, where it followed male literacy in a manner befitting

TABLE 1 Literacy in Tecamachalco, 1900–1950

	1900		1930		1940		1950	
	% Male	% Female	% Male	% Female	% Male	% Female	% Male	% Female
Tecamachalco	29	16	35	16	44	26	56	37
Quecholac	15	8	18	5	23	11	23	14
Tlacotepec	19	7	32	14	36	14	44	22
Palmar	19	9	27	14	25	15	39	26
Yehaultepec	24	5	33	9	52	18	53	25
Tochtepec	35	14	56	25	57	35	68	48
Xochitlán	22	7	33	18	56	39	54	35
Tlanepantla	26	11	57	30	57	32	65	42
F. Angeles	—	—	22	7	22	6	34	14
Total population	23	10	32	14	36	19	45	27

Youth Literacy (ages 10–14)

	1930		1940		1930	1940
	% Male	% Female	% Male	% Female	Ejidatarios % male pop.	Ejidatarios % male pop.
Tecamachalco	29	25	37	31	42	45
Quecholac	9	3	11	7	38	34
Tlacotepec	45	40	29	19	34	40
Palmar	16	17	10	11	26	26
Yehaultepec	28	14	38	26	25	44
Tochtepec	59	58	43	50	42	40
Xochitlán	54	53	77	70	14	42
Tlanepantla	65	52	60	55	0	13
F. Angeles	19	13	7	4	71	65
Total population	30	25	26	22	33	34

Sources: *Censo general de la República Mexicana*, 1900; *Quinto Censo de la Población*, 1930; *Sexto Censo de la Población*, 1940; *Séptimo Censo de la Población*, 1950 (Mexico: Dirección General de Estadística).

the district's most egalitarian county. By contrast, in Quecholac, female literacy was 8 percent in 1900.[7]

Ethnicity was not in itself an excluding factor in schooling. Tecamachalco
was one of many central Mexican regions where longtime indigenous interaction with the state and marketplace had created some demand for Spanish
literacy and a familiarity with schools. In 1900, 90 percent of Tecamachalqueños could speak Spanish. Xochitlán and Tlanepantla had the largest num-

bers of people speaking indigenous languages but average literacy rates for the region.

Because in the Porfiriato most people never attended school, the Porfirian school spread its message through patriotic festival. In towns where ritual had long regulated and enriched communal life, the liberal state seized upon it to educate an illiterate society and focused on the regionally important Fifth of May to spread its messages. Reorganized liberal space—the town plaza, streets, municipal palace, and school—became the extended theater of civic festival. Festival engaged everyone as actors and observers who "learned by doing." It promoted patriotism by teaching a vocabulary of a few key words—*patria, independencia, constitución, unión,* and *progreso.* Like the priest in church ritual, the teacher was the intellectual director of festival, subject to the jefe político's oversight. The teacher helped the Junta Patriótica, a committee of prestigious citizens selected by the jefe político, to organize the event. Like the *mayordomos* (sponsors) in religious festival, the juntas funded the event and oversaw the preparations—mobilizing people to clean streets, plant flowers in the zócalo, sew costumes, and mount fireworks.[8]

The typical fiesta began at six in the morning as the village band struck up martial music, the artillery shot off salvos, and fireworks burst into the half-light of dawn. Citizens raised the Mexican flag in the town square and unfurled national banners from the windows of public buildings. At nine o'clock, the parade began from the municipal palace as students, public employees, elected officials, locally quartered soldiers, and musicians filed through the streets to the zócalo. There the ceremony got under way with a rousing speech from the teacher eulogizing the patriot heroes—Hidalgo and Morelos, fathers of independence; Ignacio Zaragoza, general at the Battle of Puebla; Benito Juárez, father of the republic; and Porfirio Díaz, hero in the defeat of the French and Mexico's president. Schoolchildren sang songs. One or two students mounted the tribune to deliver a cornucopia of flowery rhetoric in honor of the patria and the brave poblano soldiers who had died defending Mexican soil. Orchestral music—the William Tell overture, a Bellini aria, a Sousa march—broke the monotony of speechmaking. The ceremony ended with the singing of the national anthem. In the evening, gaslights lit up public buildings and private homes on the main street. Musicians offered serenades in the plaza, a mixture of vocal solos, Viennese waltzes, *pasos dobles,* and martial trumpeting. The day's events ended at ten in an explosion of fireworks.[9]

Officials seized upon fiesta theatrics to enact the historical march of progress. As part of his mission of improvement, the jefe político led the

Cinco de Mayo procession of 1902 through the streets of Tecamachalco to the new hospital, named after the state governor. Like schools, the telegraph, and gaslights, the hospital was part of the jefe's modernizing project. The inaugural ceremony consecrated it in the blood poblanos had sacrificed to forge the Mexican nation.[10]

Although much of the ideological content of civic festival was injected from the outside and its enactment confirmed the presence and power of the state, patriotic festival, like religious festival, confirmed community identity, cohesiveness, and hierarchy. The powerful showed their largesse and won prestige. The classes mingled—the families of hacienda administrators, teachers, rancheros, mule skinners, fireworks makers, and merchants, the *peones* who swept the streets and peasant women hawking tamales and *jamaica* water, the violinists and drummers. Though its directors and beneficiaries were the small middle class, the festival was a collective work of art. In a region plagued by competition between towns and haciendas for land and water, it affirmed community identity.[11]

It also confirmed a pecking order within and between towns. The best festivals, like the municipal palaces, the flowering zócalos, and the best schools, were in the county seats. Their splendor signified wealth derived from dominion over surrounding towns. The festival, like the school, was exclusive. It relegated most people to spectator status. Its message propagated egalitarian principles and democratic hopes within a narrow, vertical system of power. It promised the comforts of modernity in the midst of want. Moreover, sponsoring festivals became burdensome. The celebration of Mexico's 1910 centennial coincided with repeated bad harvests. The jefe político exacted an exhausting toll in money and labor for the purchase of busts of Hidalgo and musical instruments and for the repair of kiosks, gardens, jails, schools, and roads. Even the largest and wealthiest towns suffered. In 1909, a majority of the Junta Patriótica of Tecamachalco resigned, claiming that they could not or would not meet their festival obligations.[12]

REVOLUTIONARY EXPECTATIONS

In Tecamachalco the revolution began in 1910 as a mostly middle-class protest against the jefe político's abuse of power, and evolved into an agrarian revolution. By 1914, peasant villagers were challenging haciendas, ranchos, and dominant towns. Outsiders egged them on as they sought support for their own projects: Constitutionalist generals redistributing land in 1915 and 1916 to wrest support from Zapata and Villa; the Comisión Nacional

Agraria (CNA) and the Partido Nacional Agrarista in the early 1920s; and sympathetic governors such as Froylan Manjarrez (1922–1923), Manuel P. Montes (1926–1927), and Leonides Andreu Almazán (1929–1932).

Tecamachalco agraristas were tough and tenacious in exploiting the absence of a strong state. When campesinos in Tochtepec learned in 1924 that Antonio Navarro, owner of the large Salvatierra hacienda, had manipulated their land request, substituting less desirable properties for the ones they had asked for, they refused the dotación. "No conviene a nuestros intereses" (It is not in our interests), they told officials. They invaded the land they wanted and stayed there until the CNA approved their occupation over Navarro's objections. Similarly, in 1914, General Prisciliano Ruiz returned to *vecinos* (villagers) of Tenango a portion of forest taken from them by the sprawling hacienda of San Francisco Aljibes. When in 1919 the owner Ismael Alvarez Sesma got President Carranza to cancel the grant, the villagers held on to it in the face of federal troops. They prohibited Alvarez Sesma's workers from using it and appealed to the CNA to sustain their original grant. Despite Alvarez Sesma's requests for protection from the army, the Puebla landowners' association, the governor, and the president, the villagers prevailed.[13]

This popular mobilization against privilege did not automatically turn into a demand for literacy. Rather, literacy followed Porfirian patterns (see table 1). In municipalities with strong schooling cultures, such as Tochtepec, literacy forged ahead: by 1930, 59 per cent of boys ages ten to fourteen and 58 percent of the girls knew how to read and write. But in Quecholac in 1930, only 9 percent of such boys and 3 percent of the girls were literate. In the absence of a regularly functioning state government and with the demise of the Porfirian political district and jefe político, villagers gained unprecedented control over schools in the 1920s. Many communities ceased to depend on the state at all and resorted to paying the teachers directly from their own contributions. But local control did not necessarily further inclusive schooling. For instance, political dispute and factionalism within towns could be as much of an impediment as weak prerevolutionary schooling cultures. In San Bartolo Tepetlacaltechco, for example, ejidatarios sporadically exchanged mortal blows with fellow villagers who chose to cultivate their small properties while renting land from a nearby hacienda.[14]

The SEP moved into Tecamachalco in the 1930s, expanding its schools from a handful in 1930 to forty in 1935. It took over existing state and local schools, created new ones, or revived schools that had been closed. Two-thirds of SEP schools were in small population centers with scanty resources and weak schooling traditions. The rest were in towns with strong schooling cultures. Wherever the schools were located, the SEP's notion of the school was distinct from that of the villagers, who in the 1920s recreated Porfirian institutions with their brief curriculum of the three Rs and patriotic history, their rote methods, and their restricted role in town life.

When he arrived in 1931, SEP inspector Jesús H. González promptly determined that Tecamachalqueños were undernourished, alcoholized creatures emaciated by an unhealthy, germ-breeding environment. He exhorted teachers and villagers to sanitize and civilize: move cemeteries out of town, introduce potable water, sweep streets, build roads and schools, install mail and telephone services, ban alcohol, persuade people to use the civil register, and fashion a civic architecture of parks and well-ordered streets adorned with the statues of patriot heroes.[15]

To villagers, González appeared less like a teacher and more like the Porfirian jefe político they had just dethroned. With their newly won autonomy, villagers were unwilling to take orders from blustery outsiders. It was their turn to decide what community projects to undertake. No, the villagers of La Portilla told the authorities, they would not build a road to Xochitlán, for it would benefit Xochitlán but not them. No, the villagers of Palmarito told Inspector González when he ordered them to renovate their dilapidated school—they had lost their harvest and could not afford it. Besides, he had to show them written authorization from the governor. Farmers in several towns shrugged their shoulders when González told them to widen the streets they had reduced to footpaths to increase cropland.[16]

Transform Tecamachalco's peasant tillers into scientific, entrepreneurial farmers? Diversify their crops, introduce new methods of fertilization, seed selection, and cooperative organization? Neither teachers nor villagers had the resources for such a transformation. The teachers made a singular effort to introduce tree seedlings to halt soil erosion and encourage fruit cultivation, but plants died for lack of water. Villagers declined to pay the cost of transporting more from the Ministry of Agriculture in Mexico City. Despite their political mobilization, Tecamachalqueños were more desperately poor in 1935 than they had been in 1910. The SEP inspector estimated that agrarista families had received an average of only 1.5 hectares from the government—most of it dry farmland without access to water. In the 1930s, repeated droughts and frosts struck so that the region resembled the Oklahoma dust bowl. Men lined up for days seeking work from the federal Secretaría de Obras Públicas on the new highway under construction from Puebla to Tehuacán. Men often left women and children to tend their milpas and animals while they searched for work in Veracruz and Tepeaca. These conditions made it difficult to listen to the SEP's prescriptions.[17]

Quickly, men saw that teachers knew less about farming than they did. It galled González that the agraristas were more likely to listen to agrarian reform officials and Ejidal Bank agents than to teachers. But it made sense. The villagers secured land from agrarian reform officials, and the bank offered incipient credit and marketing relief to fill the void left by the collapse of pre-revolutionary infrastructure. The bank, not the school, helped agraristas form producer and consumer cooperatives. González saw these emerging horizontal linkages as corrupting and inimical to the SEP's cultural prescriptions. They encouraged a notion of citizenship at odds with González's liberal republicanism and with the ideals of democracy that emanated from school texts and pedagogical plans. The Ejidal Bank fostered patron–clientelist politics, corruption, and dependence. The federal agrarian officials were incompetent and divisive. Often awarding the same land to different villages, they fomented factionalism within towns and created time-consuming bureaucratic snarls. Worse, these federal agents supported the campesinos' cultivation and processing of pulque. González had come here to sober people up, and what did they do but produce more poison for their emaciated bodies! In fact, pulque production was a rational choice. Its source, the maguey plant, thrived in the dry climate. Moreover, pulque had a guaranteed, regional market, critically important given the weakening of prerevolutionary marketing mechanisms.[18]

In 1932 and 1933, when SEP inspectors in Sonora were subordinating the school to an agrarista agenda, González was desperately trying to establish SEP authority over Tecamachalco agraristas. To do so, he stepped on the newly won rights of Comités Agrarios and Comisariados Ejidales. He claimed that, egged on by government agrarian reform agents, the agraristas disobeyed municipal officials and sought to dominate everything in their villages. They frequently seized control of the Comité de Educación, the SEP's substitute for the Porfirian Consejo de Vigilancia responsible for school upkeep. Accusing them of corruption and irresponsibility, he expelled agraristas from several comités. He then struggled to recapture control of the *parcela escolar*. Included in every ejidal dotación, the parcela was a plot of land whose proceeds were to be used to support the school. González claimed that the agraristas rented the parcel to their clientele for personal profit. He forced open-air public counting of the plot's proceeds and demanded assurance that the income would serve the school. The SEP's effort to assert its own institutional control often offended agraristas who believed the revolution entitled them, as new powerholders, to appropriate the school. The Ejidal Committee in San Martín Caltenco made this point to the teacher when they cordoned off half the schoolhouse for their business affairs.[19]

Neither González nor his teachers were consciously anti-agrarista. Huffing and puffing about the incompetence and corruption of agrarian officials, González accompanied villagers to Puebla city to secure definitive possession of their lands, upgrade village status, and resolve boundary disputes. Manuel Bravo Bañuelos and Horacio Caro, more radical and younger than González, were among many teachers engaged in similar activities. Nor were agraristas unsupportive of the federal school: they raised money for gas lamps, flags, and clocks, patched leaky roofs, and mixed adobe brick for new schoolhouses.[20]

However, both the agraristas and the SEP were caught in a situation of intensely disputed power—within and between communities, between villages and haciendas, between municipal centers and subordinate towns, between municipal councils and the new Comisariados Ejidales. To complicate matters, the SEP entered villages as the tide turned against the original agraristas. In the 1920s, the latter gained strength by exploiting the collapse of outside control. From 1929 through 1932, Governor Almazán extended the influence of the Confederación Campesina Emiliano Zapata among the campesinos and assisted them in securing land titles, amplifications of original grants, and posts on municipal councils. In 1933, the Avilacamachistas began their assault on the Almazanistas. Backing Avilacamachismo were those rancheros and hacendados who had stuck it out in the countryside after the better-heeled, absentee owners abandoned their estates. They had survived because they had fought the agraristas with armed henchmen—usually known as Defensas Rurales—and their loyal sharecroppers, renters, and workers.[21]

Under Almazán, stronger ties with municipal councils gave agraristas more access to land. Under the Law of Idle Lands, the councils rented uncultivated private property to petitioning campesinos. As the councils became more representative of Avilacamachistas after 1933, they were less likely to rent lands to agrarista tillers. When remaining Almazanista municipal presidents persisted in the practice, the state government backed the claims of private owners against the leases. When the Defensas Rurales attacked agrarista renters as "invaders," they moved with impunity and often with assistance from the federal army.[22]

At the same time as established agrarista leaders lost access to a valuable resource for their followers in rented land, they were obliged by the Law of Ejido Patrimony to parcel the ejidos definitively. As a consequence, they faced mounting opposition in their own communities from campesinos to whom the agraristas had provided no or insufficient lands. These campesinos accused agrarista leaders of corruption in the management of ejidal affairs, favoritism in parceling, and monopolization of Ejidal Bank credit. Opposition was mobilized not only by the Avilacamachistas, but by the left worker organization, the FROC, in new associations such as the Unión de Ejidatarios Carlos Marx and the Unión de Ejidatarios Flores Magón. By the mid-1930s, many villages were divided into three factions: agraristas and their conservative and radical challengers. Further weakening their cause, established agraristas could muster little regional unity because villages were fighting each other for the same resources at a moment when the Almazanista Confederación Campesina Emiliano Zapata was disintegrating.[23]

While teachers could not realize the SEP-prescribed role of organizational leadership among campesino men, they were even more distant from campesina women. The SEP inspector wanted his teachers to plunge directly through the door of the household to demand of the mother that her children be inoculated against contagious disease, be fed more nutritious food, and be more regularly washed and better clothed. The women were to clean patios, burn garbage, get the animals out of the house, and raise the hearth from ground to waist level. They were to replace their sleeping mats with beds. And yet, in Tecamachalco, villagers jealously guarded the privacy of their homes. The patriarchal separation of gender spheres made the hearth women's secluded, yet extended space. Reproductive customs of birthing, healing, cooking, and cleaning were enacted within this space and imbued with spiritual meaning. Their practice brought women secular prestige and a sense of self-worth, power, and community membership. Their practices were congruent with local resources. For instance, mothers gave children small amounts of pulque because the little water available was contaminated and because pulque was low in alcohol and nutritional.[24]

In its mission, the SEP was handicapped by a lack of women teachers, who made up only one-third of federal teachers in Tecamachalco. It was hobbled by a lack of resources, as teachers' demands for a diversified diet and improved sanitation came up against the reality of scarce water. The SEP also managed to break local rules. Whereas the SEP recognized hierarchies of leadership among men, it homogenized women in their ignorance. Teachers were not urged to seek out local specialists, who could have brokered in exotic innovations. The school's campaign to inoculate against smallpox was often tactless. Teachers took to joining the Departamento de Salubridad Federal in brigades that descended on the towns on market days to vaccinate en masse—sometimes accompanied by local police and soldiers.[25]

Tecamachalco women could have used SEP assistance. Borne by dusty winds, viruses swept regularly through towns, sickening and killing the young and old in epidemic numbers. Male migration for work left many women in charge of milpa, animals, and children. But, instead of a cooperative relationship, a big distance existed between teachers and most Tecamachalco women. Endemic violence kept the women secluded. It was dangerous to travel the roads by day or night. In Quecholac and Palmar del Bravo, robbery and kidnapping were so common that adolescent girls were whisked away in broad daylight. Rape was frequent. Few women attended night adult schools because of dangers at dusk and the fear parents had of their mixing with young men. For the most part, women left the Comités de Educación to men. They did not form anti-alcohol leagues and first aid societies. To be sure, there were variations between towns and municipalities. In progressive Tochtepec, women's active support for primary schools explained the latter's success. However, in Quecholac, mothers had little to do with schools. With the introduction of socialist education, women moved still further away. Even in Tochtepec, they deserted out of spiritual conviction or a pragmatic sense of danger.[26]

Thus, independent of local objections to socialist education as an antireligious policy, the SEP–agrarista encounter in Tecamachalco fell short of three SEP objectives. First, the SEP did not organize the campesinos politically or economically. Initial destruction of the vertical structure of rural power came from the peasants, who challenged it in sporadic association with outside groups. Now they faced a void in economic infrastructure partially filled not by the teachers but by other government agencies and private owners. Teachers were secondary also to villagers' political struggle for local representation and organizational linkage to the emerging state. Second, the SEP's modernizing prescriptions were often irrational given available resources. The experience legitimized local cultural practices in a discursive as well as a practical manner: "On the blackboard," joked the men, "no cow ever died." Finally, the SEP could do little in the short run to modernize familial patriarchy. The latter was reaffirmed by poverty, violence, and the empowerment of new male groups of agraristas, counteragraristas, and hired and self-employed gunmen.

THE CRUCIBLE OF SOCIALIST EDUCATION, 1934–1936

In the short term, local protest over the antireligious aspects of socialist education exacerbated the distances between campesinos and teachers. It drove many agraristas and the majority of women away from the school. It helped the Avilacamachistas further disarticulate the agrarian revolution. However, this campesino protest solidified, radicalized, and humbled the federal teachers. In response, the teachers salvaged what they could of the popular revolution in deeper and more sensitive dialogue with villagers.

In 1930, priests were few in Tecamachalco, but sufficient in number and sufficiently connected to the cofradías responsible for churches, chapels, and ritual to keep the district well informed by the urban-based Catholic oppositional movement. When SEP Minister Bassols reopened the religious struggle in 1932, the Catholic movement went on emergency alert. Bassols' campaign coincided with a full-scale entry of the SEP into Tecamachalco. SEP inspector González was no *comecuras*: he had no experience with the firebrand iconoclasm raging in Michoacán, Tabasco, and Sonora. Nonetheless, in the electrified atmosphere of rumor and suspicion, he provoked anxieties when he reinitiated the jefe político's campaigns to shut the schools operating in church annexes and to move the cemeteries from the churchyards to the outskirts of town.[27]

Apprehension was especially intense in the towns of Quecholac and Felipe Angeles, a new municipality that had formerly been part of Quecholac. Here, agrarianism was strong, but schooling and secular civic cultures were weak. Villagers were particularly wary of coeducation. In the Catholic discourse, coeducation was linked with sex education. The latter made rich grist for the rumor mill and its production of cataclysmic predictions. "In Tabasco, Campeche, and Yucatán," warned a leaflet from the Unión Nacional de Padres de Familia circulating in Tecamachalco, "girls eight to ten years old are found in a state of decay [putrefacción] as if we were speaking of prostitutes [mujeres de mal vivir]." The local translation was more graphic. "Down the road in San Cosme," the story went, "the teacher took down his pants to instruct the children in human anatomy." Inspector González blamed the priests for imbuing campesinos with "horror for our schools." To compete with the school's patriotic festivals, the priests introduced "doctrinas sabatinas." So successful were these and so polarized did the situation become in some villages by 1933 that even the ceremony of saluting the flag was interpreted as an act of Masonry.[28]

With the introduction of socialist education in December 1934, the opposition used the cover of night to scatter flyers through the villages. These leaflets threatened parents with excommunication if they sent their children to school. From the pulpit, priests warned of the damning consequences of state schooling. "Defend your children! Stop the state from possessing everything," read a pamphlet from the Unión Nacional de Padres de Familia, "Industry, agriculture, commerce, . . . the entire life of our Patria!" In January 1935, armed bands ran through the villages of Quecholac and Felipe Angeles, stealing horses and declaring a revolution against Article 3. Three hundred men, some in military uniform, were seen gathering in the mountains of Felipe Angeles near the hacienda of San Aljibes. By November, bands shouting "Vivas" to Christ the King marauded in neighboring Chalchicomula and Libres. They shot up towns and railroad stations.[29]

Throughout the Tecamachalco region, attendance in the federal schools plummeted. It looked to one teacher as if the Comisariados Ejidales, agrarista bailiwicks, blended in their opposition to socialist education with the religious cofradías, their theoretical enemies in the state's binary logic. Indeed, many campesinos eluded the SEP's logic. According to villagers of the ranchería La Portilla, there was no conflict between their religiosity and the revolution they had made. Accused of stealing a statue of the Virgin from the hacienda of Santa Rosa, where they had once sharecropped, they argued that they had "liberated" her. Year after year, they explained to the municipal authorities, on the pretext of sustaining the Virgin and building a new chapel for her, the landowner, Luis Ibañez, had taken two sacks of corn from each family and more from lands the families sowed for their cofradía. Ibañez never built the chapel. Instead, he sold the workers' corn to build a mezcal factory. "The image is now in our hands," the campesinos affirmed with revolutionary conviction, "and we want you to take note. After having been so exploited by the *patrones,* we believe it just to rescue what we made by our own efforts."[30]

However, not all agraristas melted into the Catholic resistance. Members of the Comisariado Ejidal in San Mateo Tlaixpan appealed to Cárdenas and Tecamachalco officials to send help to protect their teacher from harassment by a group of villagers. In La Compañia, Quecholac, many agraristas were Protestants. Their leader, Sebastian Paredes, headed the PNR Committee in Quecholac in 1935 as an Almazán partisan. The Catholic mobilization targeted them as well as the school. Similarly, Catholic protest became a pretext for assaulting teachers and Protestant ejidatarios in San Bartolo Tepetlacaltechco, Tochtepec. However, the Defensas Rurales opening fire on them in 1935 were hardly moved by faith. They were longtime henchmen for the hacienda owner Luis Ibañez.[31]

Avilacamachistas like Ibañez seized the moment to further weaken the agrarista cause. Ibañez was allied with Tecamachalco's rising political boss, General José Martínez Castro, whose job it was to subordinate local politics to the Puebla PNR machine. The Defensas Rurales did Ibañez's and Martínez Castro's bidding in eliminating resistant ejidal officers and militant agraristas. Especially singled out were those associated with Maximino Avila Camacho's nemesis, the FROC. FROC "communists," strong in Tochtepec, were the target of the Defensas Rurales. On December 5, 1936, from a parked car in the Tochtepec central plaza, Ibañez directed his men to assassinate Rafael Orea, FROC general secretary, in town to arrange his grandmother's funeral. When crowds of organized campesinos formed a protective shield around Orea, Ibañez had to retire.[32]

In the winter of 1935, the state closed its schools to protect teachers. In early 1936, the federal school in Alseseca was shut down for lack of guarantees. However, Inspector González was determined that his missionaries would tough it out against the "fanatics." Then, in February 1936, SEP teacher Castulo Meneses González was shot in Felipe Angeles. People did not know who killed him. Meneses was no *comecuras*. His brothers were priests, and he himself played the organ and sang Mass![33]

At that point, González called the federal teachers into Tecamachalco, quarantined them for two weeks and lectured vociferously about their crusade against backwardness. With the tyrannical righteousness of a true believer and the pedagogical meticulousness of an old-time Normalista, he lectured on everything: how to teach reading, writing, and arithmetic, how to vaccinate and cure snake bites. Until now, he had not been a supporter of Marxist notions of class struggle. He nonetheless recast Mexican history along lines emanating from the SEP: as a social struggle by exploited classes for rights and justice as well as modernity. The revolution, hardly a concept in González's discourse up to this time, became a decisive watershed. He compared the conquests of today with the wretchedness of Mexico before 1910. Let there be no doubt about it: the church was the enemy. The protector of the rich and the perpetrator of backwardness, it was on the wrong side in the class struggle. Emiliano Zapata, by contrast, had been on the right side, distinguished by his "love for the proletarian classes," in his fight for land and social justice. The teachers pored over the articles of the Agrarian Code and the Law on Cooperatives. They received and studied the new, campesino-oriented textbooks. The meaning of Mexico, too, was enriched and redefined by an influx of published songs and dances celebrating a diversity of local folklore and artistic expression both indigenous and mestizo. Teachers took this material to heart. They were younger than González and born of the revolution. He was a civilizer; they were Cardenistas.[34]

When the teachers ventured out again to reopen schools, they emerged with a more defined sense of ideology and purpose, and an esprit de corps. They also came out humbled and cautious. The *fiestas patrias* of 1936 became a negotiating opportunity. The Catholic campaign could not cancel this time-honored secular event, which properly belonged to the school. Teachers infused the festivals with new cultural and political messages. González was pleased. Even the women turned out in "regular numbers." González neglected to mention that no festival raised the question of religion. The villagers had censored the teachers.[35]

FESTIVAL AS NEGOTIATED CULTURAL POLITICS

The preceding should not suggest that the fiestas of 1936 were a watershed through which Tecamachalqueños joined the SEP's fold en masse—although children were in fact returning to school. Rather, festival from the early 1930s had provided a bridge between villagers and teachers and a focus for mutual construction. The SEP injected portions of its paradigm into civic ritual while villagers seized upon it to redefine themselves in the context of changing power. In the Cárdenas period, the insertion of the central state's democratic messages helped to empower the subaltern in the midst of a conservative regional consolidation.

Festival stimulated school construction that benefited both the villagers and the SEP. Given its nineteenth-century representation of hierarchy, the school was a space vital to the reordering of relations within and between communities. For small villages seeking independence from dominant county seats, pueblos, or haciendas, the school building defined empowerment. It substituted for a municipal palace and became the space where communities debated and resolved village issues. Yet poverty and political conflict impeded school construction and repair. Villagers could better overcome these obstacles when their goal was the school's inauguration in public festival on the Fifth of May or the Fifteenth–Sixteenth of September. To communities competing for the same land, water, and forests, the school was a symbol for display. Villagers of Tenango invited everyone in neighboring Santa Ursula to attend the ceremonies opening their new school. Vecinos from Santa Ursula returned home keen to finish their own schoolhouse.[36]

Villagers looked to teachers as the legitimate organizers of civic festival. Teachers' neutrality in political disputes enhanced their capacity in the role. Within communities, they used festival to promote unity between factions. At the same time, they became increasingly attentive to agrarista inclusion. They organized celebrations in the school around the giving of land titles—definitive possessions long awaited by established agraristas and land provided in ampliación to those who had been left out or shortchanged. With new didactic materials from the Cardenista SEP, teachers injected new approaches to national history and citizenship into these events and others such as the Fifth of May and Independence Day: the notion of a peasant-made revolution, the canonization of Zapata, the Agrarista Hymn, the Constitution of 1917 as a document hallowing collective rights and social justice, the sweep of Mexican history as a struggle against oppression. To peasants fighting with each other, the SEP stressed the unity of class.[37]

Villagers looked to teachers for cultural skills. Prized was the teacher who excelled at oratory and music. Horacio Caro, director of the school in Cuaucnopalan, Palmar, came from Panotla, a town of musicians in southern Tlaxcala. He played the trumpet and formed a new band for festivals in Cuaucnopalan with the children of the privileged members of the community, all of whom had been trained at the Methodist Institute in Puebla. However, festival music was democratized in the 1930s as Italian opera yielded to love songs from Michoacán and Guadalajara and "El flor de maiz" from Zacatecas. The new representation of culture encouraged the incorporation of local music so that Tecamachalqueños themselves became authors of Mexican national culture. Performance became less exclusive. Those towns unable to pay musicians for festivals made music through the newfangled machine called a victrola. Or, they relied on new dances and songs performed by schoolchildren.[38]

More than music, villagers demanded athletic competitions. The new basketball and baseball teams were a SEP innovation. The young athletes were recruited from SEP evening classes. González called them his "falange" in the crusade for hygiene, sobriety, and productivity. But sports also reflected village values and needs. They celebrated male physical prowess and dominance, prized by traditional peasant culture. Feasible under conditions of poverty, they caught on immediately in a region engulfed in competition within and between villages. Fighting between ejidatarios of La Compañia and vecinos of Santa María Actipan stopped momentarily when their basketball teams went against one another. As young players from throughout the region traveled to Tlaixpan every weekend to play, they came to know one another. Sports created a substrate for unity across an embattled, fractious terrain.[39]

As the pièce de résistence in civic festival, sports competitions democratized the event and made it more inclusive. Through them, new social groups and individuals acquired prestige in performance. Athletes supplemented or replaced musicians as festival stars. To become an athlete required less esoteric and costly training. Sports widened the circles of people who sponsored and enjoyed festival. Small towns could not always afford musicians or a victrola, but they could stage a basketball game. Even the most recalcitrant communities when it came to school attendance put up with the teacher's speeches in order to see the games. They drew female spectators because they showed off eligible young men. Young women dragged their mothers along to chaperon.[40]

The SEP seized the opportunity opened by civic festival to mobilize support for its transformational paradigm. Preparing the festival became a learning-by-doing lesson in the state's model of behavior. The streets had to be cleaned, the roads repaired, the garbage burned, and the town square spruced up with new plants, flowers, and trees. Festival was the occasion for which women teachers could mobilize mothers to try out a new, "nutritious" recipe to be served at the event. Teachers injected their model into the contents of festival, adding arithmetic and spelling contests between children of different towns to stimulate interest in schooling, and skits that explained the importance of preserving and planting trees to prevent soil erosion, castigated alcoholic fathers for abandoning their family responsibilities, and celebrated the use of soap. They tried to diversify and extend the number of civic festivals in honor of trees, birds, livestock, agricultural and craft production, teachers, and mothers.[41]

Villagers selected from and censored this repertoire. They forbade any discussion of religion. They rejected dozens of productivist celebrations to settle on four: Cinco de Mayo, Independence, a revolutionary holiday, and Mother's Day. Liquor would return, along with *charro* (rodeo) contests. Mother's Day celebrations would capture an ongoing dialogue about gender. The SEP wished to promote the new female citizen: an organizer of family life according to modern hygiene and nutrition; a producer of small crafts and garden products; a secular participant in community improvement. Teacher Victor Alva recalled the way he saw villagers enact Mother's Day celebrations in the 1940s: they became collective grieving sessions over the suffering women endured at the mercy of abusive husbands.[42]

CONSTRUCTING THE CLASSROOM AND ITS EXTENSIONS

Like festival, Tecamachalco classrooms were mutually constructed by villagers and the SEP in a blending of tradition and innovation. Villagers' agendas and priorities transformed the school before the school transformed them. The SEP itself was not one actor, but a coming together of teachers, inspector, central state directives and materials, usually resulting in innovations in method, curriculum, and social relations. The construction of school programs took place over the decade of the 1930s, before and after the explosion over socialist education, and varied according to town and teacher. The following is a composite picture of schools over the decade, with some attention to differences before and after the religious protest.[43]

In the early 1930s, most Tecamachalqueño parents sent their children to school for only a short time so they could learn the rudiments of reading, writing, arithmetic, and patriotic history. Students crowded into the first two grades of school. Enrollment depended on prerevolutionary schooling traditions. In San Martín Caltenco in Tochtepec, a majority of children attended school for at least three years in 1932–33; girls made up half the enrollment. By contrast, in Palmarito, in the literacy-poor municipality of Palmar del Bravo, the teacher could not push enrollment above 12 percent of eligible children in those years. Overall, in Tecamachalco federal schools, girls' enrollment rates were only one-third to one-half those of boys. They rose where there was a woman teacher, schooling traditions were strong, and community women actively supported the school.

Children attended irregularly. They stayed away for days at a time helping in the fields or accompanying their parents to distant markets and work sites. They entered the classroom late after completing chores. When epidemics ravaged towns, whole families left or shut themselves up in their houses. Teachers might try to embarrass the absent and the latecomers by posting their names on the school walls, as the inspector recommended. However, the unrelenting precision of the school clock and the calendar of repetitive, continuous hours of instruction organized consecutively over weeks and months had to yield to the villagers' notions of time. The SEP officially adjusted school hours to allow for work at planting and harvest time. Individual teachers developed their own imaginative ways of accommodating campesino time. In Cuaucnopalan, Horacio Caro went directly to the fathers. "Where are your children?" he asked. "I have no children," a farmer replied. "Then who is that *chamaco* hiding behind that pile of *mazorca*?" "He's my shepherd boy. I need him to watch my goats." "Well, then give him to me for a few hours in the morning and I will let you have him at midday so he can tend the goats."

Teachers had to adjust pedagogy and curriculum to the children's time and ages. They had to recognize the strength of local knowledge and difficulties of introducing knowledge about the outside world. In most Tecamachalco schools in the 1930s, children knew the animals and plants of the region but did not know what constituted a republic. How many eight-year-olds do? For their part, teachers had to cope with their own professional strengths and weaknesses. Many had had no normal school training and taught children as they had been taught. Learning new methods and materials in the inspector's seminars, they also had to deal with his traditionalism and authoritarianism. Grounded in the rigid pedagogy of late Porfirian normal schools, González was uncomfortable with the spontaneity of action education. Punctuality, work, self-control, cleanliness, and sobriety were the qualities he sought to instill in children. By nature a taskmaster, when he visited teachers' classrooms, he frequently lost patience and pushed them aside to correct their "appalling deficiencies" by demonstrating the "modern" way to teach reading, writing, and arithmetic.

Families, children, teachers, and inspector brought prerevolutionary practices to the construction of the revolutionary classroom. Pedagogy and curriculum built upon a Porfirian base of spatial organization, decoration, and schedule. The typical classroom had an earthen floor, desks, tables, benches, and a blackboard. On its walls were a clock, a map of Mexico, and a portrait of Hidalgo or Juárez. In a corner stood the national flag. Teachers moved children into contact with these national symbols through the morning assembly. The ceremony began with a salute to the flag, included the teacher's story about a patriot hero, and ended with a cleanliness inspection as children rendered up their hands, faces, and clothing before the teacher's judgment. Judged, they sang the national anthem.

But Porfirian practice was not adequate to new pedagogical demands. Teachers had to find ways to pack a substantial amount of learning into a short period of time. The SEP helped by providing textbooks, such as *Fermín, Simiente,* and *La vida rural.* Distributed in large numbers after 1935, these books condensed rudimentary science, geography, and history into well-illustrated volumes with large print. Campesino-focused texts were easier for children and adults to identify with than older readers, with their urban, middle-class models and idealizations of hacienda life. These primers honored agraristas in struggle. By teaching reading through descriptions of daily life, they probably assisted cognitive development. By converting the campesino family into historical actors and agents of change, the readers turned a male-dominated revolution into an inclusionary family event, an important technique for reaching boys and girls.

Action pedagogy could assist learning in brief periods. Its more open and participatory methods potentially softened rigid, hierarchical relations between teachers and pupils and between genders. It made school fun. According to SEP prescription, action pedagogy was ideally applied through school annexes—gardens, chicken coops, dovecotes, crafts shops, sports fields, and theaters—and through committees for production, hygiene, first aid, sobriety, and the protection of trees, birds, and children. Interaction between communities, teachers, and children determined how action pedagogy was applied.

Communities provided the resources for annexes. In Palmarito in the low-literacy municipality of Palmar del Bravo, the schoolhouse had no room for annexes and the community was slow to organize the construction of a new school. The garden was a tiny plot; the children kept some chickens in a privately owned coop. By contrast, in San Martín Caltenco, Tochtepec, the children cultivated a garden, raised birds, rabbits, and hens, and organized two cooperatives. They made fiber crafts, painted on cloth, engraved in glass, and ran a carpentry workshop. The school boasted a theater, well-equipped basketball and volleyball courts, and a museum filled with local plants, products, and minerals. They staged contests to see how many trees they could cultivate. The vecinos provided the school with water—a precious resource most villages could not or would not provide in the 1930s. Significantly, San Martín women actively backed the school before and after the 1935–36 protest.

The use of annexes for pedagogical innovation depended upon the teacher. Children could learn math by counting their garden harvest's proceeds and science through observing the conditions under which seeds sprouted. Or, annexes could simply be places where girls embroidered as they had in Porfirian schools while the teacher provided verbal instruction in math and science in the formal classroom. Maximina Márquez, an older teacher in Palmarito, taught in this manner. Younger teachers were more likely to teach "by doing" as a result of their training in rural normal schools or in the inspector's bimonthly Centros de Cooperación. Josefa Alva, for example, took pride in the garden she hoed with students, the basketball team she organized, and the gas lamps, flags, and sports equipment she purchased with the proceeds from the children's cooperative. Teachers like her set the pace for more open gender relations because they promoted girls as equal participants in farming projects and cooperatives. In many schools in Tecamachalco, girls moved from sewing classes in the 1920s to more physically expansive activities like garden cultivation, animal raising, and cooperative formation by 1940.

Whether teachers appointed them or children elected them, committees became an important expression of learning by doing. To compensate for their failure to sell their project to the community, the teachers used committees to convert the school into a microcosm of modernity. Children equipped and used medicine chests filled with iodine, alcohol, and quinine. They decorated the school walls with graphic propaganda against alcohol and in favor of hygiene and reforestation. Their committee work became identified with service to country. Members of the committee to protect birds sang a hymn binding their campaign to the well-being of the patria. In 1940, Sara Robles, teacher in Santa Rosa, formed a cooperative called the "Constructores de una Nueva Patria." Organized as a miniature ejido, it differed from Tecamachalco's adult ejidos in that it had both male and female officers.

Festival became the most widespread learning-by-doing activity for schoolchildren. It was a lesson in national culture as children tapped out the jarabe of Jalisco and drummed the Yaqui Deer Dance. They learned regional folk songs and revolutionary corridos. National history they imbibed through making altars and reciting poems to patriot heroes. They celebrated cleanliness in the drama "The Water Princess and the Soap King." In festivals, they starred as modern producers, exhibiting their lettuce and tomatoes, Leghorn hens, pottery, straw hats, and artificial flowers. Teachers excelled in festival-related skills: teaching dances, oratory, making costumes, staging skits. Today when Reyna Manzano remembers her years of teaching in Tochtepec, she does so by tapping out dance steps, acting out a sentimental dialogue between two orphaned girls, and singing tunes.

More than in the Porfiriato, the school became a relatively autonomous secular space for children where they could learn new skills, associations, activities, values, and loyalties. Because a perceptible decline in parental control over marriage and children had been associated in the revolution with kidnapping and violation of women, the school's space served as a corrective. It implicitly encouraged more egalitarian, respectful gender relations and a stronger valuing of women as active participants in the construction of the nation. However, families sought to control the school's impact on gender relations by limiting the time children spent there. One to three years remained sufficient for most boys into the 1940s, and many parents sent girls more briefly or not at all. By 1950, only 14 percent of women in Quecholac were literate, compared with 48 percent in Tochtepec.[44]

HEGEMONY, RESISTANCE, AND THE SCHOOL

Avilacamachista consolidation of Tecamachalco, accomplished between 1933 and the early 1940s, was manipulative, bloody, and coercive. This regional domination became hegemonic because it provided subaltern groups with some representation, material benefits, and avenues for registering dissent. Local popular pressure and that of national actors ensured the incorporation of portions of the agrarista agenda. SEP–community negotiations were part of this local–national linkage.

Between 1937 and 1940, Avilacamachistas integrated Tecamachalco ejidatarios into the Liga de Comunidades Agrarias, which became Puebla's branch of the CNC and as such, a member of the reformed PNR/PRM. General José Martínez Castro, regional deputy to the national congress, oversaw the integration. He carried it out on the ashes of the Confederación Campesina Emiliano Zapata, at the expense of the FROC, and by keeping Mexico City CNC organizers at a distance. To discipline Tecamachalco agraristas who objected, Martínez Castro fostered his own clientele of officials drawn from agrarista and nonpeasant ranks. He was open to negotiation with ejidatarios who strongly protested the candidates he pushed for office, and he often had to accept their objections. But he also used armed henchmen against those he judged particularly dangerous and inflexible. He rigged elections. In the 1940 presidential elections, the majority of Tecamachalqueños voted for opposition candidate Juan Andreu Almazán, brother of the popular Puebla ex-governor, rather than the PRM candidate, Manuel Avila Camacho, brother of the ignominious Maximino. However, José Martínez Castro ordered local officials to cancel Almazanista votes.[45]

Although they deformed agrarianism, the Avilacamachistas could not destroy it because of a combination of local campesino pressures and central state/party policies. The old hacienda system was destroyed and the coexistence of ejidal and private property legalized. Power relations between population centers were reordered. An agrarian political voice was guaranteed through a sharing of power at the local level between municipal institutions and Comisariados Ejidales and through guaranteed representation in local, regional, and national government via the CNC's membership in the corporately organized PRM/PRI. Nor were Tecamachalco Liga leaders all pliant cronies of Martínez Castro. They included seasoned survivors of prolonged struggle and feisty young men who had pressed for ampliaciones in the 1930s.[46]

To rule successfully, the Avilacamachistas had to partially meet the demands of campesinos, and they could do so by virtue of central government policies and resources. In the 1940s and 1950s, Liga members received tractors, plows, seeds, and credit. Federal government irrigation works, opened in the early 1940s at Valsequillo, helped to solve the age-old problem of water. In the 1950s, the government sponsored the digging of deepwater wells. Completion of the highway between Puebla and Tehuacán opened possibilities for crop diversification and marketing. As integration with the expanding urban market increased the demand for schools, central and regional governments responded by sending more teachers, raising their pay, providing materials and supplies, and sponsoring adult literacy campaigns.[47]

By the 1940s, the SEP–community negotiations of the 1930s had begun to pay off in the amplification of the campesino voice under conditions of domination. In village after village in the late 1930s and early 1940s, ejido leaders, municipal officials, schoolteachers, and Comités de Educación signed pacts guaranteeing the school parcel's harvest for school upkeep. Tensions between teachers and local powerholders eased as the SEP's original allies, the athletes, came of age and assumed office. Teachers joined villagers in pressing demands for material improvements. Teachers spent after-school hours processing water rights permits for farmers. All powerholders collaborated to form sports clubs and inaugurate projects such as the industrialization of fruit trees.[48]

As much as the federal school facilitated the linkage (indeed, the subordination of local life to external processes), villagers and teachers had constructed a school that reinforced a peasant inclination to communal organization and resistance. Like the church in the colonial period (Taylor 1979:118–19), the revolutionary school became a living arena of community decision making and activity (Ezpeleta and Rockwell 1983). The struggle to democratize the school's exclusive space was part and parcel of village politics in the 1930s. Messy and factionalized as it was, the democratic appropriation of the school—rather than rising enrollment or literacy—was the more immediate consequence of the revolution. Through it, agraristas established their place on the Comités de Educación, but often shared membership with non-ejidatario villagers. Liberated in the new order from its subordination to the Porfirian jefe político and the municipal council, the Comité de

Educación became an independent actor in community life. At the same time, the school building itself became a site where the community could resolve conflicts, articulate opinion, and contest state policies.

Schoolhouse deliberations were conducted in a political language mutually constructed by villagers, teachers, and other actors engaged in the revolutionary redistribution of resources and power. The language permitted local maneuver, dialogue, petitioning, and resistance. It drew deeply rooted local notions of justice into a new logic born of the politics and ideology of the 1930s. For example, the ejidatarios in Cuesta Blanca wrote to President Manuel Avila Camacho in 1941, in response to the governor's defense of a renter's complaint against their use of "his" water:

> Please do us the favor of dictating your final decision to grant this pueblo the use of the water as clearly explained in Article 27 of the Republic's Constitution, which says . . . : "The nation . . . has the right to impose limits on private property dictated by the public interest." Based on this law and protected by the most basic justice, we are ready to take any risk, based on the unequivocally revolutionary spirit of our present Government, which we hope will . . . hear the cry of a whole people, who without this precious liquid will perish from hunger, and will dismiss the personal interests of a single individual, who without having the necessary facts and precedent dares to claim rights that are not his . . . the people of Cuesta Blanca will go to the point of sacrifice before allowing their rights to be usurped. . . . The times when we were intimidated and subjected to brute force have long since passed. . . . We are respectful of our Supreme Government, and we know from experience and because it is a matter of justice that this decision will establish a precedent which will strengthen its prestige and the firm conviction that we are entering a new era in which we are treated as Citizens conscious of our rights. Necessity forces us to use the waters while the Supreme Government makes its favorable decision, since the time for watering crops is here and not to do so would mean the loss of the crop. We have faith in justice.[49]

The composition of the letter had its origins in colonial República de los Indios, the legal fiction that had established relations between self-governing Indian villages and the paternalistic Spanish king. The villagers justified their use of the water within a traditional peasant moral economy. They expected that the president (king) would understand their taking extralegal measures to assure survival. Nevertheless, the action was justified by more than ancient right. The authors placed their actions within the context of a popular, national, class struggle they had waged to achieve justice, citizenship, and liberation. They were no longer engaged in a defensive, local maneuver.

Their discursive context broke the boundaries of village and ejido, those of the petitionary supplication to the president/king, and even those of the written Constitution to which they appealed.

Teachers not only participated in constructing the language of local representation, they helped to write the petitions and process grievances because their moral responsibility was to foster just resistance. In the 1930s, federal teachers in Tecamachalco defined themselves as the conscience of the revolution and carved a relative autonomy from the corrupting processes of state consolidation. As Jesús González said, "Through bitter experience, we have learned that many government agents abuse their responsibility, creating mistrust in the institutions they represent." It was the teachers' role "to see to it that campesino interests do not suffer, that moral and economic fraud is avoided." Typical of teachers was Ubaldo Macías Marín, who in 1945 led San Antonio villagers in protest when the government did not fulfill its promise of a loan for planting fruit trees.[50]

But teachers could not be the conscience of revolution on the basis of a set of abstract principles issued by the SEP or by Cárdenas. They were empowered by listening to the community. The struggle over socialist education forced them to humble themselves in deference to campesino religiosity and a host of other daily practices. They learned the logic of campesino ways— why mothers gave children pulque, why men processed and sold it, why particular herbs were soothing, why local methods of planting were better suited to the soil than those taught at the Escuela Rural Normal. Faced with peasant recalcitrance and armed with Cardenista populism, teachers discovered new pride in their local knowledge and authenticity. Horacio Caro claimed to have been among the first ejidatarios of Panotla, Tlaxcala, in 1919. Reyna Manzano regularly consulted her Mixtec-speaking mother-in-law for herbal cures. Socorro Rivera made ink from local plants as her schoolteacher father had taught in their village in Oaxaca. As teachers listened, they realized that they knew more than the SEP. They knew that without their translation, SEP prescriptions had no chance. Because they experienced social mobility and individual definition through the revolution, they were mystically convinced of their role as messengers of the modern world. So they honed their skills as negotiators between two worlds (Vaughan 1990c).

Some were ineffectual and some were co-opted, seduced by salary supplements from local caciques. But the best of them acquired "el poder de hablar," the right to speak for the community, both within it and to the outside world. The democratizing process of the revolution opened this power to them on a scale unknown in the Porfiriato. Male revolutionary teachers

gained equal status with other powerholders in community affairs. Their political clout as arbitrators derived from their membership in an independent
federal agency and in the teachers' union, which became an important force
in elections.[51]

Hegemony is constructed not simply by granting representation to the
dominated or by devising a language for articulating dissent and resistance.
Hegemony has a cultural dimension. Tecamachalco's schools as products of
village–SEP negotiations were part of a cultural revolution that respected
traditions but confronted change. Perhaps the villagers who first reclaimed
lands from haciendas in 1914 were indifferent to the SEP's notions of modernity, but the traumas, miseries, and dialogues of the 1930s produced new
communities more open to externally suggested "improvements." After 1940,
life in Tecamachalco became much more integrated with the market and the
state. The newly paved highway between Puebla and Tehuacán was the artery
of integration. Along it traveled fleets of state-subsidized buses. The buses
brought cultural change, which in turn created a closer relationship between
the SEP's paradigm and daily life, and a greater demand for schooling. Young
boys wanted to be licensed as bus drivers, which required a fourth-grade
school certificate.[52] Buses allowed basketball and baseball teams to participate in new competitions in other parts of the state and nation.[53] Buses made
women's travel to market and job sites easy and safe at a time when meeting
family subsistence needs required their mobility (Friedlander 1975:1–24, 62–
64; Vaughan 1994c:117). Women's literacy increased after 1940, in part because it was useful to their new mobility.

Other "improvements" increased the capacity of families to school their
children while increasing their desire to do so. After 1940, market, state, and
school coalesced in the promotion of labor-saving devices for domestic
work: the corn-grinding mill, which eliminated hours spent at the metate
(Lewis 1951:323; Bauer 1990; Keremitsis 1983), the introduction of stoves,
manufactured cooking utensils, and the installation of water closer to home
(Vaughan 1994c:171–72; Marroni de Velázquez 1994:210–44). Mothers began
to ask for inoculation when they saw children survive epidemics. Government health programs became more effective as they identified female community leaders to facilitate innovations. Often, women respected for their
traditional healing skills helped to broker in the use of wonder drugs—antibiotics and manufactured painkillers. Inoculation, antibiotics, and finally
the availability of canned food made for more and healthier children to
whom education offered new knowledge and skills. Schooling increased
the productive capacity of family members both on the farm and off it, and

enhanced the flexibility and ingenuity of households in confronting the pressures of capitalist growth.[54]

In conclusion, the federal school was neither what was prescribed by the SEP nor what was anticipated by the villagers, but a mutual construction that, for some time after 1940, operated to sustain state/party hegemony because it articulated local interest and dissent, mobilized for community improvement, and provided knowledge, skills, and behaviors compatible with a particular form of economic modernization. At the same time, the school helped to integrate Tecamachalqueños into a national, civil society that would eventually challenge the hegemonic pact of the postrevolutionary state/party.

5

"GOOD DAY, PISTOL! WHERE ARE YOU TAKING THAT TEACHER?"
SOCIALIST EDUCATION
IN ZACAPOAXTLA

Zacapoaxtla occupies the center of the Sierra Norte, a swath of dense mountains and wild canyons in the Sierra Madre Oriental. Zacapoaxtla differed significantly from Tecamachalco. The Spaniards had barely conquered the remote region, which lacked precious metals and land suitable to estate agriculture. Lightly evangelized and administered, it served as a zone of relative autonomy and refuge for indigenous peoples (García Martínez 1987) until non-Indian immigration began in earnest at the end of the eighteenth century (Thomson 1989b:60–65). In Zacapoaxtla, Nahua villagers used the nineteenth-century civil wars of state formation to reach an accommodation with the colonizers. The Nahuas managed to keep land, cultural integrity, and a significant degree of political autonomy but had to accept non-Indian commercial and administrative control.[1]

Unlike in Tecamachalco, no strong agrarian movement emerged here in the revolution. When in the 1930s the SEP, in league with certain liberal Nahua communities, tried to promote structural and cultural change, most villagers rebuffed them to side with traditional elites, who were linked to the Avilacamachistas and championed regional autonomy from external interference. Unlike Tecamachalco, Zacapoaxtla experienced no cultural revolution in the 1930s and 1940s. Retrenched regionalism defined patriotism, shored up old power relations, shaped the politics of linkage to the new state, and distanced modernization. Nonetheless, school negotiations in the 1930s laid the foundations for post-1940 alliances between teachers and Nahuas that were forged to curb the excesses of domination and to facilitate community-initiated change.

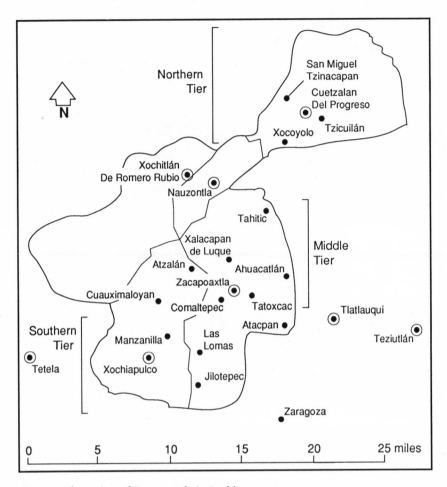

MAP 5   The region of Zacapoaxtla in Puebla

LITERACY, SCHOOLS, AND
NINETEENTH-CENTURY ACCOMMODATION

Xochiapulco, a municipality of impoverished Nahua subsistence farmers and charcoal producers located a tortuous distance from the new railroad depot at Zaragoza, boasted the highest male literacy rate in Puebla outside the capital in 1900: 44 percent knew how to read and write in Spanish (see table 2). By contrast, in the municipalities of Zacapoaxtla and Cuetzalan—by 1900 burgeoning centers in the *aguardiente* (rum) and coffee trades—male literacy rates were half those of Xochiapulco. Throughout the region, rigid patriarchal relations kept women's literacy low. Male teachers were addressed as "Ciudadano" (Citizen); the handful of women teachers were "señoritas."

Far from reflecting economic modernization, literacy differentials in 1900 are explained by accommodations Nahuas made with non-Indian settlers during the nineteenth-century civil wars, when the Sierra emerged as a critical arena for combat between Liberals and Conservatives and foreign invaders. Because these accommodations go far toward explaining distinct responses among Nahuas to socialist education in the 1930s, it is important to examine them all in detail. Three Nahua strategies, each motivated by a desire to preserve communal autonomy, are distinguishable along geographical fault lines of south (Xochiapulco), center (Zacapoaxtla), and north (Cuetzalan). For purposes of clarity, the following explanation focuses on these municipalities and is facilitated by reference to map 5.[2]

On the cold-land southern tier at the Sierra's periphery, where productive land was scarce, several villages allied with Liberals who promised tax exemption and land. To fight the Conservatives in the civil wars of 1857–1859, Liberal officers from the western district of Tetela recruited Juan Francisco Lucas, a Nahua schoolteacher, who was leading villagers in a struggle to retrieve land taken by Zacapoaxtla elites. Lucas and the villagers joined the Sixth Battalion of the Puebla National Guard. For their heroic defense of Puebla city against the French in 1862, they were rewarded with Xochiapulco, a town created from lands they had disputed with the Zacapoaxtla elites (Thomson with LaFrance 1996:44–72; Mallon 1995:27–32, 44–54; Beaucage 1973b:290–303).

In the central, middle tier, Zacapoaxtla city elites championed the Conservative, Catholic revolution, launched nationally from their town in 1855. Nahua communities around Zacapoaxtla supported them, as did key towns like Atacpan on the southern tier's eastern flank between Zacapoaxtla and the Catholic stronghold of Tlatlauqui. Thus villagers hoped to secure protection from Liberal troop levies, privatization of communal land, and anticlerical legislation (Thomson with LaFrance 1996:46, 106–14, 217–29, 252, 296–99; Mallon 1995:45–47).

To the north in the frontier, hotland municipality of Cuetzalan, communities were less accustomed to colonizers. Starting in the 1860s, two out of five villages joined local rebel "Pala" Agustín Dieguillo to prevent land privatization by Conservative settlers from Zacapoaxtla city. To meet local goals, "Pala" Agustín allied with Liberals. When he finally surrendered in 1894, full victory eluded the ambitious settlers, who had hoped to subject Indians to labor on their own plantations. Nahua communities continued as direct producers, in control of much of the land they had traditionally used (Thomson 1991b).

TABLE 2 Literacy in Zacapoaxtla, 1900–1950

	1900		1930		1940		1950	
	% Male	% Female	% Male	% Female	% Male	% Female	% Male	% Female
Zacapoaxtla	23	19	31	13	30	15	50	29
Cuetzalan	20	5	22	11	6	5	34	15
Xochitlán	19	15	19	10	35	29	29	12
Nauzontla	6	3	30	11	19	10	47	25
Xochiapulco	44	13	53	18	54	27	65	42

Youth Literacy (ages 10–14)

	1930		1940	
	% Male	% Female	% Male	% Female
Zacapoaxtla	34	16	24	18
Cuetzalan	29	22	5	3
Xochitlán	25	11	42	31
Nauzontla	45	25	16	12
Xochiapulco	65	42	53	42

Sources: *Censo general de la República Mexicana*, 1900; *Quinto Censo de la Población*, 1930; *Sexto Censo de la Población*, 1940; *Séptimo Censo de la Población*, 1950 (Mexico: Dirección General de Estadística).

On the southern tier, Xochiapulco took the name "Villa del Cinco de Mayo," commemorating its service to the nation at the Battle of Puebla. In 1864–65, Xochiapulquenses again took up arms to resist Napoleon III's Austrian troops. While their Conservative enemies in Zacapoaxtla welcomed the invaders with Te Deums, the Xochiapulquenses torched their homes, trees, and fields rather than yield to the foreign usurper. The Xochiapulquenses and other Guardsmen sent the French troops—"who had once peered at the pyramids of Egypt from the heights of victory"—limping back to traitorous Zacapoaxtla. So wrote the schoolteacher, Manuel Pozos, in his record of local history in 1904 (Pozos 1991:52–53).

Xochiapulco had a high rate of male literacy in 1900 because it was a new community, created out of several hamlets bound by years of armed struggle on behalf of patriotic liberalism. As Guy Thomson (Thomson with LaFrance 1996:175–76) has argued, Xochiapulco was a military colony constructed around ideals of freedom for male citizens, community, and nation from feudal, clerical, and political tyranny.[3] In the minds of Xochiapulco's leaders, the exercise of autonomy required education.

Principal among these leaders was Nahua General Juan Francisco Lucas (Thomson and LaFrance 1987:4–8; Thomson with LaFrance 1996:328–29; Mallon 1995:50–56, 112–28; Rivera 1991:44–45, 85–90, 164–65; SEP 1956). Lucas was one of Puebla's "Tres Juanes": the others were Tetela Generals Juan Crisóstomo Bonilla and Juan N. Méndez, who governed Puebla in the 1880s and created the state's liberal school system. Lucas stayed in the Sierra. Making Xochiapulco his home base, he turned the town into a model of liberal sociability. Dressed in peasant drill and huaraches, he personally supervised the construction of roads, bridges, and schools. In the headtown, villagers carved out wide boulevards modeled on the Spanish grid and built a town square with an imposing municipal palace and a large school. For the town hall, Lucas imported a huge clock, symbolic of nineteenth-century progress.

In Xochiapulco, men performed Masonic rites and read the Constitution of 1857 in Nahuatl. Xochiapulco had a Methodist chapel. Native religious practices persisted but without strong linkages to the Catholic Church. The only antidote to the church was the school. In the 1880s, adult men attended a night school where they learned cosmography, zoology, and botany. In the headtown, schools belonged to the community. At well-attended graduation ceremonies solemnized by music from the Cuerpo Filarmónico (village band), the juries judging teachers and students were made up of friends and equals. Schools were centers for celebrating the Fifth of May, the pivotal date in the Xochiapulquenses' mutual construction of community, state, and nation.[4]

In their analyses of popular liberalism in Xochiapulco, Guy Thomson and Florencia Mallon note the contradictions inherent in Lucas's and the schoolteachers' defense of principles of communal autonomy while they sought to impose a liberal cultural project (Thomson with LaFrance 1996:341–42; Mallon 1995:279–301). Mallon surmises that in Xochiapulco liberal institutions did not so much displace preliberal Nahua culture as they provided a "reconfiguration of boundaries of what was possible, legitimate, and desirable in village life." Reconfiguration most affected the headtown. Outlying hamlets were seemingly less transformed. Atzalan, for instance, resembled most other Nahua settlements in the region. Never subjected to the church's congregation policy, it had no center or Spanish grid. A crooked path vecinos named Calle Juan Francisco Lucas identified the town to outsiders. Extended families lived scattered through the hills. Still, the people of Atzalan shared with other Xochiapulquenses the decades-long National Guard experience in defense of the Mexican nation and communal autonomy within a locally defined liberal framework. Reciprocal relations with the headtown and the patriarch, Lucas, known affectionately as "Tata," nurtured liberal sociability.

Lucas donated his own lands to hamlets so that they could build and sustain schools. Mutually administered by cabecera officials and hamlet officers and residents, schools became symbols of communal autonomy, even when they were sparsely attended.[5]

In the second half of the nineteenth century, schoolteachers joined veteran National Guard officers as community leaders in Xochiapulco. The teachers preserved, embellished, and propagated a history of resistance linking Xochiapulco's indigenous culture to liberalism. Such was the purpose of Manuel Pozos's 1904 record of local history. Himself a non-Indian Protestant immigrant to Xochiapulco, Pozos celebrated the town as fount and protector of liberal ideals. He inspired a new generation of teachers in the central Sierra who came to study with him and share his faith in the liberating power of schooling.[6]

Pozos preached as Xochiapulco's regional power waned. Even after the municipality joined the western district of Tetela in 1870, it exercised influence in Zacapoaxtla district through General Lucas. He used the National Guard and his negotiating skills to support communities against headtown abuse in issues of taxation, electoral imposition, land division, and territorial jurisdiction. He helped Pala Agustín in Cuetzalan. Lucas derived support from the Sierra Liberals who governed the state from 1876 to 1885. After 1885, his power declined as Porfirio Díaz eliminated the Liberals from state office and demobilized the National Guard (Thomson with LaFrance 1996:370–90). In 1894, the last rebellion ended with Pala Agustín's surrender. A long period of political *continuismo* began, marked by the rapid growth of Zacapoaxtla and Cuetzalan as commercial centers. By 1900, these headtowns, with populations of 12,248 and 6,371, dwarfed Xochiapulco's headtown of 1,858 residents.

In contrast to the situation in Xochiapulco, neither teachers nor Nahua army officers held elite status in Zacapoaxtla or Cuetzalan. A handful of creole and occasionally mestizo Catholic families ruled these bustling capitals. The town of Zacapoaxtla became the center for commercial expansion into Indian territory in the rich, warmer zones of the mountain basin. The road from the railroad station at Zaragoza north to Zacapoaxtla filled with children carrying the goods of merchants from Puebla, Veracruz, and Mexico City. Zacapoaxtla's aguardiente factories, owned by families like the Sosa and Macip, received sugar grown by indigenous farmers and hauled over mountains by mestizo muleteers. Farther north in Cuetzalan, Zacapoaxtlan colonizers—the Flores, Pérez, Huidobro, and Mora families—forged ahead with development once Pala Agustín surrendered. They expanded their aguardiente processing plants, carved out ranches and small haciendas in the interstices between Indian villages, and introduced two new coffee factories, which purchased berries from hotland farmers.[7]

Elites maintained a racial, hierarchical divide between themselves and the Nahuas. They obtained land through money-lending activities—when Nahua families could not pay the high interest rates. They demanded personal, public, and religious services for which they did not pay. Cabecera officials arbitrarily arrested villagers on charges of drunkenness in order to secure labor for public projects. The headtowns kept control over the indigenous villages through appointment of the secretaries to the local town councils.[8]

The relationship between elites and villagers also contained elements of reciprocity. Complex negotiations cast the elites as "protectors" from further disruption by the expanding Mexican state and society. In this densest district of indigenous speakers in Puebla, many elites knew Nahuatl and mediated between the Nahuas and the outside world. Immigration was kept low until after 1900. The Nahuas preserved land. In Cuetzalan, many benefited from the surge of cash crop production. As market participation grew, they depended on elites for the processing and sale of their produce, for credit, and for grain, rum, and other consumer goods. In times of crisis, they turned to them for relief. The Indians kept their governing institutions: councils, religious mayordomías and cofradías. Through these, the eldest men, or *pasados,* presided and ensured cultural integrity.[9]

Unlike the Porfirian estate owners of Tecamachalco, the elites of Zacapoaxtla and Cuetzalan were entirely local and more diligent in cultivating the loyalties of those they dominated—at least in the district's middle and northern tiers. In an imaginative use of renascent Catholicism, they seized upon religious symbols, space, and associational forms to deepen ties and cement control over communities. They integrated rich local music, dance, and ritual into festivals and pilgrimages they sponsored. Priests brought together aristocratic ladies, rum magnates, Nahua councils, cofradías, and whole communities in religious construction. They built handsome wings and altars to adorn the Zacapoaxtla cathedral. Huge, imposing, whitewashed churches dwarfed the hillside barrios around the city (Sánchez Flores 1984: 224–33; Sosa, n.d.:125–33).

The jewel of local craftsmanship and collective devotion was the Sanctuary of Guadalupe, which brought God, civilization, and interracial truce to Cuetzalan. Modeled on the basílica at Lourdes, the gray Gothic structure dominated the town square and towered majestically over the mountains as they cascaded toward the Gulf of Mexico. The sanctuary's interior murals celebrated a Catholic version of Mexican history, depicting the sixteenth-century friars' loving evangelization of the Indians. The images were part of a campaign to bury all liberal associations remaining from Pala Agustín's rebellion. Although only two out of five villages had followed Agustín, the elites could leave nothing to chance.

Although non-Indian dominators could touch Indian communities through religious ceremony, priestly authority, and ritual coparenthood, the administration, practice, and meaning of religion differed starkly between headtown and village. In the headtowns, the holding of civic office was divorced from the church; in Nahua towns, the fusion of civil and religious office persisted. Catholic elite cultural campaigns and the surrender of Agustín reinforced Nahua elders' attention to religious affairs and their identification of these with communal autonomy.

In everyday life, religion in the headtowns meant attending Mass, taking Communion, and worshiping the Virgin. In Nahua barrios, religion was bound up with every living hour, from walking through the forest to planting corn to giving birth. Although we have little direct insight into the Nahua universe in 1900, that described by anthropologists in the 1970s provides us with some clues. A rigid construct built upon the imperatives of survival in a precarious world, it involved a relentless juxtaposition between the world of humans, the Sun, and Christ and a peripheral forest of night, where the meandering Devil concocted ever-new tricks for subverting order. From the rooster's crow at sunrise, the balance shifted against the Devil in favor of life. Even in daylight, the preservation of human order required constant vigilance and action. To avoid gossip and slander in the community, to practice filial obedience, to plant a cross by the stream to ward off the *duendes,* to call in a witch to retrieve a child's lost soul, to act out excesses of anger in the marriage ceremony through the night in order to repress them in a sacred commitment to unity at dawn—these acts maintained the world of humans, the Sun, and Christ. In a hierarchical structure based on age and gender— the dead over the living, the elders over the young, men over women, and parents over children—whole communities and families went into excruciating debt to pay for the fruit, aguardiente, meat, and *mole* that fed the ancestors on the Day of the Dead.[10]

In a rigorous world of few words but constant, didactic, symbolic action, Nahua children learned by doing from their parents—weeding the milpa, grinding corn, sewing costumes, learning prayers and dances, the flute and the drum. In such an environment, Spanish-language schooling appeared to be of little use. Families distant from schools and needing children for work kept their offspring's names from the school rosters to escape fines.

Nor were schools places where Nahua children felt comfortable. Because cabecera elites relied on religion and trade to cement their ties with villagers, they were less concerned than their Xochiapulco counterparts with schooling as a tool of interethnic sociability. They set up boys' schools in many hamlets, but the schools were instruments of discrimination and condescension. In contrast to the experience in Xochiapulco, schools were not appropriated as symbols of community construction and were even more sparingly used. Often housed in rented spaces, they were poorly supplied with texts, paper, and ink. Teachers earned a pittance. The town council secretary, sent to represent cabecera interests, often doubled as teacher. Graduation exercises took place in the headtown. Cabecera officials, not villagers, made up the jury. Even when, after 1900, examinations began to be held in villages, the presiding judge represented the cabecera. He often overlooked poor performances because the teacher was his *compadre* and because not much was expected of the "indios chamacos" (little Indian children).[11]

Despite these barriers, with advancing commercialization after 1900, indigenous boys' use of schools increased in major towns. Between 1900 and 1910, the number of monolingual Nahua speakers in the district declined from 22,166 to 17,642. By 1905, an average of thirty-eight boys took final examinations in the beginning course (*curso inferior*) in each barrio school near Zacapoaxtla city and on the southern tier. With prosperity, school-building also accelerated in Cuetzalan. The town of Tzicuilán even created a girls' school—making it and Jilotepec on the southern tier the only villages with girls' schools in the Zacapoaxtla district. By contrast, Xochiapulco's hamlet schools were all coeducational.[12]

In central Zacapoaxtla, music acted as another catalyst for boys' schooling. Music had been vital to indigenous culture and to the sealing of interracial relations in colonial society. Postindependence civil wars encouraged the proliferation of village bands with secular repertoires and purposes (Thomson 1989a:51–61; Thompson with LaFrance 1996:316–22). Becoming a musician and playing in the Cuerpo Filarmónico freed one from the head tax and from military and community service. The Catholic Escuela Glorias de Mayo in Zacapoaxtla attracted young men from the barrios; there, they learned the three Rs, Christian doctrine, oratory, and music and trained to join the prestigious thirty-five-member Cuerpo Filarmónico, subsidized by the *ayuntamiento* (city council).[13]

Music in Zacapoaxtla served both religious and secular purposes. Catholicism alone was insufficient to create and sustain the Zacapoaxtlan elite's exercise of hegemony. The state was their engine of domination. To rule, they had to poeticize state and nation. In their symbols of rule, Zacapoaxtlans stood between Xochiapulco, where liberal ideology dominated, and Cuetzalan, where priests reigned as local intellectuals. Indicative of their ambivalence is the fact that the Zacapoaxtlans mounted the town clock, that indispensable fetish of Porfirian modernity, on the Cathedral. In the Fifth of May celebrations, directors of the Catholic boys' school and the public boys' school alternated as orators.[14] As in Xochiapulco, Fifth of May rituals celebrated local participation in the victory over the French in 1862. They provided rich opportunities for the emerging middle class to engage in artistic expression. Teachers, musicians, conductors, and composers competed to turn out patriotic poetry, waltzes, hymns, and marching tunes. Like the mist enshrouding the hills and hamlets, their oratory trapped patriotism in a setting of utopian rusticity. The discourse also ranged above the mist to embrace a national ideology of progress. The festivals were occasions to inaugurate a school, gaslights, an aqueduct, or a bridge. They were moments for composing and singing a "Hymn to the Sciences." Just as they were opportunities for Nahua musical groups to compete with one another, so were they moments for the multiracial Filarmónico to perform Schubert's "Poet and the Peasant."[15]

THE SEP'S FAILED REVOLUTION IN ZACAPOAXTLA, 1923–1938

On the eve of the revolution, two tensions rustled Zacapoaxtla's peace. The first was between elites and villagers in places where wealthy families such as the Macips, Sosas, and Varelas had expanded their landholdings at the expense of village subsistence: this expansion most affected southern-tier towns and Atzalan in Xochiapulco. The second tension was between elites and the middle classes and was born of economic prosperity, state expansion, schooling, and immigration. Members of this growing middle class had little hope for mobility in a region of increasingly closed, familial power. While some sought access to the world of the elites, others—including many schoolteachers—were offended by the servitude imposed on native peoples. These tensions played themselves out in the course of the revolution in Zacapoaxtla and reached their climax in the 1930s when the SEP, backed by the Almazán government, joined forces with regional teachers, middle-class liberals, agrarista villagers, and the Xochiapulquenses to integrate the region into the new state via radical reforms. This project met defeat at the hands of another faction of the middle class, allied with the old elites, Avilaca-machismo, and many Nahua villagers alarmed at the SEP's assault on their integrity.

Predictably, Xochiapulquenses joined the revolution of 1910. They served in the armies of Juan Francisco Lucas. The old cacique entered the fray to safeguard Sierra autonomy. Before he died in 1917, he had declared for the Constitutionalists. Xochiapulquenses leaped at the opportunity to defend the "sacred rights of man." Among the many local boys who won rank in battle were Jorge Washington Sánchez, Juan Pablo Mirabeau, and schoolteachers Manuel Rivera and Sergio "The Squirrel" Gutiérrez. In February 1913, when it was rumored that the federal garrison at Zacapoaxtla would attack Xochiapulco, the entire community—"hasta las mujeres" (even the women)—took the opportunity to trounce their old enemy (Rivera 1991:196–97). They marched over the mountains armed with old rifles, machetes, sticks, stones, and clubs. Descending upon Zacapoaxtla, they swarmed onto the plaza and invaded the stores. The Indians struck terror into the hearts of city merchants and alerted them to the fragility of their interracial peace.

In 1914, Xochiapulquenses, led by the teacher-officers Rivera and Gutiérrez, helped the vecinos of Atzalan redeem a portion of the Varela family's Papalocuautla ranch and advance claim to part of the Sosa family's Apulco hacienda. In 1925, Sergio "The Squirrel" Gutiérrez and Atzalan vecinos invited the government agrarian reform engineer to survey Apulco lands. They were dispersed by the gunmen of Julio Lobato, ambitious mestizo manager of the Apulco hacienda. When the engineer sought police protection in Zacapoaxtla, the municipal president turned him down. The engineer left town. No agrarian reform official returned to help the Atzalan villagers until 1932.[16]

While Julio Lobato represented one option for middle-sector upward mobility, Rafael Molina Betancourt represented another. The son of a merchant who owned a butcher shop in Zacapoaxtla, Molina Betancourt had graduated from the public boys' school, where his uncle taught music. His ideals drew from the liberal wellspring of Xochiapulco and his own schooling. His studies at the normal schools in Puebla and Mexico City during the heady revolutionary years deepened his convictions. He had joined the armies. When Vasconcelos launched his educational crusade, Molina Betancourt signed on. Sent to Zacapoaxtla in 1923, he intended to civilize the indigenous peoples while liberating them from the yoke of local elites.

Molina Betancourt broke traditional headtown control over schools when he placed several of the bankrupt institutions under SEP jurisdiction. He mobilized young male teachers around a new radical project. On Saturdays they met to discuss action pedagogy. Several were indigenous in background; most were sons of the middle class; all were bilingual. Securing villagers' help in building an aqueduct to a new school garden, setting up chicken coops, discussing cooperativism, these teachers became political actors who threatened to empower new individuals and groups in Nahua towns. Local officials often blocked them. They refused to enforce attendance laws. They declined to set aside land to support the school, and where such land existed they withheld its proceeds. Teacher Lauro Molina Arriaga got shot in the leg. The Molina Betancourt home was torched.[17]

When the SEP transferred Molina Betancourt in late 1923, Manuel Rivera, teacher and revolutionary officer from Xochiapulco, became SEP inspector. Xochiapulco became pivotal to the federal project. In 1923, Xochiapulquenses asked the SEP to federalize their central school. Their town, they argued, had long defended the patria with little compensation. They were convinced of the importance of schooling to create "men of conviction, apt and capable so that our beloved Patria is respected by the most civilized nations of the world." They asked the federal government to invest in their teachers' salaries. They requested agronomists and craftsmen to promote fruit cultivation and ceramics. They wanted help to build a new road to the railroad station at Zaragoza. The Xochiapulco school opened as a SEP Centro Escolar in 1923 under the direction of General Sergio "The Squirrel" Gutiérrez. It served to train rural teachers in action techniques and revolutionary ideology.[18]

When Moisés Sáenz, undersecretary of education, visited in 1927, he recognized Xochiapulco's main school as the Sierra's jewel. Its students excelled in arithmetic and reading. Children entered speaking only Nahuatl and were taught in that language in the first year. The 130 children filled five grades. The school boasted "magnificent" annexes: a library, a playground, chicken coops, bee hives, rabbit hutches, a dovecote, a garden, an orchard, carpentry shops, and two hectares of land sown to support it (Sáenz 1927:68–72). Youth literacy jumped to 65 percent for boys in 1930, indicating the growth of literacy in outlying hamlets. A further revolutionary advance was the inclusion of girls, whose literacy rose to 42 percent.

Federal schools in Jilotepec and Comaltepec, south and west of Zacapoaxtla, also delighted Sáenz with their flourishing gardens and craft shops making artificial flowers, batik fabrics, ixtle baskets, and leather goods. In Jilotepec, Ernesto Castillo, with the help of his mother, taught seventy-two children in the day and many adults at night, including some "señoritas." At Comaltepec, Humberto Uribe Guerrero experimented with fertilizers in the school garden and oversaw the stitching of shirts on sewing machines (Sáenz 1927:72, 91–93). By 1930, boys' literacy had risen to 34 percent in Zacapoaxtla, fueled mostly by communities like these (see table 2). Girls' literacy lagged at 16 percent.

Sáenz noted that Jilotepec and Comaltepec schools functioned despite the indifference of municipal authorities. Indifference sometimes turned to hostility in the middle tier around Zacapoaxtla. In Xalticpac, where Spanish speakers were few, the teacher ran a dismal school with a few "dirty, apathetic" children. The teacher complained of harassment from elite families in Zacapoaxtla (Sáenz 1927:71–72, 88–89). North of the city in the municipalities of Cuetzalan, Nauzontla, and Xochitlán, the federal effort hardly penetrated.

In 1929, the federal school project took on new militance when Governor Almazán exiled General Gabriel Barrios, the regional strongman who had protected the Sierra from outside interference. Almazán meant to build a popular base for the PNR in the Sierra by sponsoring agrarian organization, schools, and new groups in municipal office. Unlike Inspector González in Tecamachalco, SEP officials assisted Almazán's effort and continued it after his resignation in 1933.

Rafael Molina Betancourt, *oficial mayor* in the SEP under Bassols, and his brother Fausto, now SEP inspector in Zacapoaxtla, were instrumental in creating the Escuela Rural Normal at Tlatlauqui in 1932. Even before the national adoption of socialist education, students at the Normal were creating "Cartillas de Divulgación Socialista" to teach reading through such concepts as surplus value, class struggle, and exploitation. Discouraged by the clerical "fanaticism" of Tlatlauqui, they moved the Normal to Xochiapulco in 1935. In bidding for the Normal, Xochiapulco spokesmen had stressed "the absolute absence of the Catholic religion" in their town. They donated fifteen hectares of land and opened the municipal palace to classes until proper quarters could be built. For some time, the municipal president rotated his office between private homes.[19]

Rafael Molina Betancourt sent Raul Isidro Burgos to direct the Normal. One of those seasoned architects of the revolutionary school, Burgos had created and worked at rural normal schools in Chiapas and Guerrero. A native of Morelos, he was at heart a Zapatista. A man of charismatic humility, dressed in peasant drill and huaraches, he invested his salary in his schools and gave anything extra he had to the poor. With his students and the Xochiapulquenses he built the Normal, hauling lime, mixing mortar, baking bricks.

With them he plowed and weeded the school's fields and planted seedlings in new orchards. He never admonished a pupil except through discussion. He inspired awe and mystical enthusiasm. To his students, he was a "holy man."[20]

Although Burgos's students came from different parts of Puebla, many were local. Eduardo Ramírez Díaz was from Nauzontla, north of Zacapo-axtla; his mother had studied to be a teacher with Manuel Pozos of Xochia-pulco. His father served on the committee that bid for an agricultural school in Nauzontla. Faustino Hernández from Cuetzalan had followed his youth-ful dreams to Mexico City, where he hoped to become an airplane pilot. Dis-appointed, he went home to train with Burgos. Burgos also went from village to village recruiting young people whose campesino and indigenous roots were deeper. He convinced Carlos Vázquez, emerging agrarista leader in Jilo-tepec, to give him his son Filadelfo. Defying his Nahua parents, who did not want him to continue his studies, Juan Cuamatzin took refuge in the normal school at Xochiapulco, where, in his own words, he became "civilized." These young men wed themselves to an ideological project. When they woke in the morning, they sang the "International." As they worked in the fields, studied agrarian law, learned revolutionary corridos, and built a new kiosk for the plaza, they came to see themselves as "social gladiators" destined to change the world.[21]

On the southern tier, the Molina Betancourt brothers, Raul Isidro Burgos, and the Xochiapulco leaders used their Masonic ties to cement alliances with agrarista activists, who in turn won municipal office: Carlos Vázquez in Jilo-tepec, Margarito Ibarro in Las Lomas, and Herón Lima in Zaragoza. These men led villagers in retrieving land from the Macip family's haciendas. A further radicalizing impulse on the southern tier came from a new element in regional politics: the railroad workers' union in Zaragoza. Agraristas also got support from the statewide Confederación Campesina Emiliano Zapata (CCEZ).[22]

North of the southern tier, the Almazanista effort challenged Zacapoaxtla elites and their upwardly mobile recruits gathered around Julio Lobato, mu-nicipal president in 1931. Almazanismo relied on more radical young men— among them, federal schoolteachers. With them was Celerino Toral, em-ployee of the state tax collector's office, a consummate violinist who played in the Filarmónico, a dark-skinned, energetic young man who had declared his opposition to the Lobato–elite alliance.[23]

These radicals publicized federal agrarian and labor laws and organized the local CCEZ. People responded. Grievances negotiated or suffered in the din and shadows of daily life gained public visibility and legitimation. Campesinos from barrios near and north of Zacapoaxtla asked for land that had been taken by elite families. As the SEP entered Cuetzalan, villagers spoke up against illegal land grabs, excessive taxation, and arbitrary arrests. Zacapo-axtla workers who were owed back pay and claimed physical abuse by their employers began to organize. Prisoners demanded better rations and wages for their work.[24]

Between 1932 and 1935, the agraristas Herón Lima, Carlos Vázquez, and Margarito Ibarra controlled town councils in Zaragoza, Jilotepec, and Las Lomas. Teacher Lauro Molina Arriaga won the municipal presidency in Zacapoaxtla. Celerino Toral became head of the local PNR Committee. The "men of words" (hombres de las palabras), as they called themselves, had triumphed over the "men with guns and money" (hombres de pistolas y billetes).

The "hombres de pistolas y billetes" had no intention of surrendering power. Lobato's armed men kept Atzalan families from cultivating land ceded them by the government from the Apulco hacienda. Eliseo Bonilla, lo-cal officer of the Ministerio Público, kept agrarian reform authorities from measuring his property of Ejecayo, solicited by the "ejidatarios comunistas." In Xochitlán, municipal authorities forced a newly formed campesino group to sign a paper agreeing that there was no land in the area that could legally be affected by land reform. In Cuetzalan, delegates were blocked from at-tending a campesino congress in Puebla. In Xaltetela, Lobato's men stopped a man from ceding land to the school. Throughout the ex-district of Zaca-poaxtla, elites promoted or took advantage of inter- and intravillage disputes to splinter the redistributive movement. On the southern tier, they resur-rected old Conservative alliances to set Atacpan against Xochiapulco and its allies: both sides laid claim to the same hacienda lands. Internal disputes broke out in middle-tier towns: in Tatoxcac, a faction of vecinos accused the justice of the peace of pressuring them to join the agraristas, pocketing their money, and harassing the village elders.[25]

In their campaign against "los comunistas," the Lobato group found a winning issue in socialist education. SEP promotion of agrarianism in Zaca-poaxtla coincided with a more aggressive SEP policy toward traditional cul-ture and an influx of new teachers, not all of whom were local. Even when they were, Burgos's protégés were committed to the SEP project. They had difficulty distinguishing between liberating people from their structural op-pressors and freeing them from their daily cultural practices.

In their righteous zeal, teachers offended local customs. SEP insistence on coeducation riled both mestizo and indigenous societies. Outside Xochiapulco, the region had no experience with coeducational schools. Female teachers usually made coeducation less threatening to parents, but the SEP here employed few women. A veteran state teacher in Nauzontla instigated a revolt in the town council over the principle of coeducation. Porfirio Cordero, SEP inspector, found the root cause for low female enrollment in the widespread Indian belief in women's inferiority and marginalization: the sexes had to be separated because women were guilty of "original sin."[26] Teachers did not have to be raving iconoclasts to arouse hostility. In indigenous communities, when teachers threatened to move the cemetery, they ventured into a minefield. Nahuas venerated their ancestors. Death had intricate, vivid meaning, sustained through daily ritual, symbolism, and beliefs relating the human body and soul to nature and the Devil. When teachers launched anti-alcohol campaigns, they seemed oblivious to liquor's intimate role in sacralizing every event in the life cycle from birth to death. Mixed with music and dance, it made life meaningful, safe, and enjoyable. When teachers denounced religious festival and church maintenance as wasted time and money, they did not see that ritual labor was as vital to community sustenance as productive work. They stepped directly on the toes of male elders, who controlled both secular and religious dimensions of community life.[27]

The policy of socialist education dealt the elites a winning hand at an ideal moment. They could cast themselves as protectors of both non-Indians and Indians from a foreign project cooked up by the Devil. With priests from Tlatlauqui, Zacapoaxtla, and Cuetzalan reputedly leading the legions against the godless school, nightmarish rumors spread through the hamlets. One teacher was reported to seduce men's wives while they were off tending their animals—a politically convenient story concocted to alarm indigenous men. In the federal schools, girls and boys were said to undress in front of one another to demonstrate the teachings of sexual education. The government was kidnapping children. They were being sent to the United States and turned into oil for airplanes. In a region where forced military recruitment had perennially terrorized communities and the Devil turned men into animals or elements, such stories struck like lightning. In 1935, federal schools emptied.[28]

One early morning in the fall of 1935, three teachers were murdered in Teziutlán villages southeast of Zacapoaxtla. With his machete, cristero leader Clemente Mendoza nearly severed the head of teacher Carlos Pastraña. The three schools were torched, doors and furniture destroyed, supplies and archives burned, and human excrement smeared across the walls. Nearby, on

Zacapoaxtla's southern tier, federal teachers began to fear for their lives. In Las Lomas, Ebundio Carreón and his brother Rafael, the teacher, stood guard with rifles, holed up in the schoolhouse, until Margarito Ibarro, local agrarista leader, took them into his home. No one dared venture out at night: doors were locked with balls and chains. In Comaltepec, three men were arrested for plotting to assassinate teachers.[29]

Local wisdom attributed Mendoza's hacking of teachers and schools not to his love for Christ but to orders from Teziutlán priests and from Maximino Avila Camacho's mother, a longtime Teziutlán resident. Perhaps this conclusion was reached because a few weeks after Mendoza's attack, the state PNR, now controlled by the Avila Camachos, orchestrated a full-scale rout of Almazanistas in municipal elections throughout the Sierra. To win, the Avilacamachistas manipulated local PNR committee composition and vote tabulation. Julio Lobato returned to power. In rapid blows from the state PNR and its local allies, the systematic dismantling of agrarismo began on the southern tier. Competition for land between villages hastened the debacle.[30]

In December, SEP teachers in the Zacapoaxtla region asked to leave their communities and be concentrated in the cabecera. Throughout 1935 and 1936, SEP inspector Porfirio Cordero ran from village to village holding assemblies to counteract opposition. He insisted that socialist education was not antireligious. As President Cárdenas had said in Guadalajara, its purpose was to combat the errors and lies invented to exploit the campesinos, in order to ensure them justice and better lives. In the summer of 1936, Cordero sent teachers to a Cultural Mission for thirty-five days to assure their safety and buoy their spirits. They returned in September to empty classrooms and accusations from parents and local authorities that they had shirked their duties and abandoned their schools. In Tatoxcac, no one would lift a finger to finish building the *casa del maestro*. Elsewhere, teachers were denied food and a place to live. The school in Tzicuilán was torched. Vecinos who were trying to set up an agricultural school in Nauzontla fled town in fear of their lives. In Xocoyolo in Cuetzalan, men and women burned incense around the teacher Eduardo Ramírez Díaz: they believed he had been sent by the Devil to seize their children for the government. Into Cuetzalan rode the cristero bands, ex-soldiers of the deposed General Barrios. They attacked villages, schools, and agraristas. In San Miguel Tzinacapan, they kidnapped the teacher Faustino Hernández and held him for eight hours. Resistance in some places, wrote Cordero, reached the point of rebellion.[31]

For the most part, Xochiapulco towns—and southern agrarista strongholds like Jilotepec and Las Lomas—stayed with the SEP. Although literacy declined slightly here in the 1930s, Xochiapulquenses continued to work closely with Burgos and the Normal (see table 2). Young people formed socialist leagues and basketball teams. Women organized Ligas de Madres Proletarias. Accused by some government spokespersons of lacking command of the Spanish language, the Xochiapulquenses turned out for Independence Day celebrations in 1935 decked out in workers' blue and practicing their Spanish. The Frente Unico Popular Regional Xochiapulco, whose members included the teachers, kept up their drive for land resolutions for southern-tier towns.[32]

Support from Xochiapulco emboldened the federal teachers, as did their nucleus of support in Zacapoaxtla. They proudly armed themselves to resist the reaction. Cirilo Contes, a pint-sized teacher with a big gun, became the brunt of local humor. Neighbors greeted him as he crossed the Plaza, "¡Buenos días, pistola! ¿Donde te llevas al maestro?" (Good day, pistol! Where are you taking that teacher?) Teachers gathered in the Zócalo to sing the socialist hymn:

> They say that I am a socialist,
> That I go against capital,
> That I am a propagandist of social revolution,
> What they say is true and I will never deny it,
> I am content being so even if they shoot me.[33]

But their revolution failed. In 1938, Julio Lobato was elected to represent the central Sierra in the national Congress. Governor Maximino Avila Camacho backed him. His deputyship marked the beginning of a local cacicazgo that lasted until 1957. With the exception of Atzalan, land petitions above the southern tier were never honored. On the southern tier, the beneficiaries were few and land was granted mostly at the expense of ejidos awarded in the Almazán period. Xochiapulco was isolated. When the Frente Unico Popular requested aid from the federal government to complete a road to the railroad depot, it was turned down. When in 1939 Rafael Molina Betancourt appealed to Cárdenas to arm the Xochiapulquenses to fight the ex-general Barrios's cristeros, he got no reply.[34]

MINIMIZING SCHOOLS, REGIONALIZING FESTIVAL

In the agrarista stronghold of Tecamachalco, revolutionary appropriation of the federal school was socially conservative but democratic. Appropriated by new powerholders, the school could introduce novel values, behaviors, symbols of national identity, and linkages with the outside world. The revolutionary state institutionalized these changes; the market facilitated them. In Zacapoaxtla, no profound transformation in the regional power structure and its external linkages occurred. The school's potential to introduce new values, behaviors, and identities was limited. How deeply could the Spanish-language curriculum penetrate the minds of Nahuatl-speaking children who stayed only briefly in school? How could team sports move to center stage in communities still governed by aged patriarchs? What meaning did the figure of Zapata have in towns where agrarianism was akin to communism and the Devil? How successful could Mother's Day celebrations be in hamlets where women stayed clear of schools? What color could the Yaqui Deer Dance add to festivals already vivid with the Quetzales in their red, green, and gold dress, their crowns of feathers once plucked from the sacred quetzal bird? In Zacapoaxtla, Indian communities, local elites, and schoolteachers constructed a minimal school and regionalized patriotic festival. The revolution provoked a turning inward, a rejection of outside linkages and innovations. It stymied a process of capitalist development in order to preserve precapitalist, servile, but ethnically integral practices. Official literacy statistics may exaggerate regional declines, but they are indicative of a tumultuous encounter between the SEP and local society in the 1930s.[35]

In 1935, Inspector Porfirio Cordero wrote of the "mutual poverty" of school and community. He referred to the lack of resources to realize the SEP's project. Because of the presence of the Normal Rural, Zacapoaxtlan teachers had more formal training than their Tecamachalco counterparts. However, the Normal Rural at Tlatlauqui had lacked land and staff to carry out agriculture. While agricultural training and recruitment of students with campesino roots began under Maestro Burgos's direction at Xochiapulco, federal teachers were under attack, their channels of communication blocked. Moreover, the federal government provided no resources—little land and no credit, seeds, tools, marketing mechanisms, or roads. As in Tecamachalco, the teachers' faithful governmental allies were the health agents, whose inoculation campaigns caused the same alarm they had in Tecamachalco.

Schools resembled those in Tecamachalco, with portraits of Juárez, Hidalgo, and Morelos hung on the walls. School inventories show the same influx of populist texts in the mid-1930s: *Fermín, La vida rural,* and *Simiente.* Annexes for gardening, animal raising, and crafts were often stronger in the municipalities of Zacapoaxtla and Xochiapulco than in Tecamachalco because the region had more water and an artisan tradition, and because the

SEP had begun intensive work there in the 1920s. On the northern tier, annexes were rare.

In the 1930s, above the southern tier, indigenous communities remained distant from the school. To some, it was simply unfamiliar. Tahitic, a remote town, had never celebrated a patriotic holiday. In 1931, Inspector Fausto Molina Betancourt had to address the townfolk in Nahuatl in the open air in the company of the municipal president because people would not approach the school where he wanted to greet them. Built in the Porfiriato, Tahitic's school had hardly been used.

At least it had a building. In many towns, mobilizing school construction was more difficult than in Tecamachalco. Xochiapulco and southern towns were an exception: vecinos from Atzalan were fined by the forest inspector for illegally cutting wood to renovate their school and build the teacher's house. Villagers of Cuaximaloyan, a barrio of Xochiapulco, bankrupted themselves and solicited help from surrounding towns, teachers, and normal school students to complete an impressive two-story school. In La Manzanilla, Xochiapulco, the community went into debt building a new school with garden, basketball court, and chicken coops. In southern towns, land grants facilitated appropriation of the school by new power groups. In Jilotepec, the teacher organized the ceremony, awarding land titles in the schoolhouse.

Language was a barrier to schooling. In 1930, only 41 percent of the population knew Spanish. Many teachers did not know indigenous languages, and many children did not stay in school long enough to learn Spanish. Most crowded into the preparatory course for non–Spanish speakers and the first year of instruction. Teaching by committees or by the project method was difficult. The language barrier and the short time spent in school limited exposure to the social and natural sciences as teachers focused on teaching to read in Spanish. Again, the Xochiapulco communities were distinct: there, Nahuatl speakers did not find language a barrier and parents often encouraged children to finish several grades.

Outside the southern tier and the municipal headtowns, women's participation in schooling was extremely low. In the Zacapoaxtla region excluding Xochiapulco, official statistics suggest that literacy among girls fell from 18 to 11 percent between 1930 and 1940. In Ahuacatlán, girls were 13 percent of students in 1931 and 15 percent in 1938; in Xochitepec, 4 percent in 1933 and in 1938. Although girls' attendance improved with female teachers, the latter taught mainly in mestizo towns. Few bridges were being built between the school and Nahua women. In Xochiapulco and southern-tier towns, female enrollments were consistently higher. Some women attended night school and joined anti-alcohol campaigns and Ligas de Madres Proletarias. They did not serve on the Comités de Educación. Even in Xochiapulco, "parents" were still fathers.

The strength of resistance in the middle and northern tiers made teachers entirely beholden to local society. The situation sometimes soured them on the SEP's lofty discourse. Eduardo Ramírez Díaz recalled how much work, ingenuity, and time it took to establish trust with parents. He came to resent much of his training:

> We left the Normal Rural with mostly theoretical knowledge. Any empirical teacher, a mechanic, a shoemaker, a carpenter with no normal training was better than we were. I saw immediately that our Normal School professors had sent us out without knowing anything useful. Socialism, communism, *progresistas, grupos avanzados,* what good did these do us? The SEP authorities were not helpful either because they wanted us to go by the book and we had to adapt to the context. The problem was to teach people to read. I grouped all the pupils who did not know how to read into one class and only when I found out some knew more than others did I divide them. We had learned two methods of teaching reading—the natural method and the onomatopoeic of Torres Quintero. Using the latter, I had children reading in three months without understanding anything. The next year I used the natural method; it was extremely difficult and took a lot of work, but this was the one I used to teach Spanish. Parents were very pleased when their children knew how to read after the first year and that gave me a certain acceptance.

It helped that Ramírez Díaz's family was well known in the region and that he helped vecinos paint the church.

As in Tecamachalco, teachers compensated for their minimal schools through celebrating festival. Festival performance was even more important here. While verbal communication was fraught with difficulty, aesthetic expression was strongly woven into the fabric of social relations. As Porfirio Cordero said, "If you do not know the spoken language, what better language than that of ritual and music?" He was particularly attuned to the pedagogical value of patriotic arts, for he had learned his skills from his father, José María Cordero, teacher, violinist, and festival promoter in central Puebla. As a Normalista student in Puebla, Porfirio Cordero had acquired oratorical skills that he perfected as he accompanied revolutionary leaders through Mexico.

In constructing revolutionary cultural festival in Zacapoaxtla, teachers had abundant artistic talent and collective art forms at their disposal and could select from local indigenous and mestizo music, dance, theater, and poetic oratory. Artistic expressions were not only pre-Hispanic and colonial. Zacapoaxtla as a multiracial social formation was created in the nineteenth century through foreign invasions and civil wars, or rather through the ways these experiences were crafted into collective aesthetics. Music permeated the religious and patriotic festivals that bonded Indian and non-Indian societies. While the families of Cuetzalan coffee barons socialized to the strains of Viennese waltzes at the Flores hacienda known as "Eden," the flute, drum, and violin were also part of every indigenous marriage celebration. In a region where communities had fought French and Austrian invaders on their own soil, patriotic oratory and lyrical poetry wed Mexican patriotism to a mountain utopia sealed from the outside world by thick mists.

The SEP wanted to appropriate portions of this regional aesthetic for inclusion in its construction of a national popular culture. They also wanted to pierce the cloud cover to inject new messages, identities, and linkages to the outside world. Teachers wanted local festival to mix traditional regional culture with the new plays, poems, and songs they composed at the Normal Rural and the Cultural Missions. Raul Isidro Burgos's song "El metate" (SEP 1956) was representative of the attempt to innovate through traditional performance:

> "Indita del paliacate"
> Slave of the metate
> When will you abandon it?
> Leave the wretched metate
> that harms you
> Let the mill grind the corn
> For that it is made of metal.
> The metate is jealous of your husband Miguel
> It won't give you rest
> To sleep with him.
> Dedicate yourself to your children,
> to your husband, your home,
> Give them good care
> And teach them to work.

However, the SEP construction of a patriotic cultural repertoire in Zacapoaxtla was influenced more by local culture than by revolutionary messages. New identities, values, and linkages were marginal to a renewed celebration of regional exceptionalism and isolation. Festival could inaugurate a school, embellish the town square, or celebrate a new public work. It was possible to establish Independence Day as a major holiday competing with the Fifth of May, but, north of the southern tier, where neither agrarian reform nor the revolution had much meaning, it was difficult to engender new notions of identity and inclusion—especially around a modernizing paradigm that opened the *patria chica* to the magic and wonder of modernity. On the contrary, teachers did not import culture. They exported local art through SEP publications into the mainstream of a new national culture. In Zacapoaxtla itself, they reinforced the image of a rustic utopia, a closed patriotic construction. Typical was Profesor Agustín Limón's song, *Sierra de Puebla*, with lyrics in Spanish and Nahuatl:

> *The clouds are descending,*
> *Grace is near,*
> *The breeze wets the rooftops,*
> *The afternoon has begun to weep.*
> *So it is in the Sierra de Puebla*
> *So it is in my native land*
> *The place of beautiful women and brave men,*
> *Who took charge of history,*
> *With neither screams nor blustering,*
> *They humiliated the foreigner.*
> *When the dawn breaks, the moon dies*
> *The stars go out and the sky catches fire.*
> *The birds sing, the turkeys flap their wings,*
> *The lambs gambol and the children play.*
> *There in the distance at the foot of the mountain*
> *Is my little house warmed with smoke,*
> *There is the love of my life, my heart, my woman.*[36]

Even Raul Isidro Burgos succumbed to the mist. He composed a song describing the humble homes of Xochiapulco adorned with plants and flowers:

> *Skies of indigo, skies of blue,*
> *Submerged in an endless fragrance*
> *Of rosemary and balm.*
> *Gray mists and white crests of snow,*
> *This is the Sierra of Puebla, simple and content.*

The final verse of Burgos's song depended upon the town in which it was sung. Xochiapulquenses ended this way:

> *Xochiapulco, Xochiapulco,*
> *Hideaway of dreams,*
> *Your men have shown themselves*
> *to be of stout heart.*[37]

Zacapoaxtlans ended differently, in metaphors confirming the postrevolutionary construction of power:

> *Zacapoaxtla, Xochiapulco*
> *Magnificent in history,*
> *One the Sparta of the Sierra*
> *The other our Athens.*
> *Zacapoaxtla, Xochiapulco,*
> *Hideaways of dreams*
> *You are the pearls of the Sierra,*
> *The pride of the nation.*[38]

SCHOOLS, HEGEMONY, AND RESISTANCE IN ZACAPOAXTLA

School building began in earnest in the 1940s with government support and local elite patronage. Julio Lobato embraced the rhetoric of schooling. In his 1937 campaign for Congress, he pledged to foster education so that the old "privileges of culture would disappear and enlightenment grace all social classes." Indigenous communities chimed in: the vecinos of Tahitic asked for a teacher—"amante del progreso y de la cultura popular" (a lover of progress and of the people's culture)—to "elevate us socially and culturally and lift our *poblado* out of the vulgarity of ignorance." But the words were mouthed as part of a negotiating process that had snubbed the SEP's paradigm. The encounter had privileged ethnic difference over assimilation; regional autonomy over national integration.[39]

In Zacapoaxtla, the school appeared to have been subordinated to a regional hegemonic project at odds with the SEP's national discourse of social justice, inclusion, and progress. Precapitalist social relations, based upon a strong racial divide, exaggerated patriarchy, and abundant consumption of alcohol had been reinforced. The central state did relatively little to undermine these entrenched conditions, because local pressure from below and political will from outside had not been sufficient to create a campesino sector within the PNR/PRM/PRI strong enough to break the political monopoly of local elites. Campesino organization was not robust enough to attract the National Ejido Bank as a credit source to offset dependence on local merchants.

The road got paved not from Zaragoza to Xochiapulco: it was paved from Zaragoza to Zacapoaxtla to Cuetzalan, widening paths of power cut before the revolution. Even with the road, Nahuas and non-Indians constructed a socioeconomic fabric that narrowed the passageway for modernity's entry to a mere footpath. Indicative of the region's retreat, regional literacy outside of Xochiapulco was no higher in 1940 than it had been in 1900. The population of Zacapoaxtla city had fallen from 12,000 to 2,163. The once bustling commercial center became an economic backwater.

In such a milieu, teachers easily became "absorbed by the environment." Natalia Molina, the most celebrated woman teacher in Zacapoaxtla, lived in her old age in a rustic house on the city's main street. The house fully contradicted the urban order of space and decoration so meticulously prescribed by the SEP. It resembled a warehouse, its undifferentiated rooms filled with piles of paper, books, and letters stacked upon home-crafted wooden chairs and tables. Narciso Bassols would have glowered to see the Pope's portrait hanging on a wall alongside multiple calendars. Turkeys, chickens, parrots, doves, and cats roamed the patio overgrown with plants, bushes, vines, and flowers. Cornstalk crosses over the doors warded off evil spirits.[40]

Logically, teachers befriended caciques. The elites supported school construction, financed civic festival, and seemed to determine the margin of maneuver open to everyone else. In interviews, veteran teachers mouthed a discourse challenging caciquismo. Such was their mission, learned from Maestro Burgos. However, when asked about a particular powerholder, the teacher inevitably responded with pride, "He was a good friend of mine. We drank together. He respected me. He helped with the school." To help the indígenas, argued León Ramírez, it was less effective to challenge the cacique than to implore him for a "pedacito de tierra" (little piece of land) for a needy family. The relationship could become corrupt. Recognizing the teacher's relatively high status and meager income, the cacique might offer an "extra" salary to the teacher or his wife, sell him a house or property at a low price, lend money, or contract him to manage a livestock finca.[41]

How then can it be argued that the negotiations over federal schooling in Zacapoaxtla in the 1930s contributed to the construction of national hegemony, which by definition must balance consensus with coercion, incorporate some aspects of the popular agenda, and allow for the articulation of dissent? How can domination be consensual when the use of violence, repression, and electoral fraud is rampant? How can one argue for national hegemony in a region that closed its encounter with the revolution by insulating itself from the state's modernization program?

First, despite his violent and illegal tactics, Lobato enjoyed considerable subaltern support and incorporated some popular demands. Communities recognized the contradictions in SEP policy. Within the short time period during which they could choose sides, powerful factions (the elders in the center and north, traditional enemies of Xochiapulco in the south) opted against the radical national project and its local agents. Lobato and his goons were not the only ones to use coercion against the radicals. Communities themselves coerced teachers into tempering their rhetoric and altering their project. Community action ensured that the state would incorporate a popular demand it had ignored: respect for local culture and customs. Only after the state accepted this demand could communities begin a dialogue with teachers and appropriate schools.

Second, once in power, Lobato could not rule by force. He had to use his connections with the Mexican state to provide benefits for the region while simultaneously shielding it from outsiders. Paving roads, constructing schools and clinics—these were material improvements the cacique secured from the state.

Third, the Lobato cacicazgo achieved regional hegemony for a time precisely because it functioned within a larger context. The overall state structure and the imagined national community permitted some dissent, incorporated some popular demands, and emitted a discourse of social justice and inclusion. For several decades after 1940, that larger structure and discourse were represented in the Zacapoaxtla region by the federal teachers. As an organized group, teachers became Lobato's nemesis. The nascent liberal opposition in Xochiapulco and Zacapoaxtla solidified as a political tendency in the 1930s. Federal teachers were crucial to its expansion after 1940. As in Tecamachalco, their power derived from their employment by a national agency independent of local and regional jurisdiction and their corporate solidarity, nourished by their national trade union. Their power was greater in Zacapoaxtla politics than in Tecamachalco because they substituted for absent or weak popular organizations. In the more differentiated populist politics of agrarista Tecamachalco, they were among several competing groups.

In the 1940s, teachers continued to struggle with Xochiapulquenses and the vecinos of Atzalan to win a portion of the Apulco hacienda, a goal they finally achieved in 1951. With Zacapoaxtla progressives, teachers formed a union of craftsmen and miscellaneous employees in Zacapoaxtla city, published a paper critical of local politics, and encouraged communities to resist cacique intervention in elections. They were instrumental in dismantling the Lobato cacicazgo in the 1950s and in ensuring thereafter that the progressive faction would contend in municipal politics on equal footing with Lobato's heirs.[42]

Teachers were not above the corruption of clientelism, nor were they removed from the servile relations characteristic of the region. The feisty, mestizo violinist Celerino Toral emerged as the progressive faction's leader. Effective at mobilizing Indian discontent, winning municipal elections, and financing public works projects in indigenous towns, he made his fortune contracting Indian labor to companies in the hotlands of Tabasco and Veracruz. In other words, he was an *enganchador,* a satanic figure in official revolutionary rhetoric. His behavior appeared more contradictory to outsiders than to local people. The old patriarch Juan Francisco Lucas had been similarly enterprising. He had enriched himself through land, commerce, and money lending but used his wealth and power responsibly—to protect indigenous interests and meet indigenous needs. Toral made his fortune finding Nahuas jobs. He enjoyed his wealth and used it to create political space for the Nahuas. Toral, like Lucas, seems to have achieved the status of "good patriarch," described by Guy Thomson and Florencia Mallon in their analyses of popular liberalism in the Sierra.[43]

The progressives' politics were complex and sullied, but they came to be seen by many groups within communities as a force through which Nahua dissent could be heard and processed. Teachers were allies in struggles for barrio independence from headtowns and in the procurement of fairer terms of taxation, trade, and landholding. Honorio Cortés, a former student of Burgos at Xochiapulco, founded Tosepan Titataniske, a cooperative of Indian coffee producers in Cuetzalan. Tosepan Titataniske eventually extended throughout the northern Sierra; it represented the first significant break with the traditional elite commercial monopoly and a meaningful step toward solidarity between Indian communities.[44]

The major difference between Toral and Lucas as progressive caciques lay in the institutional framework within which they operated. Thomson has noted that Lucas's popular liberalism failed because it could not be institutionalized in a peacetime setting. Once Díaz removed the liberals from the state government and demobilized the National Guard, popular liberalism retreated in the Sierra before the stronger force of authoritarian *continuismo* and economic growth characteristic of the Porfirian regime after 1890. As much as one might be tempted to argue that this process repeated itself in

Mexico after 1940, it did not. Despite the warts it was born with and those that appeared with age, the postrevolutionary state provided a political party, popular associations, public agencies, a legal framework, and an ideological discourse for institutional renewal and the articulation of dissent. Because this structure was less complex in Zacapoaxtla, federal teachers between 1940 and 1970 came to be more salient there as the articulators of its dissenting functions than in any other region examined in this study.

EPILOGUE

I conclude this chapter with a story. In 1937, Faustino Hernández went to teach in the Nahua village of San Miguel Tzinacapan, a few kilometers down the mountain from Cuetzalan. A native of Cuetzalan and a would-be airplane pilot, Hernández had become one of Raul Isidro Burgos's "social gladiators." Upon entering San Miguel, he was taken prisoner by cristero rebels. Although the cristeros were from the other side of the Sierra, the Migueleños probably protected them. San Miguel was not one of the Cuetzalan towns that had followed Pala Agustín's Liberal rebels in the nineteenth century. In the 1930s, vecinos looked upon the school and teacher with great mistrust. When the Hernández family arrived, community women kept Señora Hernández away from the well: they were sure she would poison the water.

For years, Hernández stuck it out, teaching a handful of children and using his relations with the Cuetzalan elites to negotiate lower interest rates for vecinos' loans, to referee property disputes, and to support San Miguel's complaints against excessive taxation. After seven years, Hernández recounted,

> An old Indian named Miguel took me to a meeting with his compadres. It was an assembly presided over by the elders, and after the women cleansed me with incense to force out the evil spirits and after the presentations, the oldest man told me: "We are convinced that you respect us and from now on, you command." They gave me the cane of justice. After this consecration, I was the "amo" and I had the greatest satisfaction: I had no more problems with the people. My biggest problem was that I had over 120 students.[45]

Thus did the local governors appropriate the energies of Hernández to serve their interests. They conferred upon him "the power of words." As secretary of the Junta Auxiliar, he had to broker community interests with outside powerholders—obtaining through his racial and class privileges benefits they might not have been able to obtain for themselves. Turning over 120 students to him was an act of community self-interest—a recognition of the growing importance of Spanish literacy to survival. But far from an offering to the school's model of transformation, it was an act of trust binding Hernández to serve the community.

The elders of San Miguel then joined with Maestro Hernández in orchestrating the construction of a magnificent two-story school building. As the sons of the elders tell the story today, the building required the labor of men, women, and children over four years. Great quantities of timber, stones, and sand had to be hauled by mule from mountainsides and distant quarries. It was the largest construction the village had undertaken since the building of the church in the sixteenth century. The imposing new school, built to look like a palacio municipal, symbol of community power and autonomy, was placed like one, adjacent to the church on what villagers were fashioning into a town square.[46]

Inside the school on the second floor, two giant murals filled the walls at opposite ends of a spacious room. In one, an oversized, sinewy Indian painted in the style of muralist David Alfaro Siqueiros cries out in agony as he strains to break his chains. In the other mural, an old man with flowing white hair and beard and a gentle, wise face sits center stage flanked by four men, two to his left and two to his right. Little children at his knees and behind him offer him fruit. This aged Christlike figure is Raul Isidro Burgos. The men flanking him in the style of disciples are the elders of San Miguel and the teacher Faustino Hernández. The Migueleños painted Raul Isidro Burgos as Christ to protect their own, not the national, Western culture; to empower their town, not the state. No cacique from Cuetzalan flanked Maestro Burgos—only the elders and Maestro Hernández.

The mural is not the last signal that the school is a mutual construction of town and teachers. In front of the school, on what is today the town square, is a marble work of art. It is not a statue of Juárez or Hidalgo, nor is it San Miguel. It is a Masonic obelisk. Under it, say the vecinos, are the ashes of Maestro Raul Isidro Burgos.[47]

Thus did the Migueleños build the revolutionary school to cut themselves a pathway out of servility without sacrificing their culture. Today, the school has become the municipal palace, and community children attend several schools. San Migueleños have astutely utilized the inroads of modernity in a tricky game that does not forfeit an ancient culture. They have used Tosepan Titataniske, the government coffee-purchasing institute (IMECAFE), Catholic liberation theologians, anthropologists, folklorists, feminists—and consistently, federal teachers. Today, community women spearhead the regional women's artisan and livestock cooperative headquartered in Cuetzalan. They are a breakaway organization from the male-dominated Tosepan Titata-niske. Armed with a fax machine, catalogs, and electronic calculators, they are penetrating the international market. They hope to do it on their own terms.

6

"EDUCATED BY BULLETS"
THE YAQUIS OF SONORA,
THE MEXICAN SCHOOL,
AND THE MEXICAN STATE

The antireligious frenzy of socialist educators in Sonora barely affected the Yaquis. SEP officials surmised that if teachers challenged the saints here, they risked a full-scale rebellion. Sonorans feared the Yaquis, who, since 1825, had defended their valley lands from the grasp of the state and capitalist developers. Unlike the Nahuas of the Sierra Norte, the Yaquis reached no accommodation with the colonizers. Beaten back, deported, dispersed, after 1900 they witnessed their homeland's rapid penetration by the Yoris, as Yaquis called the non-Yaqui settlers. To stop this invasion, they joined the Mexican Revolution. Disappointed in the government's refusal to meet their demands, they rebelled again in 1926, only to have Mexican airplanes bomb them. By 1930, the recalcitrant Yaquis were cordoned off on the Yaqui River's right bank in a camp policed by the Mexican army.

This occupying force and the SEP's better wisdom protected the Yaquis from the voracity of the Sonoran "priest-eaters" in 1935, but not entirely. Revolutionary youth organizations, the Bloques Juveniles, desecrated some Yaqui churches. In Potam, the Yaqui governor took a SEP delegate into the church and showed him a wall smeared with obscene graffiti. "Do you see this?" he asked the visitor (Fabila 1940:247). "Yoris did this. Now tell me: if we did this in your churches, would you condone it? We have issued orders that these not be erased so it can be seen who are the more savage: the Yaquis when they make war to defend themselves and kill to protect their Nation, or those who do this, certain they will never be punished. Tell me, who are the savages?"

Between 1935 and 1939, Lázaro Cárdenas negotiated a settlement with the Yaquis that went a long way to meeting their demands. He recognized the authority of the Yaqui governors and allocated more than four hundred fifty thousand hectares of land on the river's right bank in what was the revolution's only tribal land grant. He promised water, technical assistance, schools, and infrastructural support to transform material life. Although Cárdenas had genuine sympathy for the Yaquis, his endowment also conformed to the interests of the state. He assisted the Yaquis not only to ameliorate the blatant injustices they had suffered but to gain national control over the relatively autonomous political region of Sonora and to terminate the Yaquis' capacity for revolt.

More than the Puebla communities previously described, the Yaquis received state economic and political assistance intended to realize the SEP's notion of modern Indians: productive farm families adopting modern hygienic and consumer practices, members of the Mexican nation with a distinct, artistic heritage. However, the Yaquis used the state's resources to preserve ethnic autonomy and to restore a culture dedicated not to productivity but to ritual labor and to social cohesiveness achieved through religious practice. In pursuit of this goal, they temporarily marginalized the Mexican school. Nonetheless, their settlement with the state produced new linkages, identities, and empowerments that implied membership in the Mexican state and nation. Yaqui ability to create and sustain ethnic autonomy depended upon relations with the central government. The latter protected Yaqui territory and institutions from the aggressive, racist society around them. After 1960, the Yaquis began to use the school. They no longer viewed it as a threat to their culture, but as a tool for survival.

PREREVOLUTIONARY TRADITIONS OF SCHOOLING AND LITERACY

Of the rural societies examined in this study, the Yaquis were the most literate. Congregated by the Jesuits in the seventeenth century, they built the Eight Pueblos of Vicam, Potam, Bacum, Rahum, Huirivis, Torim, Belem, and Cocorit on the floodplain of the Yaqui River (see map 6). Overflowing twice annually, the river allowed them to sow corn, beans, and squash. They constructed the pueblos around a ceremonial culture. The Jesuits transcribed the Yaqui language to the Roman alphabet, created schools, and participated in the formation of a Yaqui religious hierarchy, thereby stimulating a rich religious literacy. Yaqui religious officers, especially the maestros, practiced and transmitted this literacy. The maestros' notebooks combined Yaqui, Spanish, and Latin transcriptions of prayers, chants, and credos, which were handed

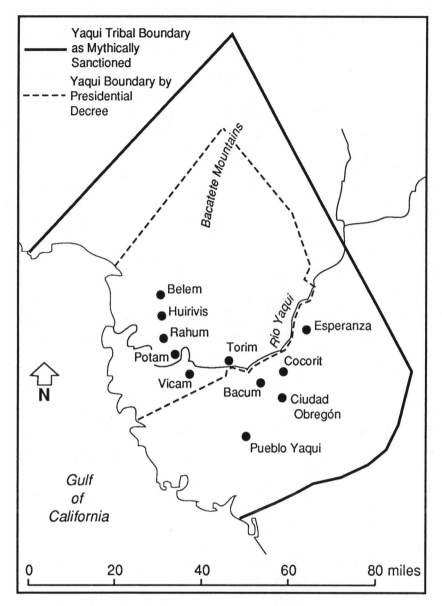

MAP 6   The Yaqui Valley in Sonora

down and elaborated upon from generation to generation. In the nineteenth
century, church authorities reinforced the maestros' role as teachers when
they sent them catechism manuals for teaching children.[1]

Yaqui profane tales, music, poetry, and song—known as the Pascola arts—
were also written down and transmitted orally; they entertained during the

sacred Lenten season and in every Yaqui household throughout the year. In the Yaqui home, the oldest woman preserved the Books of the Dead. In them were inscribed the names of the family's ancestors. Women kept them on the household altar and took them to church in handkerchiefs to be blessed with chants and song (Spicer 1954:124).

Although Yaqui literacy was a restricted, religious literacy, it glued the society and it was mobile. In the wars of the late nineteenth century, as Mexican armies dislodged the Yaquis from their pueblos, the maestros took their books into the hills to continue ritual and education. In their forced exodus, in deportations to the sisal plantations of Yucatán, and in treks across the desert to Arizona, the maestros kept the prayer books and guarded religious practices even when portions of ceremonial life had to be curtailed. Religious literacy in the hands of Yaqui intellectuals became a tool for the creation and preservation of a separate, non-Mexican cultural identity at a time when a sense of Mexicanness was taking root elsewhere in the incipient national society. Unlike the Nahuas of Zacapoaxtla, who built ties of reciprocity with local elites through religion, the Yaquis in the late nineteenth century used religion to define their separation from the dominant society. As Mexicans waged war on them, Yaqui intellectuals independent of the official Catholic Church kept Yaqui faith alive. Religion turned forced migrations into a diaspora of cultural preservation—in contrast to the cultural fragmentation or assimilation that characterized the migration experiences of so many Mexicans in the late Porfiriato.[2]

War and the diaspora encouraged a secularization of Yaqui literacy. Warfare required written negotiations and communications. The diaspora encouraged literacy among ordinary Yaquis. In many cases, hardship impeded the acquisition of literacy as families were broken up, forced to work exhausting hours on plantations, or kept constantly on the move. But as the Yaquis became the most traveled ethnic group in Mexico, their exposure to secular literacy grew. They maintained ties across great distances through letter writing. Children might learn to read from a maestro, from their father, from a mayordomo on a Sonoran hacienda, or in an Arizona or Hermosillo school. Many eventually attended the school founded in 1923 by Ms. Thalmar Richey in Pascua Village, the Yaqui settlement in Tucson. Ms. Richey's school exclusively served Yaqui children, many of whom went on to attend Davis Elementary School. Rosalio Moisés, one of several diaspora survivors to have recorded his personal history, recalled how he was in and out of schools in Arizona depending upon where his father worked. At one point, his father enrolled him at Davis Elementary. When his father worked in the Sasco smelter, the mine boss put the boy in school.[3]

However, there is a difference between learning to read and write and education. In the late nineteenth century, as the anthropologist Alfonso Fabila said, Yaquis were "educated by bullets" shot from Mexican guns (Fabila 1940: 148). They did not appropriate local Mexican schools, even on a restricted basis, in their Eight Pueblos, because they were either at war or in mandatory exile. Instead, their nineteenth-century experience fostered a literature and an oral tradition oppositional to the Mexican school. Just as nineteenth-century foreign invasions stimulated a Mexican patriotic literature that issued forth in civic festival in Puebla, the wars against the Yaquis in Sonora fostered a Yaqui patriotic literature and oral tradition that cast the Mexican as enemy. The wars created a new Yaqui intelligentsia. A small but significant number of maestros, captains, and governors became avid historians: keepers and transcribers of their own historical record and critical readers of Mexican historical texts, especially those written about the Yaqui wars. These historians reinvented their origins to cancel any debt to the non-Yaqui. As Juan Valenzuela, the mystical *kobenau* (governor) of Rahum, told the anthropologist Edward Spicer, the Yaquis had been conquered long before the Spanish arrived. It had happened when Jesus came and the Eight Pueblos were formed. The Great One Above, not some earthly government, had ordered the pueblos to exist. The Spanish king had merely recognized the Yaquis' divine right to their lands. The Yaquis drew their boundaries not in relation to the Spanish empire but in relation to the surrounding Pima, Seris, and Mayos.[4]

They celebrated their prowess in war against the Mexicans. They remembered the bitter battles, how they suffered in the mountains without food, water, or clothes because they believed that "better our land go into the hands of any other nation than into the hands of the Mexican." Men, women, and children had jumped off mountain cliffs at the battle of Mazocoba in 1900, for suicide was preferable to surrender to the hated Yori. Battles with the Mexicans were always unfair, because Mexican troops always outnumbered the Yaqui. But Yaqui soldiers made up in bravery what the cowardly Mexicans lacked. Ambrosio Castro, Yaqui poet and historian, described a battle near Oros where forty Yaquis confronted three thousand federal troops. The Yaquis lost three men. The *federales* lost hundreds. Juan Valenzuela recalled the peace at Pitahaya negotiated in 1909 between Yaqui General Luis Buli, Sonoran Governor Izábal, and Generals Lorenzo and Torres. The treacherous Mexicans had broken the agreement and begun to disarm the Yaquis when two men in Buli's guard drew their bayonets to the neck of Izábal and said to him, "Keep your word as the peace was made!" Izábal and Torres gaped in terror as Yaqui men surrounded them. They "defended their beloved mother soil, putting their bayonets to the breasts of those men, and Izábal defecated in his pants. This is very positive in our history," Juan Valenzuela mused. The two guards, Santiago Guicoyoi and Tiburcio Agraciamacqui, became honored as "second to God."[5]

The intellectuals constructed the tragedy of the diaspora together with every Yaqui who lived it. Lucas Chávez was fourteen when his parents were shot dead at the Battle of Batachive. He and the other children were hustled off to work on haciendas for rations of clothing, food, and blankets. Here, Yaquis worked from sunup to sundown. At night people were too exhausted to sit and visit. Ceremonial life was often circumscribed because of work and because to the hacienda owners, the rituals made "too much noise." Treatment was harsh and cruel. Suspecting families of helping the Yaqui guerrillas, the patron often locked them up at night and came by at two in the morning, cracking his whip and shouting at the women to get back to their huts to prepare food for their men's workday. In 1901, people recalled how Yaquis on the haciendas were rounded up and taken to the jail of Tetakari in Hermosillo, where they were beaten, shot, or shipped off to Yucatán. When Mexican soldiers invaded the Yaqui barrio of Mariachi in Hermosillo, they hanged defenseless men and bashed the heads of babies against the rocks. Women were killed so they would not bring Yaquis into this world; girls were kidnapped to be Mexicans' wives. Little boys were torn from their mothers' arms and sent to homes of the rich as slaves. Colonel Luis Medina, it was said, sold them to the wealthy of Guaymas like dogs. Those who could headed north for Arizona. If the rural police caught them, they were hanged from telephone poles and mesquite trees.[6]

This oppositional history was more than the fabrication of a few intellectuals. It was constructed, embellished, spread, and ingrained through joking and storytelling during men's evening card games at Sasco smelter and household celebrations of babies' baptisms on Yucatán sisal plantations. It sparked the imagination of children and forged their identity. In Hermosillo, Yaqui boys played cowboys and Indians with their own cast of characters: they shared mud figures of Mexicans, then destroyed them with slingshots and blowguns (Moisés, Kelley, and Holden 1971:8–9, 15, 22).

Out of their construction of recent history, Yaquis wove together the bases of their own perceived racial superiority. They looked down on the Pimas and Opatas, who had lost their language, and on the Seris, who were savages without religion. As for the Mexicans, they were treacherous, cowardly, and money-grubbing. Most despicably, they were irreligious. They shirked their obligations to God, the saints, and humankind. They were inferior in the eyes of God. The Yaquis had been made from brown clay, the Yoris from gray ash cast in a pile of rubbish.[7] Such a literate and oral tradition, freshly reworked in the midst of battle and terror, did not mesh easily with the Mexican revolutionary school's goals of creating a homogeneous citizenry loyal to the Mexican nation and committed to economic modernization.

CULTURAL REDEMPTION THROUGH REVOLUTION: SIDELINING THE SCHOOL

Between 1880 and 1910, the Mexican army expelled the Yaquis from their homeland (Dabdoub 1964:139–57; Radding 1989:340–42; Hu-DeHart 1984: 155–200). From an estimated twenty thousand Yaquis in 1860, some three thousand remained in 1910 (Spicer 1980:158; Fabila 1940:110). The valley became a vast military camp. From their towered forts, Mexican soldiers stood guard against the remaining Yaquis and protected invading Yoris. The army surveyed the land, then carved it up in huge grants for officers and entrepreneurs. A major concession to Carlos Conant passed to the Richardson brothers of Los Angeles. They began digging canals and sold the irrigated land to investors and colonists. At the end of the Porfiriato, trainloads of Californians arrived daily. Settlers flocked in from other parts of Sonora. In 1904, the army fractioned and sold the lands of the southern pueblos, Bacum and Cocorit. These sacred towns became Yori settlements. To the north, the army made Torim its headquarters. By 1907, it was the largest city in Sonora with twelve thousand people; the lands around it were sown by the Yori to new cash crops: tomatoes, tobacco, cotton, sugarcane, rice, and hops.

In the Mexican Revolution of 1910, the Yaquis rose up in hopes of retrieving their ethnic lands and expelling the Yori. With their vast military experience, they and their southern neighbors, the Mayos, joined the Constitutionalist armies of Sonora under Generals Obregón and Calles and helped to catapult those men to national power. In 1920, the beleaguered Yaquis became hopeful when Sonoran governor Adolfo de la Huerta promised them repatriation to their homeland, the withdrawal of federal troops, and the evacuation of non-Yaquis from the pueblos of Vicam and Potam. He negotiated with Yaqui governors and agreed to assist them in rebuilding the Eight Pueblos. Yaquis began to return home (Fabila 1940:101; Figueroa Valenzuela 1992:69–71; Hu-DeHart 1988:166–67).

But in Mexico City, Presidents Obregón and Calles reneged on de la Huerta's promise to slow colonization. They implemented their developmentalist dreams. In 1926, the central government purchased the Richardson Construction Company, accelerated canal construction, and facilitated private development of the Yaqui River's left bank. The town of Cajeme, named for the Yaqui chief, grew into a burgeoning agribusiness center and was renamed Ciudad Obregón. There, natives of Germany, Yugoslavia, China, California, northern Sonora, and Italy rubbed shoulders in a frenzied race to turn the land to profit. In 1925, the Yaqui chief Pluma Blanca asked the government for the lands of Bacum under the constitutional provision for restitution of usurped property. The authorities turned him down.[8]

In 1926, the Yaquis once again protested the government and its broken promises. The state's response was swift and brutal. General Yocupicio invaded the area with twenty thousand troops. As the Mexican soldiers opened fire, streams of Yaquis sought refuge in the Bacatete mountains. Government airplanes bombed the Bacatetes to chase the Yaquis from their hiding places. Federal troops captured the fleeing Yaquis and drafted them into the army, sending them to Yucatán, Veracruz, and Mexico City. The Mexican army permanently occupied Yaqui country in an encampment named Colonias Yaquis (Hu-DeHart 1988:167–68; Figueroa Valenzuela 1992:74; Spicer 1980: 261–62; Radding 1989:349).

In the early 1930s, remaining Yaqui families came straggling down from the mountains. Those drafted into service in the far corners of the Republic began to return. Others came home from Arizona. All faced an embittering situation. Yori settlers had chased them out of Bacum and Cocorit. They had to desert Belen, Huirivis, and Rahum as Yori irrigation works diverted water upstream and left the towns dry. The churches they had begun to repair in 1920 were once again in ruins. The Forty-sixth Cavalry Regiment had turned the church at Bacum into a barracks. All Yaquis were under military surveillance; most men were dependents of the army and its payroll.[9]

Returning families sought refuge in Potam, Vicam, Torim, and smaller settlements scattered through the mesquite.[10] From riverbeds, they gathered carrizo cane to rebuild their homes and spacious ramadas. They whittled wooden crosses and placed them in every yard. With hoes and mules, they cleared the brush to plant their corn, beans, and squash. The drums of the Yaqui military society greeted the dawn and beat through the day to announce church services for Yaqui soldiers. Decked out in headdresses of foxskin, feathers, and seashells, the soldiers carried old Springfield rifles and bows and arrows. They held high the image of the Virgin of Guadalupe, their supreme commander. Church bells once again called people to household and communal ceremonies. Through the cactus scrub traveled "men in blankets and torn overcoats carrying masks, harps, violins in little bags, painted sticks, stuffed badgers and foxes, cocoon rattles." They were on the way to a pueblo to make a fiesta. Life was beginning again.[11]

As they reconstructed their society, the Yaquis had options. They could build a society on the principles of their own ethnic organization, separate from the Mexican, or they could opt for a more flexible, assimilationist approach. Broadly, they were divided into two groups that reflected an old division between "broncos" and "mansos"—the militants and the tamed. Traditionally, Yaquis could pass from one group to another just as people in opposing groups could hold similar opinions. The broncos believed the Yaquis should hold out for a complete return of valley lands and a restoration of the Eight Pueblos, to be governed by Yaqui institutions. They opposed fusing local government with Sonoran municipal institutions. They were committed to a society in which land did not yield profit but was a sacred entity providing the wherewithal to sustain ceremonial work. As Edward Spicer observed, their project was not one of unconscious traditionalism but a deliberate reconstruction of Yaqui history based upon recent institutional practices and tragedies.[12]

The broncos, or Restorationists, condemned as Torocoyoris, or traitors, those who would compromise with the Mexicans. Torocoyoris opened themselves to the dangers of acculturation and assimilation. The potential for multiplying the Torocoyoris was great in 1934. Most families were government dependents. Hundreds were returning from varied experiences in Hermosillo, Mexico City, Empalme, Tucson, Los Angeles, Yucatán, and Veracruz. Those who had been in the United States had worked with Europeans, Chinese, Mexicans, African Americans, Papagos, and Navajos clearing land, building the desert's irrigation works and Tucson's sewers, chopping cotton and picking pecans. Many returned with stoves, sewing machines, victrolas, and a love for the New York Yankees. Others had been posted in the army throughout Mexico. Dominga Ramírez, a young girl when the revolution rescued her from a Yucatán plantation, had had the time of her life in Mexico City as the stepdaughter of a Yaqui officer in the Mexican army: there she had leisure, fine dresses, and high-heeled shoes (Kelley 1978:162–72).

Diverse experience outside the Yaqui Valley created divided opinions about modernity and Mexican schools. Rosalio Moisés, who had grown to manhood in the United States, was appalled at conditions in the valley: rampant tuberculosis, dirt, rats, insects, and mosquitos; no food except corn tortillas, salt, and coffee; no beds or pillows; skinflint wages. He found the Yaqui Restorationist leader, Juan María Santiamea, "very stupid." Santiamea was always repeating that "Jesus Christ was born here in Belem pueblo," which, according to Rosalio, no one believed. Moisés condemned the Yaqui governors for neglecting issues of health and sanitation. In his opinion, the Yaquis needed tractors, water pumps, and doctors—not festivals, which always ended up bankrupting the poor. Similarly, Juan Aguilar was one of many Yaquis who returned to the valley to take up market-oriented farming. He had brought with him a large collection of books and newspapers dealing with world and Mexican politics. He moved to Cuesta Alta, away from the Eight Pueblos, and wanted a school there.[13]

Many Yaquis shared some commitment to modernization and assimilation, but they were not organized as a group. In Potam in 1934, those who shared such values lived scattered through separate barrios. One barrio belonged to the Merideños, Yaquis who had been posted in the army in Yucatán since 1914 and had returned in 1934. In another lived the Veracruzeños, who had been drafted following the 1926 uprising and sent to Veracruz. In a third were the Aguileños, who had left the pueblos to work on a hacienda near Empalme in the early 1920s. They now formed a Mexican army battalion charged with keeping the fourth barrio of broncos under control. These were the Santiameas, members of the authentic Yaqui Military Society loyal to Juan María Santiamea, Potam governor and Restorationist.[14]

In the balance of forces among the Yaquis, the Restorationists had a lot going for them. They controlled the interlocking Yaqui institutions of government: the military societies, the pueblo councils, and the church organization. They were the governors, elected yearly by the adults of their pueblos and attentive to the opinions of the council of elders. Among the Restorationists were the tribe's organic intellectuals, the keepers and makers of written and oral traditions. Religious maestros like Cenobio and Juan Valenzuela of Rahum, Uj Ujllolimea of Potam, Heraclio Tadeo of Huirivis, and Ambrosio Castro were poets, historians, chanters, and teachers. They had their typewriters, books, and newspapers. They corresponded with chiefs of tribes north of the Mexican border. They could discuss many topics in current world affairs, from the U.S. reservation system to Adolf Hitler.[15]

More important than their opinions about world politics, their articulation of Yaqui history touched every Yaqui heart. Rosalio Moisés may have despaired at their disregard for technology, but their tragic tale of persecution was his story too. His mother's family had been slaughtered in the hills at Mazocoba. In Hermosillo, with his grandparents, he felt helpless, "like a blind boy," when the soldiers took his grandfather, the tribe's last shoemaker, and shipped him out to Yucatán in a boxcar. Like other Yaqui children, he faced hunger and shame in Hermosillo. Mexican boys attacked him with rocks and stones; they spat at him while their mothers laughed.[16]

The Restorationists' fervent racial pride was a strong antidote to the unrelenting racism that nagged at Yaqui everyday life. For the Yoris around them, the Yaquis were savages born to the warpath; assassins of Mexican children; practitioners of superstition, perpetually parading around saintly images and given to excessive dancing and drumming; improvident squanderers of resources and time; irrational enemies of progress, torching modern farms and scientific equipment. They burned alive those their trials condemned as criminals. There was not a sonorense who did not have a tale to tell of Yaqui savagery. Colonists remembered their terrorizing new settlements and massacring at random. Up in the northern mining country, the yarns spread about Yaquis cutting the soles off the feet of Mexican travelers and making them walk on cactus spines, tearing out eyes and severing limbs, attacking trains and kidnapping girls. Every week with amazing regularity in the 1930s, the U.S. consul at Guaymas reported an impending Yaqui uprising. It was a persistent prognosis in the press, in cafés, in governing circles. Any minute, the Yaquis could revert to a fighting mode.[17]

These were the attitudes that greeted the Yaquis as they came down from the Bacatete. In 1933, Yaquis who had once lived in Bacum installed themselves at El Lencho, waiting to return home to clean up the church in time for Lent. They had stopped fighting because they had been promised their sacred homelands, they told President Abelardo Rodríguez. At all costs, Governor Rodolfo Elías Calles responded to the president, these families should not be allowed to return to Bacum. They would only harass the progressive colonists. Tell the Yaquis there was no available land in Bacum. If they did not have enough lands where they were, it was their fault because they did not want to work. If they *did* want to work, let them clean out the canal at El Lencho.[18]

It was easy to repress other images of the Yaquis—working alongside the *colonos* in the fields, nursing and cuddling Yori children, teaching the Yoris how to deal with the snake-infested mesquite and pitahaya cactus. It was easy to forget the debt Sonorans owed them for working their households, mines, haciendas, and railroads. It was easy to repress these images because the

Sonorans' model of identity, avidly promoted by Governor Rodolfo Elías Calles, rested upon their contrasting themselves with the Yaquis: primitive, fanatical, wasteful, brutal, dirty.

The two societies lived in bitter antagonism. When Celia Ruedeflores's Yaqui mother married a Yori in Cocorit, his parents shunned her, his cows were slaughtered, and his grocery store was boycotted. Yori opinion justified such discrimination. It explained the Mexican authorities' sense of superiority and their refusal to learn the Yaqui language or anything about the culture. It forgave the Mexican officials for trafficking right and left in Yaqui resources: renting their lands without permission and pocketing the payments; appropriating the land for themselves and making the soldiers work it; cutting wood illegally; reaping profits from bootleg liquor. Yori racism strengthened the hand of the Yaqui Restorationists and gave them the moral high ground. They could easily shame as Torocoyori—traitor—any Yaqui who cooperated with the Mexicans and put up with their abuse.[19]

The deepest source of Restorationist strength lay in their control over religious practices. In the midst of Yaqui division and unprecedented Mexican control, at a moment when tribal political and military institutions were weak, religion created unity. Despite differences among Yaquis, the church, said maestro Juan Valenzuela of Rahum, "is the Mother of us all." For all his travels and interethnic experience, Rosalio Moisés could not forget that he was a Fariseo, or a Judas, member of one of two brotherhoods that governed during Lent.[20]

Each village was a ceremonial unit. All Yaquis belonged to a brotherhood or sisterhood. Authority in the church was shared. From childhood, most men and women played critical roles in ceremonial societies as dancers, musicians, singers, poets, storytellers, jokesters, or flag bearers. As in the case of the Sierra Norte Nahuas, the Yaquis learned and taught through participatory, collective ritual. And as in the case of the Nahuas, religion was not restricted to the church's space. It penetrated households, yards, and thoroughfares (Fabila 1940:250–51; Spicer 1954:83–85, 183; Erasmus 1978:32–33, 43).

The full weight of the Yaquis' didactic, ceremonial organization was felt during Lent, when the elected governors surrendered their canes of office to the Societies of Judases (Fariseos) and Horsemen (Caballeros). The societies became the teachers of Yaqui history and ethics as they guided people through a participatory dramatization of the time when Jesus lived as a healer in the Yaqui Valley, where the evil Judases pursued and crucified him. This prolonged passion play became a period of intensive training for young people in the ceremonial societies. With their masks, harps, violins, and headdresses, the Judases traveled from pueblo to pueblo, taunting and mocking the faithful as they searched for Jesus. Families opened their homes to the image of the Christ child, giving him shelter at the household altar and holding fiestas in his honor. The Judases pursued Jesus until they tracked him down in the Garden of Gethsemane, where his protectors, the Horsemen, had fallen asleep on the job. The Crucifixion was enacted as a period of intense oppression and penance after which Mary saved Christ by turning herself into a tree, and took him to Heaven as a newborn child. On Saturday morning, the Judases attacked the church, which was defended from within by the "forces of good": the church groups, the Horsemen, the Military Society, the governors, elders, *pascolas,* and *cantoras,* and the children dressed as "angelitos." To the wild ringing of bells, the "good forces" fought off the Judases with dancing, flowers, and switches. On the third try, the Judases surrendered, flinging their masks onto a huge fire and igniting the effigy of Judas. Repentant, they rushed into the church and pushed toward the altar, where they were rebaptized as Yaquis, or human beings. This dramatic and joyous event of reunification and redemption, known as La Gloria, was talked about for months before and after: it was the moment for which people planned all year.[21]

Doing penance through Lent was arduous. It required enormous expenditure in energy, time, and resources. Productive work in the fields, on the canals, and making carrizo baskets was admired not for the profit and higher standard of living it might bring, but for its ability to sustain families, sponsor fiestas, and permit ceremonial work. In the United States, men left jobs in California and New Mexico and whole families headed back from the Arizona cotton harvest for the Lenten celebrations in Tucson.[22]

In the diaspora, many Yaquis had rarely if ever experienced a full Lenten season. Nonetheless, because the Yaqui religion was one of everyday sociability, in its simplest forms it had served to sustain individual spirits and group identity. On Yucatán plantations and in Mexican army camps, Yaquis drew strength from ritualized household celebrations girded by an elaborate system of fictive kinship, or *compadrazgo.* These rituals encouraged a life-sustaining flexibility in household membership and human relationships amid dislocation, impoverishment, disease, and death. Thus many Yaquis who knew nothing of the Easter liturgy were supportive of religious revival as they returned home in the 1930s. Dominga Ramírez was representative. Having grown up in La Colorada mine and in Yucatán, her exposure to Yaqui ceremony was superficial. Once back in the valley, she sought for her son a traditional girl from a religious, bronco family, monolingual in Yaqui.[23]

Nonetheless, the Restorationist project was not a sure bet. General Gutiérrez Cázares, Yaqui Military Zone commander from 1931 to 1935, despised it. A Sonoran born in the Mayo Valley, Gutiérrez Cázares ran the Yaqui Zone like a hacienda. In fact, he had his own ranch at Aguacaliente in Yaqui territory. He saw the Yaquis as alcoholic, lazy, barbarous, and poisoned by an "odio ancestral contra los blancos" (ancestral hatred of white people). In the deepest Obregón-Calles tradition, he held that Yaquis would be incorporated into civilization by working for Yori entrepreneurs like himself. He considered the Yaqui governors and the Restorationist faction to be backward, retrograde, meddlesome enemies of progress. He wanted them relegated to religious functions. They fought him over timber cutting on Yaqui lands. Gutiérrez Cázares protected a Mexican entrepreneur who employed Yaquis and non-Yaquis to chop wood for railroad ties. The governors believed this exercise in modern enterprise to be an infringement of sacred tribal land rights. The commander justified it because it gave Yaquis honest work and took them off the government dole.[24]

The Restorationists came to prevail because President Cárdenas supported them. In the fall of 1935, Cárdenas made Gutiérrez Cázares Sonoran interim governor and named Juventino Espinosa Sonoran military zone commander. A progressive officer from Nayarit, Espinosa had commanded the Yaqui Zone in 1931 and was sympathetic to the Yaquis.[25] Colonel José Dozal Guzmán, also partial to Yaqui rights, was sent to head the Yaqui Colonies. In October 1937, Cárdenas recognized the authority of the Yaqui governors. He granted to them as representatives of the tribe nearly the entire right bank of the Yaqui River. This unprecedented tribal land grant endorsed the governors' control over land use and recognized the elected pueblo representatives as civil authorities.

Cárdenas followed the accord with an integral development plan, which he subsequently discussed and revised with the governors at Vicam in June 1939. The government provided mules, seeds, reapers, tractors, trucks, machetes, hatchets, barbed wire, plows, water pumps, and shovels. The capable army engineer, Guillermo de la Garza, took charge of expanding an incipient network of canals. Cárdenas promised the Yaquis half the waters from the Angostura Dam, then under construction. To offset commercial exploitation, a new Comité Regulador de Subsistencia and the Comisión de Fomento Agrícola del Yaqui provided credit and purchased wheat at sustainable prices. Schools, health facilities, and an agricultural experiment station were projected as part of a development project that would engage state agencies of agriculture, education, welfare, indigenous matters, and the army. Central government officials helped the Yaquis defeat a strong campaign undertaken by agribusinessmen at Ciudad Obregón to stop this land reform and development project.[26]

Although Cárdenas empowered the Restorationists, his goals differed from theirs. Like the SEP, Cárdenas believed that the Indian "problem" was a material one. Land, schools, and economic resources would assure Yaqui integration into the Mexican nation. Market-oriented Yaquis would preserve their artistic heritage and capacity for cooperative work. From the Restorationist perspective, Cárdenas provided the material capacity and political recognition to fortify an autonomous tribal culture. The Restorationists were not interested in becoming Mexicans; they sought the right to be fully Yaqui.[27]

This conflict between the state and the Restorationists lay at the heart of the struggle over federal schools in the 1930s. Entering the Yaqui Colonies in 1935, the SEP assumed control of military and state schools and immediately articulated its nationalizing, incorporative project. Leonardo Magaña, the SEP inspector, was a progressive man in the eyes of the railroad unionists of Empalme and the agraristas on river's left bank. He championed socialist education as a redistributive, empowering policy from a class perspective. But he became oppressive when he reflected on "el problema Yaqui:"

> A minimum part of the tribe is identified with the whites . . . but even they are little interested in the school. . . . Yaqui children speak little Spanish and when they speak some, they do it incorrectly . . . one of the main reasons for low attendance is because the pupils do not understand the teacher and get bored. Once we have overcome this problem, we will have gained something but the problem will not be resolved since much has to be overcome, such as their immense apathy, race hatred, and fanaticism. The Yaqui man is lazy despite being physically strong. Today he works because he is militarily coerced. . . . Almost all are so vice-ridden that a large share of their income goes for drink. They continue to think of the mestizos and whites as invaders and hate us so much that among them there is not a single sentiment of gratitude as exists among other indigenous tribes. They seldom or never thank us for our services. Their religious fanaticism is tremendous. They spend most of their time preparing for fiestas and ceremonies. . . . This vice has to be corrected little by little since in any formal campaign, the teachers would perish and perhaps there would be a new rebellion. For now our school campaigns are to teach the Spanish language and combat those who sell alcohol, beer, and mezcal in order to get hold of Yaqui paychecks.[28]

The Mexican school program and its teachers meshed a local racist construction of the Yaqui with the SEP's colonizing zeal to forge a national culture. This project the SEP foisted upon the Yaquis at a moment when traumatized anti-Mexican feeling was being fed by the ascendant Restorationists. The dominant group and the SEP represented two nations at war. Because Cárdenas took a special interest in the Yaquis, polarization was briefly alleviated by an enlightened SEP effort to train Yaqui teachers and technicians and to incorporate local culture into curriculum through the creation of an Internado (boarding school). But when this effort foundered in 1939, schools again became an arena of misunderstanding.

BUILDING COMMUNITY: SIDELINING SCHOOLS, 1935–1942

The Mexican federal school could not be appropriated by the Yaqui Restorationists' postrevolutionary reconstruction of community. Unlike those of the Sierra Norte or Tecamachalco, Yaqui governing institutions were not undergoing a process of interpenetration with those of the dominator. The Yaquis wanted to reconstruct them as separate institutions. They wanted to rebuild the Eight Pueblos, which dated from the time Jesus had been in the valley, and Mexican schools were not part of them. Mexican schools belonged to occupying, Yori forces: the Mexican army, the state of Sonora, and the SEP. The Mexican officers commanded Yaqui soldiers to build the schools. To the Restorationists, these were not community efforts but forced constructions carried out by the Torocoyori and belonging to the dominators' space. Yaqui space consisted of the *guardia* (headquarters of the civil governors and military society), the church, and the household.

When in October 1935 SEP inspector Magaña asked the governors to mobilize support for the schools, they told him, "We do not want schools because they make youth shameless [*sinvergüenzas*]." The schools turned children into Torocoyori. Inspector Magaña belittled the governors. He called them *comanaguas*, men obsessed with their traditions, who objected to any association with the Yoris.[29] He was convinced that Yaqui children had to mix with Yoris in order to destroy race hatred, to better customs, and to integrate them as rapidly as possible into national culture. But when the SEP in Potam integrated the Mexican military's school, attended only by children of the Santiamea faction, with the state school, attended by children of Torocoyori soldiers and the non-Yaquis, the results were disastrous. The children of the Santiameas stopped attending school. When Magaña merged a school for Yaquis with the Yori school in Vicam Station, the Yaquis deserted.[30]

Teachers contributed to Yaqui alienation. In contrast to Puebla teachers, those in Yaqui pueblos were largely indifferent to community welfare and culture. In 1935–36, the anthropologist Alfonso Fabila noted "real caste antagonism" between teachers and Yaquis. Not one teacher spoke Yaqui; not one was Yaqui. Teachers, he said, were poorly trained and supervised. They were irresponsible and abandoned their work regularly. They had little to work with in the way of books, desks, benches, blackboards, or tables. Occasionally, but rarely, a dedicated teacher created a garden, playground, or basketball court. Even after federal schools were transferred to the Department of Indigenous Affairs in 1938 in order to improve Yaqui–school relations, the ambience in primary schools did not change. The director of the Potam school told anthropologist Edward Spicer in 1942 that the "indios" were shiftless and lazy. He spent his noon break strumming a guitar under a tree by the school. He seemed unhappy all the time. A fellow teacher found Potam "very ugly and sad" and preferred Ciudad Obregón.[31]

Teachers' attitudes and those of non-Yaqui students made the cost of attending schools high for Yaqui youngsters. Mexican pupils ridiculed them for their lack of proper clothing and ignorance of proper Spanish. They beat them up. The inspector dismissed allegations of mistreatment as lies and excuses. "The reality," he said, "is they are lazy, they do not like school, they are always looking for a pretext not to go. Parents are not concerned with educating their children, just with instilling in them sentiments of hatred and fanaticism."[32]

Teachers conducted classes in dingy rooms behind closed doors. They were oblivious to important goings-on in the surrounding Yaqui space, or they misinterpreted and deprecated them. They seldom attempted to engage mothers. Yaqui women, their maternal instinct sharpened by experience, were said to inculcate fear of the Yori in their children. In the few instances in which home visits were attempted—to vaccinate families—angry people frequently fled their households. They were not opposed to shots. The Yaquis were a worldly people. They feared the Mexicans were coming once again to draft or kill them. Women might take children to a clinic, but they barred health personnel from their homes.[33]

Yaqui society and the school clashed over gender values and behavior. Many Yaquis in the diaspora had experienced coeducation, secular dancing, and competitive team sports. But in the mid-1930s as Yaquis reunited in the valley they lived a moment of ascendant conservatism. Coeducation and the federal school's secular dances for men and women became problematic subjects of contention. Yaqui governors did not object to the surging popularity of baseball, but they opposed the SEP's uses of it. Inspector Magaña promoted sports to foster interracial understanding. After spirited games between Yaqui players and the railroad workers' team at Empalme, the governors told the SEP there would be no more mixing with the Yoris.[34]

Patriotic festival, essential to construction of community and nation in

Puebla, was antithetical to the Yaqui creation of community. The Mexican school celebrated a different history using a different symbolic repertoire. The SEP's Mexican history had little positive meaning here. The indigenous people of Mexico were reduced to the glorious Aztec and Mayan past. Yaquis were like the Apaches: savages subdued for the sake of progress. Nor could one take the SEP's construction of the agrarista Zapata, plop him down in Potam, and anticipate a heartfelt response.

Edward Spicer described the celebration of Mexican Flag Day in Potam in 1942:

> Toward noon, a few people began gathering in front of the school. Gradually a procession was formed consisting of the civil authorities bearing the flag in front, the musicians immediately behind playing the national anthem, behind them the officers of the regular army . . . and behind them the Yaqui officers of the Aguileños, Merideños, and Vera Cruzeños. The school children with the four teachers lined up in two lines behind these, the boys separate from the girls. A few of the girls had faded Mexican tricolors. . . . The procession started out and marched off to the music up the street between the pool hall and the garrison. It marched through the Aguileño, Mérida and Vera Cruz sections of town, but did not visit the Santiamea area. Mexican military and civil authorities, but only a few Yaquis attended the evening program where the director of the school gave a reading on the meaning of the Mexican flag, its colors, symbols, and history as three dark-skinned boys held the flag at attention behind him. The school boys and girls then imitated an Apache dance with feathers in their hair. A [Yaqui] deer dancer came in half naked with a rattle in each hand and did a crouching dance. The crowd roared. . . . [He] struck everybody as burlesque and was laughed at accordingly.

The program, Spicer concluded, was "miles away from life in the village."[35]

Despite the antagonisms, Yaqui school attendance showed interesting patterns in 1935. Attendance improved outside the centers with sizable Mexican populations. Yaqui attendance ranged from 0 to 14 percent of eligible children in Potam, Vicam Station, and Bataconcica, but rose to 40 percent in Pitahaya, Palo Parado, Torim, Vicam Pueblo, and Compuertas.[36] Three factors may explain variation in attendance. Where both Mexican and Yaqui authorities were concentrated, their conflicts negatively affected school attendance. Where Mexicans were present, Yaquis shunned the schools. The more Yaqui they could make the schools, the more they used them. Finally, many Yaquis who favored schooling probably settled outside the major centers where the Restorationists were powerful: they were more interested in clearing the scrub and making a go of their small farms.[37]

The possibility of having a truly Yaqui school that would mutually serve the interests of the Restorationists and the modernizers presented itself in 1935. In January, the SEP began to press for the creation of an Internado Indígena to train Yaqui technicians for the tribe's self-development: teachers, agronomists, nurses, and hygienists. Yaqui Zone commander Gutiérrez Cázares stalled the effort. The governors agreed to cooperate with the SEP if the SEP would pressure the central government to stop Gutiérrez Cázares's protection of Yori logging. Both SEP representatives and the Yaqui governors telegraphed Cárdenas to have the cutting suspended, but Gutiérrez Cázares intercepted the telegrams and stopped the dialogue. At that point, Cárdenas appointed Gutiérrez Cázares interim governor of Sonora. The SEP then appealed to the new military zone commander, the progressive Juventino Espinosa. Espinosa met the Yaqui governors' demands and supported the creation of the Internado.[38]

Juan Aguayo, a teacher at the Escuela Rural Normal at Ures, spearheaded the effort to build the Internado and nurtured a close relationship with the Yaqui maestros and governors. The school opened in the home of Vicam maestro Ignacio Mendoza in 1935, then moved to its own quarters where it was equipped with workshops, a sports field, orchards, and irrigated land for experimentation. In 1938, it was still unfinished and understaffed: there were no baths, dormitories, kitchen utensils, or tools for the workshops and no teachers of agriculture, small industries, or crafts. In preparation for Cárdenas's visit in June 1939, a frantic attempt was made to install potable water. During his visit, Cárdenas promised the Yaquis that teachers would be trained in the Yaqui language. That was Cárdenas's logic in transferring the Internado to the Departamento de Asuntos Indígenas and bringing in the linguistic anthropologist Morris Swadesh.[39]

Briefly, under Aguayo's leadership, the Internado flourished, not as a center for technical training but as the flagship for a possible Yaqui-fication of schools. Aguayo worked with local advisors to incorporate Yaqui history into the school's design and curriculum. Murals on the walls celebrated the Yaqui family, Yaqui territory (in vistas of the Bacatete mountains), and heroism (in the figure of the nineteenth-century military leader Tetabiate). Enthusiasm grew. The SEP had commissioned anthropologist Alfonso Fabila to study Yaqui Valley schools in 1935. He came to the valley with the deprecating attitude of Magaña, but in prolonged discussions with the Yaqui maestros and governors, he became a convert to Yaqui culture and a supporter of their rights of self-determination. He participated in the "discovery" of Yaqui poetry, songs, stories, and myths. There was talk of writing textbooks in Yaqui and publishing a Yaqui dictionary. The first Yaqui teachers were hired in primary schools. The Yaquis began to use the Internado for tribal affairs. A Mother's Society formed.[40]

But as early as 1939, the tide began to turn against the Internado. As Cárdenas tempered his radical policies, he reappointed Gutiérrez Cázares as military zone commander of Sonora. Understandably, the Yaqui governors objected. Gutiérrez Cázares quickly maneuvered to remove those government officials most identified with the Yaquis: Juan Aguayo of the Internado, irrigation engineer Guillermo de la Garza, and General Dozal, Yaqui Zone commander. He accused them of fomenting race hatred, alcoholic excess, and a collapse of discipline that had culminated in renewed assaults against non-Yaquis. The problem lay in the officials' collaboration with the "old and decrepit ones," the elders and governors, with their retrograde ideas and systematic opposition to progress. He claimed that Dozal's stewardship had left roads, telephones, schools, and irrigation works in a state of disrepair; that agricultural production had fallen and wood cutting had stopped. Sonoran merchants at Vicam Station eagerly supported Cázares's indictment. They claimed that Dozal had told the Yaquis not to pay their debts. They argued that their rights as Mexican citizens were being violated because Yaquis restricted the materials they could use to build houses and prohibited them from exploiting the area's timber, land, and salt resources.[41]

The generals who replaced Dozal returned to the Gutiérrez Cázares policy of market-driven assimilation. Mexican entrepreneurs exploiting Yaqui resources would serve as role models for the shiftless Indians. Once again, the generals trafficked in Yaqui lands, forests, water, labor, and the very tools and machinery provided the Yaquis by the government. They attempted to sideline the governors.[42] The generals' dominion did not eliminate the Restorationists, for the Yaqui governors nominally controlled the use of the land and local politics and could appeal directly to the Mexican president against abuse. But the political transition doomed the Internado as an institution committed simultaneously to the promotion of material development and of tribal culture.

Neither Aguayo's successors nor his fellow teachers were as committed as he. In Fabila's opinion, their "imprudence" and alienation from Yaqui culture cost them local trust. The attempt to incorporate Yaqui culture into the curriculum faltered. In 1940, the school was losing Yaqui students because it had accepted too many non-Yaquis: only twenty-one of fifty-two students were Yaquis. The coeducational nature of the institution vexed the Yaquis because it meant the mixing of adolescent boys and girls. Rumors of illicit relations between male and female students undermined local support. Yaquis withdrew their children from school when one of the male teachers married a student.[43]

In 1942, jurisdiction over the Internado was taken from the Department of Indigenous Affairs and returned to the SEP. In 1943, the Yaqui Military Zone commander reported that the Internado was in ruins, without towels, sheets, mattresses, electricity, and water: its teachers had not been paid in months and only two of its thirty students were Yaquis. In 1946, 194 Yaquis, led by the governors, addressed a petition to the Mexican president complaining that the Internado taught nothing useful and that the teachers made the students work like "peones." Of the signers, only 23 percent were literate. By 1950, there was not a single Yaqui with a normal school certificate.[44]

HEGEMONY, RESISTANCE AND SCHOOLS

In the late 1930s, the Yaquis of Sonora and the central government reached an agreement whereby the Yaquis could maintain a separate cultural and political identity within the context of the modernizing Mexican state and economy. Informally, this agreement meant marginalizing federal schools with their assimilative goals and discriminatory practices. The settlement can be understood as part of the Mexican postrevolutionary state's hegemonic construction. To argue that the relationship between Yaquis and the state was characterized by hegemony—that is, a degree of consensus on the part of the dominated with provision for the effective registering of dissent—is to dispute the opinions of anthropologists and historians who see the relationship as one of ongoing antipathy, either because they view Yaqui culture as intrinsically opposed to the modernizing national society (Spicer 1980:328–30) or because they see Yaquis primarily as victims of advancing capitalism (Hu-DeHart 1988:167–79). Though these positions have been eloquently argued by eminent scholars of the Yaqui, my understanding of the cultural politics between Yaquis and the state in the 1930s suggests the need to explore the institutional relationship established between the central government and Yaqui authorities, to differentiate among actors, both dominators and dominated, and to understand cultural change within the dominated group.

First, the central state permitted the solidification of Yaqui culture and identity at a moment when military defeat and Yori encroachment threatened ethnic survival. The central government made the Yaqui governors representatives of a whole ethnic group—not a part or a faction of the Yaquis, not a town in Yaqui territory, not an appendage of the Mexican army or the state of Sonora. The ultimate representative of the central government was the Mexican president, to whom grievances could be registered against abusive government agencies and Yori entrepreneurs. This relationship provided the Yaquis with some protection from the voracious racism and aggressive capitalism surrounding them. The state provided economic resources, infrastructural support, and jurisdictional and representational integrity sufficient to allow the survival of a ceremonial culture in a rapidly modernizing region. The relationship was created by Lázaro Cárdenas. As Vicam governor Miguel Valencia said after lengthy discussions between the governors and Cárdenas at Vicam in June 1939: "In the spirit of all his words, we found respect for our racial personality."[45] Creating trust that had never existed, the Mexican president and the governors forged linkages that were then institutionalized through subsequent practice.

In recognizing Cárdenas as president of Mexico and themselves as members of the Mexican Republic, the Yaqui governors created obligations for him. They described Lázaro Cárdenas as the president "eminently chosen by the majority of the republic to attend to the complaints of evil that befall us . . . that we all may enjoy the guarantees of well-being as dictated by the Holy Law of our Mexican Republic." Their use of revolutionary terminology such as "the struggle for justice on the part of the oppressed" differs from that of the agraristas of Tecamachalco or the Nahuas of the Sierra Norte. The Yaquis were entitled to justice because they had been wronged not as members of a class, a peasant community, or even an ethnic group, but as a whole race destined by God to occupy a sacred territory. As the governors wrote to President Manuel Avila Camacho in 1941: "Our struggle for self-preservation dates from the year 1533 when the Spaniards first stepped on our lands; it continued in 1838 when they redoubled their spirit of destruction as we tried to conserve the lands of the tribe; it continued afterward in the period of the dictatorship when they thought they could destroy our long-suffering race by exploitation and extermination." To retrieve this land—"a holy jurisdiction bordering those of the Mayo, Pima and Seri"—they had joined the revolution. In the revolution, they had sacrificed themselves not just for their own cause, but also for the Mexican nation. Their own cause, while separate, became enmeshed with the struggle of the whole Mexican nation against oppression. That struggle created the federal government's revolutionary mandate and obligation. The government had to recognize the Yaquis' rights as a separate people—"our race which now more than ever needs the fulfillment of the promises of the Revolution." If the government fulfilled its "contractual obligations," wrote the governors, the Yaquis would "positively form part of the Mexican Nationality." They would be "un pueblo tranquilo, feliz, y amante del trabajo" (a peaceful, happy, and work-loving people).[46]

This was the language of negotiation and resistance within the context of domination. The Yaquis were in no position to withdraw from the Mexican republic in 1940 if their demands were not met, and the Mexican government without Cárdenas was less than eager to respond to their demands. It was not a happy relationship, but neither was it a hopelessly repressive one.

To protect the Yaquis from Sonoran predators, the government sent frequently avaricious federal bureaucrats. Between 1940 and 1956, the dominant power was the Mexican army. Its rule was marred by extortion, corruption, and profiteering and aggravated by lack of water. Waters from the Angostura Dam, promised by Cárdenas, were diverted upstream to serve the Yoris. Through the 1940s the Yaquis had little water. Between 1949 and 1952, they were inundated with torrential rains. The army persistently attempted to silence the governors and to marginalize Yaqui institutions.

In its attempts to break Yaqui political autonomy the army was unsuccessful. In 1956, after years of complaints from the governors, the Mexican army left and the Banco de Crédito Ejidal became the major government administrator. In that year, the Yaquis began to receive water from the new Alvaro Obregón Dam. The Ejidal Bank recognized Yaqui governing institutions. New ejidal cooperative credit societies respected tribal authority. The bank adjusted to Yaqui priorities, providing income for fiestas and credit during Holy Week, and arranging work schedules to permit ceremonial work.[47]

The Yaquis' relationships with on-site bureaucracies, whether under army or Ejidal Bank administration, bred dependency, clientelism, and corruption. Although the greed of state agents was largely responsible, the Yaquis were not innocent. Neither economic autonomy nor empowerment in and of itself had been a major Restorationist goal. At the practical level of daily life, they might be separated from control over sacred territory, which the Yaquis formally retained. For the Restorationists, economic autonomy was a means to an end—the preservation of Yaqui culture—and if the end could be achieved by other means, the means might be modified. Yaquis yielded control over their work process and resources to government agencies. In time they came to produce not for themselves but for the market: most of what they themselves consumed, they purchased. Most were organized in cooperative societies that worked for the Bank. It would be generations before they produced their own technical cadres.[48]

On the other hand, the relationship between the central state and the

Yaquis, even under these distorted conditions, allowed the Yaquis to fortify a distinct ethnic identity and solidarity. They used their own political institutions and channels of communication with the central government to seek redress of grievances and to obtain benefits. The Yaquis played one government agency off against another in order to widen their own space for maneuver. They used the SEP in the 1930s and the Department of Indigenous Affairs in the 1940s to curtail the abuses of the generals, to "inform" the president of "real conditions," and to obtain favors from him.[49]

Out of the ideological and institutional settlement of the 1930s the Yaquis forged an us-versus-them mentality that became the wellspring of Yaqui resistance in the context of post-1940 domination. This dichotomizing discourse was useful in preventing tribal fissure and in maximizing bargaining power (Figueroa Valenzuela 1992:143–48). Factionalism, historically familiar to Yaqui society, was inevitable given the rapidly changing society surrounding the Yaquis, the diversity of government agencies in Yaqui territory, and the long-range impracticability of the Restorationist solution. The institutional apparatus and discursive content of hegemonic relations encouraged struggle within Yaqui society simultaneous with the presentation of a united front to outsiders.

In his study of Yaqui politics and culture in the 1970s, Thomas McGuire noted that religion was no longer the defining characteristic of Yaqui identity or the unifying cultural element Edward Spicer had found it to be in the 1940s and 1950s. McGuire found the dynamic faction in the Yaqui Fishermen's Cooperative, whose members abjured religiosity. Nonetheless they identified as Yaquis through Yaqui political institutions and in their defense of tribal territorial rights. I would argue that the institutional apparatus that sustained Yaqui identity in the midst of cultural change was the result of Yaqui–state negotiations in the 1930s.[50]

In the 1930s, the settlement between Yaquis and the state required the sidelining of the federal school because the latter was incompatible with the settlement's focus on Yaqui cultural autonomy. Gilbert Bartell, who studied the Fisherman's Cooperative in 1961, believed that Yaqui literacy declined between 1940 and 1960 along with their knowledge about and contact with the outside world. The Yaquis turned inward, expressing little interest in international and national politics, not voting in elections other than their own. However, Bartell reported that in 1960, 62 percent of Yaqui adults could read and write, a percentage higher than in Tecamachalco or Zacapoaxtla. He observed that in each pueblo and settlement a significant group of households favored schooling for purposes of self-defense in the modern world. By 1960, young Yaqui families had determined that their children needed schooling (Bartell 1965:37–45, 63, 106, 174–75, 283–88). In 1971, the primary school in Potam could no longer accommodate the large number of children seeking entry (Hewitt Alcántara 1978:261). In the mid-1970s, McGuire noted that children of Fishermen's Cooperative members finished high school (McGuire 1986:140).

Yaqui society had undergone a process of secularization that involved coming to terms with Mexican schools. Dominga Ramírez and her family were representative of this process. Once a secular-minded young woman who missed her dancing days in the Mexican army camps, she had become religious upon her return to the valley in the 1930s. By 1960, she was a proud matriarch deeply invested in Yaqui religious institutions. Her son Anselmo, whom she had married to a devout, Restorationist girl in 1940, no longer attended ceremonies: he saw them as a major cause of poverty and drunkenness. By 1960, he was an overseer of the Yaqui Cattle Cooperative for the Ejidal Bank. An early school dropout because of his tattered clothing, Anselmo had taught himself to read. Both he and his religious mother were strong supporters of schooling (Kelley 1978:183, 191–96).

When Yaqui children began to attend school in large numbers and for extended periods of time, at least two factors helped to mitigate conflict between their culture and the schools. First, Yaquis produced their own bilingual teachers, in consonance with changing government policy. Second, the multiethnic approach to national culture within the schools acted as a bridge. In the post-1960 world of reduced racial tensions in the Yaqui Valley, the school's presentation of multiethnicity was more acceptable and pleasing to Yaquis than it had been in the more racially tense and divided world of the 1930s. By the 1980s, both Yaquis and Sonorans enjoyed Yaqui religious celebration as part of a national and regional theater of cultural performance (McGuire 1986:71–88; 1989:172–73). Similarly, Yaqui men, as Alejandro Figueroa has noted, had become avid participants in another form of national cultural performance: Mexican football (Figueroa Valenzuela 1992: 352–53.)

By the 1990s, the Yaquis had produced their first generation of university-educated leadership. Yaqui primary school teachers were already middle-aged. Through the twentieth century, the Yaquis kept their identity while accommodating cultural change. They continued to believe in their own cultural superiority. This in turn kept their political mobilization and their critical assessment of Mexican government policy forever pitched. They were always ready to do battle and to ally with history's progressives, for they knew beyond doubt that they were a wronged people on the right side. As the somewhat astonished Claudio Dabdoub wrote in his history of the Yaqui Valley (1964:14): "The Yaquis have a personality which better corresponds to the white race in their self-confidence, dash, and arrogance, qualities they never lose even in defeat; in fact, the Yaquis have never felt defeated." At the end of the twentieth century, such social organization and cultural consciousness are, as they are for the San Migueleños of Tzinacapan, political and economic capital in a world atomized by modernity.

7

Weaving Fantasies of Modernity, Eating "Tortillas Filled with Faith"

The Cultural Politics of Schooling in a Sonoran Immigrant Society

When socialist education came to Pueblo Yaqui, a new Yori settlement on the left bank of the Yaqui River, Marcelina Saldívar remembers that there was not much fuss.[1] She was in the third grade. "The saints do not exist," the teacher, Rosario Tapia de Nuñez, announced to the children. Tapia spoke with uncharacteristic hesitation, for she was one of those self-confident women indefatigably committed to civilizing the frontier. She was also a devout Callista, so she instructed her students to "fight fanaticism." After their daily chores of sweeping the street and burning the garbage, they would go into the homes to search for wooden crosses. The children were naive about the dangers. They had grown up without priests or churches. Many did not know their prayers and had had no one to bless them. When they attempted their search mission, the adults whisked them away from their doorways. They did so not out of fear or hostility but with a sense of humor. They had a special *cariño* (affection) for the schoolchildren and for doña Rosario.[2]

Socialist education and the school's paradigm were well received on the left bank of the Yaqui River. In contrast to other regions examined in this study, official statistics show an increase in literacy from 54 to 71 percent for boys ages ten to fourteen and from 59 to 79 percent for girls.[3] Educational policy was well received because it converged with the fantasies and hopes of uprooted families who had come to the valley in search of a better future. The school promised such a future. Teachers helped to organize for it, and the government provided the material and political resources for its realization. Here, it might be possible to accept the state's paradigm in a manner consistent with the state's expectations. Teachers, vecinos, and the central government were equal partners in the construction of community and individual identity. The school was part of a package that created national linkages around a class ethos, strengthened a regional identity, and transformed local social relations.

CULTURES OF SCHOOLING ON THE LEFT BANK OF THE YAQUI RIVER

On the left bank of the Yaqui River, Mexican society was new. From a few hundred colonists and soldiers at the turn of the century, the population grew to more than thirty-three thousand in 1940.[4] Foreigners poured in: Germans, Yugoslavs, Greeks, Chinese, Lebanese, and Yankees. They came lured by propaganda advertising the valley as the world's most fertile land. It would yield harvests in six weeks, compared with three hundred days in California's Imperial Valley. "Leave your troubles and double your profits!" the ads read. Most immigrants were Mexican peasants driven by poverty or the revolution from elsewhere in Sonora, Chihuahua, Sinaloa, and the western states of Jalisco, Nayarit, and Zacatecas. Many were part of the mobile labor force that had developed in Sonora in the late nineteenth century: families or individuals who moved from mining camps to haciendas to railroad work, across the border to Arizona, then back again to flimsy ranches in the high sierra. In buggies and mule wagons, on burro and horseback, by train and foot, they came to the valley in search of work, land, and a better life. Most worked for or rented from foreign and Mexican entrepreneurs; others bought and staked out small farms. They fought off rattlesnakes and mosquitos to clear the cactus and mesquite. They heaped the brush into fires that drove the desert temperatures upward of 150 degrees. Their bare feet burned and cactus spines pierced their clothing and limbs. They chopped wood and hauled it to build and fuel flour and rice mills. They made tortillas, laundered, and sewed. In mud up to their knees, they pitched shovels to dig the canals they made flow with the glistening, cool waters of the Yaqui River. Then on the virgin fields, they planted and picked amazing harvests of lettuce, wheat, rice, beans, and tomatoes.[5]

Although many were illiterate, they carried within them a culture of schooling. Marcelina Saldívar's parents, Eulalia and Domingo, came from Zacatecas via Nayarit to Nogales on the Sonoran border, where Domingo worked on the railroad. Seeking a job on "the other side," he was turned back by U.S. authorities because he could not read or write. In the early 1920s, the family headed for the Yaqui Valley. When they first came to the valley, the family wandered like gypsies from camp to camp until Eulalia put her foot down in Pueblo Yaqui: "Here I stop because the children are growing and need to go to school." So Domingo went to work in the camps, returning every eight days, and the children went to school in Pueblo Yaqui. Lina's mother sent her to school to give her an opportunity she herself had been denied. Eulalia's parents had forbid her to go to school because they thought she would learn to write love letters to boyfriends. Eulalia deeply admired the teacher Rosario Tapia for her dedication and skills. Lina worshiped her and decided to become a schoolteacher.[6]

In the Yaqui Valley, children worked as they did elsewhere in rural Mexico—clearing, sowing, and harvesting. After the age of twelve, most young men looked for permanent work—cutting rice, digging canals, selling dried meat in the camps. Before the age of twelve and between harvests, they went to school—usually for about two years and sometimes more.[7] Life in the valley promoted a culture of schooling because it kindled fantasies of modernity and hopes of improvement. To people living the valley's stunning transformation, schooling was like a machete to the farmer, the olla to his wife. Plain and simple, it enabled.

In contrast to the other societies examined here, entrepreneurs served as role models to young people in the Yaqui. In part, they became models because, unlike most central Mexican hacendados, they reduced the distance between themselves and their workers. Many foreigners rolled up their pant legs and shirtsleeves and sweated shoulder to shoulder with their employees in pursuit of a common project: to conquer nature and overcome Indian savagery in the name of progress. And they served as role models because there was as yet no strong community ethos binding workers, renters, and small farmers and setting them off from the big owners. What tended to unite the little folk were longings for equality and improvement, and dreams of being as competent and successful as Mr. McGriffith, who taught many how to harvest rice. Entrepreneurs brought modern technology and know-how. True, human muscle and thousands of mules built modern agriculture in the Yaqui prior to 1940, but what mesmerized people were the wonders of modernity appearing one right after the other, the next one bigger than the last—combines, reapers, tractors. Mr. McGriffith had a tractor as big as a locomotor that hauled five disks with twenty-five shells. Domingo Pérez's cotton-ginning plant near Cocorit was a marvel. Alvaro Obregón had an airplane fumigator that bathed his properties in insecticide. After leaving the presidency in 1924, Obregón devoted himself full-time to introducing modern agriculture to the Yaqui: bringing in U.S. suppliers, inviting Anderson Clayton to experiment in cotton production, welcoming Hindu and U.S. vegetable producers. To valley settlers, Alvaro Obregón was a paragon of modern morality.[8]

Although the valley roads filled with mule wagons carrying produce to packing plants, processing mills, and the railroad station at Cajeme, workers saw the source of power transform before their eyes as Standard Oil of California and Sinclair set up pumps and shops. The gringo inspectors on the Richardson canal scooted around on motorbikes. As soon as they could, successful owners bought Model T Fords. In their "Fordsitos," they jauntily plied the roads, honking their way passed the mule wagons and leaving them in great clouds of choking dust.[9]

As Mexicans in the valley participated in the transformation of the world around them, they flocked to the seductions of consumer culture. As the canals advanced, wooden hotels and supply stores went up in Esperanza and Cocorit. Almost overnight in the 1920s, Cajeme, appropriately renamed Ciudad Obregón, was on its way to becoming a showplace of modernity. Its hardware stores carried the latest tools, gadgets, lubricating oils, and machinery from the United States. Other stores sold sewing machines. In new, spacious windows, they displayed the latest fashions from Paris—or at least from Tucson. Traveling salesmen, Chinese and Lebanese, plied the roads in their wagons, trucks, and Fordsitos, bringing to the newly sprung towns and agricultural camps overalls, yards of percale, shoes, perfume, lard, flour, and canned sardines.[10] In the middle of the scrub and the pitahaya, the dust and the wheat fields, between harvests of cucumber and potatoes, an essentially urban culture took shape.

Because valley settlers produced for the market rather than for themselves, they bought the goods they consumed. Women might still launder with ash or soothe stomachaches with water boiled with cinnamon and husks of *guamúchil*. They might grind corn at the metate or stitch by hand, but quickly they took to sewing machines, oil stoves, corn-grinding mills, and medicines. If workers and settlers could not afford all the marvels of modernity, they were obliged by necessity to purchase some of them and could dream about one day acquiring more. Many remembered surviving on roots and rattlers in the Sierra. Mountain life was noble, but hard. It was something folks wanted to leave behind: they wanted to eat meat and sleep on beds. When in the mid-1930s young agrarista militants were confident they would receive land, they invested in America farm machinery manuals.[11]

The new cultural goods the settlers consumed were threads for spinning dreams and keys to an imagined liberty: mechanical and fashion catalogs, radios, victrolas, and, above all, the movies. This was a society suddenly caught in the grips of Hollywood. As Julio Sotero traveled through the camps with his film projector, he introduced new heroes and heroines to enthusiastic crowds: King Kong, Clark Gable, Charlie Chaplin, Tarzan, María Felix, Mae West. Boys went out to pick the potato harvest with thoughts of Tom Mix dancing in their heads: "Watch out for your back! There he is behind you! That's right, give it to him!"[12]

For young girls, the emerging culture opened a whole new life. During the revolutionary years, Manuela Cano Valenzuela worked with her mother on the ranch of don Epifano Palomares in the more conservative Mayo Valley to the south. At night, the mistress gathered the workers and read to them about Jesus. When Manuela left with her mother to cook in Camp 26 in the Yaqui Valley in 1923, she was mortally shocked. A young man put a song on the victrola for her. The crooner sang, "I was the first to kiss your lips, look into your eyes, see you smile." Fifteen years old, she hid in terror. But at her metate, she quickly learned to flirt with the mule skinners—grinding up a masa of "pura coquetería."[13]

Then Manuela began to dance. Every Saturday night the camps danced. Whole families came to kick up their heels on the hard ground beneath oil lamps to the music of Pancho Amavisca's band, the Orquesta Juárez of Cajeme, or Juventino Arreola's musicians from Cocorit. The music was different here from the folk dances of the Sierra Norte or the Yaqui pascolas: it was sexy, romantic, and individualized. Young people soon abandoned polkas and waltzes for the foxtrot and the Charleston. "Religious women like Julia Gallegos," recalled Viviano Alatorre Valenzuela, "prayed that the dances would keep the young girls free of temptation." But the cat was out of the bag in the Yaqui Valley. When Toña la Negra appeared on the screen in nothing more than a halter and a miniskirt of banana leaves, the audience from Cocorit, "devout to the point of fanaticism," abandoned the theater. But the young girls of Pueblo Yaqui kept sewing their dancing frocks, copying them from the ones they had seen at the movies and in fashion magazines.[14]

The cat was out of the bag because society in the Yaqui Valley lacked the centuries-old communal glue that safeguarded morality and traditions in Tecamachalco, Zacapoaxtla, and Potam. Mexicans in the Yaqui were constructing new communities motivated by necessity and fantasies of the future, not by the customs of the past. The material organization of family life nurtured outwardness and openness. These were not households organized around subsistence production under the male elder's management. Husband, wife, and youth might work at a variety of wage-paying jobs: clearing and planting the fields, cooking, laundering, and sewing in the camps, repairing machinery, working in the mills, teaching school, sorting vegetables in the canneries and packing plants, or working on the railroad. These work situations reduced the power of the male head of household, who was no longer its production manager. They increased the cultural capital, experience, and independence of other family members. Young women as well as young men got involved in union organizing.[15]

This more flexible family organization opened up vistas and created role models and opportunities made tangible in a period of economic growth and rapid social change. Lina Saldívar's role model was her teacher. Her uncle, Saturnino Saldívar, who worked in the flour mill in Campo 65, was rapidly becoming a political leader. When Lina was ten, in order to continue her studies she went to live with Uncle Julio, a barber in nearby Esperanza. Esperanza opened a new set of dreams for Lina. The streets were paved. Water came out of a tap. She could read by an electric light. She had begun to read history books and novels recounting the formation of workers' unions in Europe.[16]

Material conditions fostered a separate space for youth. In Tecamachalco in the 1930s, that space was only partially won. In Zacapoaxtla and Potam, it was staunchly resisted. On the Yaqui River's left bank, it was dynamized and expanded by dances, victrolas, fashion store windows, union meetings, movies, and school festivals. Young men and women mingled as a matter of course. Coeducation was not even an issue. Life promoted an independence for women unheard-of in the other three societies explored here. Many plied the valley alone with their children. They were able to sustain themselves and school their children because they found jobs in the collectivized domestic work of the camps and in the canneries of Cajeme. A single woman with children could not only survive, she could enjoy herself.[17]

But the more liberated life of the valley had its dark and seamy side. Like mining towns, the farm camps bred depravity. Men gambled at night and whiled away hours in billiard halls. Women were used and abandoned. People flocked to horse races, cockfights, rodeos—those blood sports that symbolized savagery and backwardness to the Mexican educators. When there was not Prohibition and even when there was, men drank heavily—not the traditional mezcal or pulque, but beer. Saturday dances always ended with bullet-ridden bodies floating in the canals: "Si no había muerto, no servía el baile" (If no one gets killed, the dance wasn't worth it). Such perversity demanded that women come to the fore as civilizers and moralizers. In this role, they attached themselves to the school—as students, teachers, and members of Ligas Femeniles, anti-alcohol leagues, hygiene crusades, and mother's clubs. If schooling in the Yaqui was a necessary tool to advance modernity, it was also a force to moralize behavior in the creation of community. In the 1920s, a group of zealous young women from Pueblo Yaqui formed the Coalición Pro-escuela del Yaqui. "In the buggy of don Pascual Ayón we went through the camps of the Germans and Yankees raising funds for our school."[18]

Doña Rosario Tapia, Pueblo Yaqui's teacher, was the Sonoran equivalent of the North American suffragette and prohibitionist. She organized adults into the Sociedad de Padres and improvement crusades. Every two weeks, she put on a festival to which people came from the surrounding camps. They watched athletic events and listened to oratory celebrating motherhood. Lina Saldívar, a major actress in these festivals at the age of nine, remembers:

> We danced the jarabe tapatío. We set up scenery and a curtain in the bandstand in front of don Pascual Ayón's carpentry shop. In the opening scene, a mother with her children waited for her husband, who arrived drunk with a bottle, wanting to beat her in front of the frightened children. The curtain closed and another scene opened with a man and a woman seated at a table, waiting for the teacher to show them how to write. . . . For the Twentieth of November, the anniversary of the Revolution, we carried banners against illiteracy and alcoholism in parades through the Yaqui. I recited a poem about an orphan dressed in rags. The audience cried and congratulated my parents. The teacher taught us to cry and to mimic. She was so very luchadora.[19]

What made the moralizing role of schooling so functional in places like Pueblo Yaqui was the absence of the organized Catholic Church or another competing authority of virtue. People in the Yaqui carried their religious beliefs inside them. They might have altars and religious objects in the home; they took advantage of the presence of a priest to receive the sacraments, to baptize a child, or to marry. But the priests they saw were few and far between. There were Mexican churches in the older settlements of Cocorit, Bacum, and Buenavista, but not in Pueblo Yaqui, which was little more than a spate of houses near a canal. In 1934, when people began to demonstrate in other cities of Sonora against socialist education, no one raised an eyebrow in Ciudad Obregón. In this bustling center of tomorrow, people were more upset that the sale of liquor would once again be curtailed.[20]

The Mexican community under construction in the Yaqui was, as social chroniclers Mayo Murrieta and María Elena Graff have so aptly described, one committed to modernity without a past. Their motivation was to leave the past—the dearth they associated with life in the high sierra—and to overcome the backwardness they identified with their Yaqui neighbors. The Yaquis became the dreaded and despised other: those who had ravaged the colonists' carefully tended fields, run them out of Potam and Torim in 1921, torched Pueblo Yaqui in 1915, and burned down the Agricultural Experimental Station, destroying years of research, hybrid seeds, and water registers. In the evening, settlers would sit under the ramadas, fighting mosquitos and spinning tales of Yaqui witches wandering the wild scrub at night and talking with each other and the animals in cackles and squawks. The world of the settlers could tolerate the "tamed Yaquis," who helped them clear cactus with awesome strength and skill. But the settlers forged their world on the principle of tomorrow. Yaqui ways were part of the past.[21]

The valley was also a place where plans were hatched about how to get to this secular promised land. It was not simply a question of imitating Misters Bruss and McGriffith, working hard and buckling under to the boss's command, and fantasizing about Hollywood in off-hours. On the contrary, by the early 1930s people were discussing social revolution, unions, and land reform.

GOING AFTER THE FANTASY

As a group, people working in the valley camps and staking claims to land had not participated in the Mexican Revolution. Most of the early colonists remembered the years of fighting as no more than Yaqui attacks. The Mexican Revolution came to the river's left bank long after the years of military struggle. It came in the 1930s, when demographics, state-building politics, and people's imaginations met in a synergistic convergence.

What became a class identity among the small farmers, renters, and workers of the valley began as a nationalist feeling—not the sort promoted by school textbooks, but a rancor that grew from working with the Richardson Construction Company. Foreign entrepreneurs might serve as role models. but Mexicans chafed at what they perceived to be the Richardson's preference for foreigners. Through its 1911 contract with the government, the Richardson received an annual fourteen thousand million cubic meters of water from the river to irrigate company land on both banks. It had an obligation to fraction and sell land susceptible to irrigation in lots of four hundred to two thousand hectares. Those receiving land automatically got water.

In 1921, Pascual Ayón, a carpenter from Durango who had settled at Pueblo Yaqui, denounced the Richardson's concession. He said that foreign ownership of land so close to Mexican beaches went against Article 27 of the Constitution. He requested land for Pueblo Yaqui. Ayón became the leader of the Yaqui Valley branch of the Partido Nacional Agrarista, supported by the Obregón government in Mexico City.[22]

On the Fifth of May 1923, a group of field workers invaded Richardson lands. The company protested loudly, arguing exemption from agrarian law on the grounds that theirs was a colonization project. President Obregón proposed that the government purchase some Richardson land for the agrarians. As a result, in October the first government land grant was made to the congregation of Cajeme. In 1926, the government bought the Richardson stock. The company's rights to water and to unsold irrigated lands, its credit, plant, and equipment passed to the Banco Nacional de Crédito Agrícola. This nationalization raised hopes and spurred the agraristas to write more petitions, but it was a chimera. The Richardson continued as a company in liquidation, with a colonization contract good until 1947. Its North American and Sonoran management controlled the use and sale of water and land. In 1926, President Calles reaffirmed the exemption of Richardson lands from ejidal dotación. At the same time he encouraged private purchase of the lands. During his presidency, an influential handful of Sonoran families bought them: the Salidos, Bórquezes, Esquers, Campoys, Paradas, Astiazaráns, and others. They became the base for the Calles cacicazgo in Sonora and a counterweight to Alvaro Obregón's claque of Mayo Valley owners.[23]

Under the leadership of Pascual Ayón, agrarista sentiment grew. Although skirmishes multiplied between land petitioners and the owners and renters of Richardson lands, the government of Plutarco Elías Calles spurned the agraristas. In 1929, their fortunes turned as a result of the intersection between national and regional politics and the onset of the Great Depression. The formation of the PNR in Sonora required the Callistas to build a popular base of support separate from the Obregonistas. How they maneuvered in the southern valleys was critical because the Obregonistas were strong here. One Obregonist was Pascual Ayón, who in 1929, became secretary of the new PNR branch in the Yaqui Valley. In part to capture his loyalty, the Callista state government made a provisional ejidal dotación from Richardson property to Ayón's settlement at Pueblo Yaqui. The company protested the legality of the move, which nonetheless served the Calles' political interests.[24]

In 1931, when Rodolfo Elías Calles became governor, he had to build a party apparatus while coping with the effects of the Great Depression. Refugees from northern mines and from Arizona swelled the agricultural camps. By the mid-1930s, 90 percent of Sonora's labor force was concentrated in the southern valleys. The immigrants destabilized the Yaqui Valley, contributing to wage wars between camps, provoking owners to denounce robberies of produce, stimulating competition among political organizers, and multiplying land petitions. These workers would be the backbone of young Calles's populist party-building in Sonora. He won over Pascual Ayón and sponsored the rise of a new group of militant leaders in the valley. Jacinto López, a shoemaker from Cananea, and Francisco Figueroa, a teacher, came to the valley out of El Huarache, the radical group formed in Hermosillo and early won to Calles's organizing efforts. Saturnino Saldívar, Manuel Bobadilla, and Mauricio Moreno began work together on the Richardson Lower Canal, then found jobs at the flour mill of Campo 65 owned by the German Hermann Bruss. Buki Contreras, Vicente Padilla, and Machi López got hired there as well. All were between the ages of twenty and twenty-five. Organizing began in the mill when Ramón H. Olivarria brought them together to study the new labor codes. They began to read voraciously: magazines, periodicals, labor history, and reports on owner abuse of workers.[25]

One day in 1932, seventy workers at the mill went public in the schoolhouse. They formed the Sindicato Central del Valle. Their goal was to end illegal hours of work and implement the new labor and agrarian laws. The Sindicato Central became the nucleus for the Unión de Obreros y Campesinos, which would in turn become part of the Federación Obrera y Campesina del Sur de Sonora (FOCSS). Organizers moved from camp to camp, creating unions, negotiating work contracts, and proposing land reform.[26]

Rodolfo Elías Calles sought the implementation of federal labor and land laws, but not at the expense of his friends. His policies aimed to strengthen these entrepreneurs. By expelling the Chinese merchants, he expanded his allies' business opportunities and capitalized the Banco Agrícola Sonorense. The bank supplied credit to the farmers, whom Calles organized into separate producer cooperatives according to the crops they produced. He brought the societies together into the Confederación de Asociaciones Agrícolas del Valle Yaqui. They shared storage facilities and regulated production and sales while lobbying for reduced transportation fees and other profit-enhancing benefits. Calles helped by improving the valley's road system and creating an agricultural experiment station in conjunction with the Secretaría de Agricultura.[27]

Given his commitment to the Mexican owners, Calles hardly intended to disturb private holdings in the valley. What he sought was a solution similar to his project in the Mayo: the colonization of new lands opened through ir-rigation.[28] Something had to be done because the Six-Year Plan of 1934 and the subsequent Agrarian Code opened land reform to agricultural workers. During his presidential campaign, Lázaro Cárdenas visited the Yaqui with the national labor leader Vicente Lombardo Toledano. With FOCSS organiz-ers Padilla, Saldívar, and Machi and Jacinto López, they discussed land re-form. In the same visit to Ciudad Obregón, Cárdenas talked with Plutarco Elías Calles and his son Rodolfo about plans for building the Angostura Dam. The dam would retain the waters of the Bavispe River in a canyon south of Douglas, Arizona. It would regulate the flow of water to the valley and vastly increase farm acreage. It would greatly strengthen the hand of the federal government in the distribution of water and land at the expense of the Richardson Company. The new farm acreage might be used to meet agrarista demands—or, existing properties in the hands of the Richardson and other owners might be divided.

In August 1934, following the Cárdenas election, the governor of Sonora declared the Richardson exemption canceled by the Agrarian Law of March 21, 1929. To agraristas at Bacum, the governor allocated Richardson lands and a portion of the properties of Jesús Antonio Parada, one of the largest land-owners. The owners and Richardson managers protested loudly into the spring of 1935. President Cárdenas stood firm. In March, he signed the defin-itive presidential resolution.[29] Sonoran authorities dawdled: the state's Agrar-ian Commission could not find an engineer. The state government backed the municipal president of Ciudad Obregón, Flavio Bórquez, one of the val-ley's richest entrepreneurs, when he evicted the ejidatarios from the lands they had been promised.[30]

But in Mexico City, Cárdenas had given the green light to Yaqui Valley militants. In the fall, petitions for land began to pour in. According to the U.S. consul at Guaymas, the agraristas requested choice developed lands, most belonging to United States citizens. In March 1936, the consul observed that although the agrarian movement was directed against close friends of the Calles family, it would affect virtually every owner in the valley. The own-ers joked grimly that they had more to dread from new "revolutionists" than they had ever had to fear from Yaqui "broncos."[31]

In October 1936, when Cárdenas announced a massive redistribution in the Laguna region of Coahuila, hopes soared in the Yaqui farm camps. The agraristas sent a delegation to see Cárdenas in Mexico City and request an immediate distribution of valley estates. Petitions, marches, conventions, and demonstrations proliferated in the valley. So did the recalcitrance of the capitalists. Owners' White Guards stalked the camps in armed motorcars in the style of Chicago gangsters. Agraristas were thrown out of their homes in the camps. In November, Pascual Ayón asked President Cárdenas that the agraristas be given the right to bear arms to protect themselves.[32]

In December 1936, Cárdenas issued a decree annulling the Richardson's status as a colonization project and making the lands it originally and currently owned subject to ejidal claims. In January, he announced new federal investment for the Angostura Dam, which would open more acreage. American and Mexican owners rushed to find a favorable solution. U.S. owners appointed the entrepreneur Z. O. Stocker and the consul at Guaymas to secure their exemption; in return, they would partially finance new lands for the petitioners. For their part, Mexican owners also proposed a colonization project but formed a common front against the Richardson, in hopes of profiting at the expense of the Americans from any changes that would take place.[33]

Inaugurated governor in January 1937, Román Yocupicio immediately championed all owners. Colonization of new lands was acceptable; a division of private property was not. Yocupicio wasted no time in going after the agraristas. In February, he deposed them from the town councils they had won in Ciudad Obregón and Huatabampo. When Machi López of the FOCSS called a campesino unification convention, Yocupicio arrested him and denounced the leaders for dividing the state's campesinos, whom he intended to organize into his own Sonoran branch of the CNC. Into the autumn, Yocupicio waged an unrelenting campaign against militant trade unionists, agrarista organizers, schoolteachers, and SEP inspectors.[34]

But the militants, vehemently supported by the CTM, moved forward. In June in Ciudad Obregón, they held a worker-campesino unification congress, at which the FOCSS became a CTM affiliate. Yocupicio arrested the meeting's leaders for subversion. When thousands of campesinos and urban workers marched out of Ciudad Obregón to demand their release, Yocupicio relented. Despite harassment and arrest of agraristas and teachers through the summer, the FOCSS forged ahead, pressing with the CTM for a division of Yaqui and Mayo Valley lands. In July, Cárdenas sent engineers to survey the land and conduct the census.[35]

On September 6, 1937, Cárdenas announced that he would divide the Yaqui Valley camps. The owners stopped preparatory work for the next growing cycle and suspended discussions over collective contracts with workers. Laborers began to leave to avoid starvation.

Machi López, Buki Contreras, Aurelio "El Negro" García, and other leaders hurried to Mexico City to receive instructions from Cárdenas. Upon their return, they traveled through the camps, organizing commissions to receive land. Eulalia Saldívar sent her husband to get on the lists: he was one of hundreds to sign up. On October 31, 1937, Cárdenas expropriated 17,000 hectares of irrigated land and 36,000 hectares of desert from the biggest owners. Land went to 2,160 campesino families, to be farmed in collective ejidos in conjunction with the Banco de Crédito Ejidal. The decree affected 21,179 hectares in U.S. holdings. Cárdenas tried to reduce the power of Mexican owners by limiting properties to 100 hectares.[36]

The president postponed his visit until June 1939. Provisional possession was carried out in 1937 by the agraristas themselves. Vicente Padilla recalled the drama: "We hardly recognized the peones' faces: they were transformed by hope. They greeted us with the excitement of children, plain and unschooled, with only their love for the land, their shovels and plows. They couldn't imagine that they were going to be owners. We informed them by congregation and settlement. They cleaned the streets. Workers and campesinos built the official stage. The state government was nowhere in sight. It was an act of 'puro agraristas.'" When Cárdenas came in June 1939, the crowds were so imploring that he got out of his car and rode on a truck to make better contact with the people. In the official ceremony, the heads of each agrarian committee paraded before him, turning over petitions from their ejidos—31 de Octubre, Providencia, Primer de Mayo, Javier Mina, Cuauhtemoc, Morelos, Guadalupe Victoria, Francisco I. Madero, and Progreso. With each resolution the president presented, the cries went up: "¡Viva Cárdenas! ¡Uno, dos, y tres! ¡Yocupicio es una res [beast]!" The president lifted his hand: "Make good on the Agrarian Reform, don't let it go sour, help me! Make the land produce more or the same as the hacendados!" The musicians played: "¡Viva Cárdenas, muchachos! ¡Viva la Revolución!" They slaughtered cows, barbecued the meat, and danced for a week.[37]

THE SEP AND THE CONSTRUCTION OF COMMUNITY IN THE YAQUI VALLEY

The redistribution of power and resources in the Yaqui Valley would not have occurred without the support of the central government. The president empowered the campesinos of the Yaqui Valley. He did so through the CTM, his appointed military commanders, and the Secretaría de Educación Pública. The SEP helped to build a popular base for nationalizing politics in a region famous for its aloofness. At the same time, the SEP helped construct communities around principles of modernity, social justice, science, and class.

The SEP was a central actor in the reparto. It entered the agricultural camps for political reasons. In January 1935 when Sonoran Callismo was still allied with Cárdenas, SEP director Lamberto Moreno created a new school zone in the Yaqui Valley in order to "cure" workers of religious superstition and to mobilize them for "collective proletarian revindication against their exploiters." Shortly after founding the school zone, Moreno began to plan with the Mayo Valley branch of the Federación Obrera y Campesina and the Unión Campesina de Empalme for an agrarian unification congress with local, state, and federal representatives. The anti-Callista rebellion postponed this event, but SEP teachers and personnel (such as Hermenegildo Peña and Heriberto Salazar) were active in the campesino conference called by Machi López in February 1937 and in the FOCSS-CTM unification congress of June 1937. Federal teachers, in their capacity as SEP employees and unionists affiliated with the CTM's STERM, were among those Yocupicio repeatedly harassed and jailed.[38]

In the fall of 1935, Lamberto Moreno appointed Leonardo Magaña as school inspector for the Yaqui Valley. His choice fit his political goals. Although Magaña never rose above local racism in his work with the Yaquis, he inspired teachers and families of the Yori camps and settlements. A longtime unionist, he had taken part in the 1930 teachers' strike in Alamos, which had generated leadership for the Huarache circle in Hermosillo. He then headed the highly successful Article 123 School of the Southern Pacific Railroad workers, paid for by the railroad company. Located in Empalme near Guaymas, the school served a thousand students, many of them enrolled in adult evening classes. It worked closely with Section Eight of the National Union of Railroad Workers and the Unión Campesina de Empalme. The school's Mother's Union served hundreds of poor children daily breakfast in the school. Its baseball teams were superb, regularly competing with those from Ciudad Obregón, Navojoa, and Guaymas. Its cultural events drew large numbers of people, who were entertained as much by the jarabe tapatío as by skits satirizing priests. Teachers and railroad workers actively backed Ramón Ramos's PNR candidacy for governor in 1935.[39]

Magaña's work strengthened the connection between urban industrial trade unionists and the nascent organization of farm workers and small farmers in the Yaqui Valley. When he began his inspectorship, teachers were already engaged in such organization. In the fall of 1934, Governor Calles had set up schools in the agricultural camps, paid for by the Asociación de

Agricultores. Five of these functioned under the SEP and eleven under the state government. Taken over by the SEP in 1935, they became Article 123 schools: schools set up at employers' expense in order to bring about owner compliance with the Federal Labor Law of 1931—not simply its requirement that workers' children be schooled, but its stipulations in relation to wages, hours, housing, health, indemnizations, and labor contracts. With the changes in agrarian law opening land reform to agricultural workers, teachers were also expected to organize them to solicit land. Thus, even more than the SEP rural school, Article 123 schools were intended to alter the local distribution of wealth, power, and resources. The Article 123 schools were not the only SEP schools on the left bank of the Yaqui River, but they became the heart of its operation there.[40]

In the camps, the SEP became part of the construction of community. The heterogeneity of the population created a homogeneity of purpose: a commitment to the future. The school here did not have to fit a predefined communal space and ritual. It did not crash against a wall of established custom and interest. It did not demand community expenditure. It was paid for by employers, and where it was not, the state government promised assistance in school construction. Instead of an intrusive institution that made demands on scarce time and energy, the school was a tool deemed necessary by many to achieve self-realization. The believers created a model for the rest to follow. In the camps and in other settlements where community institutions were absent, were weak, or belonged to the property owners, the school became the political, economic, social, and cultural center of a community under construction. It was a community based upon principles of class identity. In 1935–36, when owners, alarmed by rumors of an impending reparto, refused to make repairs on the schools or to pay for additional teachers, their recalcitrance simply contributed to an emerging class cohesion among families in the camps. The owners were shirking their duty to the workers.[41]

In the fall of 1935, as Indians chased teachers out of villages in the Mayo Valley to stop their sacking of saints and churches, teachers in the camps in the Yaqui municipalities of Ciudad Obregón and Bacum organized campesinos into cooperatives and worked in tandem with trade union organizations and Comités Agrarios. Perhaps it was the wisdom of Magaña, or the lesson of the Mayo, Ximello's after-the-fact disciplining of the SEP, or the lack of religious iconography in the camps, but the teachers there were not avidly antireligious. Where opportune, Magaña encouraged them to develop defanaticizing themes in the classroom and the cultural festivals, but this campaign was peripheral to their major objective.[42]

Although women predominated slightly over men in the teacher corps of the Yaqui Valley, male teachers assumed political leadership in the camps. Three teachers, Eusebio Morales of Campo 7, Jesús S. Madrigal of Campo 27, and Cornelio Ramírez Vázquez of Campo 6, were the core of the effort. They worked with Magaña, other teachers, and the local nuclei of the FOCSS to form Comités Agrarios. In the fall of 1935, these comités formulated petitions in Campos 6 and 7 and in Pueblo Yaqui for land. The teachers also maneuvered to secure the signing in the spring of 1936 of a valleywide labor contract ensuring payment of the minimum wage, a seventh day of work, vacation pay, and medical care. In their Centros de Cooperación Pedagógica, teachers studied agrarian and labor law, cooperativism, and the subordination of Mexico's economy to the imperialism of other nations. They explored their own role in campesino and worker organization. When the teachers, with Magaña's blessing, formed the Yaqui Valley branch of the federal teachers' union in Ciudad Obregón in January 1936, they did so in solidarity with the FOCSS. As part of their founding conference, the teachers marched with FOCSS members to Campo 6, the problematic property of Asa Brunk, one of the valley's first gringo settlers. Arriving penniless, he had made it rich, but his workers continued to live in hovels without hygiene. The school, although well attended, was in bad condition. The teachers and workers gathered at Campo 6 to lend their moral support to teacher Cornelio Ramírez Vázquez's campaign to improve conditions. They confronted Brunk, who promised he would repair the school if his lands were not divided.[43]

Along with leaders like Saturnino Saldívar, Machi López, and Jacinto López, SEP teachers became the organic intellectuals of a political movement. In the camps, they could win leadership denied them in Puebla and the Yaqui pueblos. They could do so because they built a new movement with little previous history and vested interest. Second, little social distance separated them from the people they organized. And third, they shared goals and values with their communities. They were not imposers, and insofar as they were transformers, the transformation they sought was coveted by the people they taught. Under these conditions, they were able not simply to assist and facilitate a political movement. They were also able to move it forward—to give ideological and social content to its raw, emerging militance.

The teachers shaped a new sociability around class association and identity. Through their union, they published a periodical dedicated to political and pedagogical issues. Their evening classes became centers for literacy, political education, and technical empowerment. Flour mill employees in Campo 65 learned how to type and keep accounts. Unions and Comités

Agrarios used the schoolhouse for meetings. The teachers built their school programs with the support of the unions. The school's artistic performance became an organizing tool. In the spring of 1936, Magaña conducted his Centro de Cooperación Pedagógica in Campo 7, where the energetic Eusebio Morales ran the school. The union subsidized the teachers' food and lodging—partially through a donation it secured from the owner. Teachers discussed with union members questions of cooperativism and their own role in union and campesino organizing. The union and the teachers mutually sponsored a cultural velada combining the usual themes of class struggle, defanaticization, hygiene, and sobriety. The velada ended with a dance, which drew people from all the surrounding camps. When the teachers originally formed their union, they not only marched with FOCSS leaders to Brunk's wretched Campo 6, they marched through all the camps. They met with parents, organizers, and schoolchildren, discussing the salient problems of each locale, admiring the magnificent school garden in Campo 34 and the prowess of Campo 65's sports club, and watching the children perform their songs, dances, recitations, and gymnastic exercises.[44]

In the hands of the unions and the teachers, sports became a tool for raising class as well as national consciousness. People took to baseball with zeal here, as they did in the rest of the state. But in the Yaqui Valley, the camp teams competed with those of Empalme railroad workers and the FOCSS affiliates in Navojoa and Huatabampo in the nearby Mayo Valley. Similarly, school teams were closely associated with the political organizations.[45]

Teachers developed with campesinos and workers a mutual language of modern legality. They based their claims to legitimacy, social justice, and citizenship not on the traditional campesino moral economy that informed the farmers of Tecamachalco, not on the regionally defined, informal reciprocities that sustained relations between Nahuas and their dominators in Zacapoaxtla, and not on the sacred foundations of Yaqui political thought. Valley peasants and workers spoke the language of collective rights as expressed in the Mexican Constitution of 1917 and in subsequent labor and agrarian law. As the agraristas of Bacum wrote in 1934 in an appeal for the "Emancipación Social del Campesino," addressed to the president in September 1934: "We note with sadness the failure to fulfill our petition. Our group has suffered a general demoralization noting that the time period indicated by the Law of Dotations and Restitutions of Land and Waters has passed, as well as the time period stipulated in the Agrarian Code of the United Mexican States, signed by yourself as president."[46] Their notion of legality incorporated a modern notion of class. May First, the international workers' holiday commemorating the anarchist martyrs of Haymarket Square in Chicago, was a far more important holiday here in the 1930s than the Fifth of May.[47] So the agraristas of Bacum told the president: "The workers' unions have helped us present petitions to the governor. This is our right under Article 27 of the Constitution. We have 333 members . . . and would have many more were it not for the delay in the resolution . . . and the fact that people see that much of the land we have asked for is being solicited by the estate managers and their *peones acasillados* as idle lands . . . depriving the Organized Class of its rights."[48]

At the same time, teachers participated in the construction of a modern notion of the social subject, especially around concepts of the human body. They strongly promoted an array of athletic activities, from basketball and volleyball to calisthenics and track. Anti-alcoholism was a consistent theme linked with sports, and it probably took among some people. Vaccination, vigorously promoted in cooperation with the authorities of Salubridad Pública, was not questioned. Women led hygiene campaigns. On the river's left bank, these campaigns made a great deal more sense than they did in Tecamachalco. Trucks picked up the garbage the schoolchildren and parents gathered, or the teachers burned it. It was feasible to put metal screening on the doors and windows to keep out flies and mosquitos. Outside Ciudad Obregón and Cocorit, there was still little potable water, but there was plenty of water in the river and the canals for bathing and cooking. The building of latrines was part and parcel of the school project, already having been initiated by most camp owners.[49]

As elsewhere, the federal teachers were not trained agriculturalists or artisans, except for those who had graduated from the Normal Rural at Ures. School annexes were relatively rare here, compared with Puebla. Craft production was superfluous to a society already dependent on market consumption. School gardens were scarce also. Teachers were less concerned about teaching people how to work the land than about helping them to get the land they did not yet have. The teachers' technical weaknesses in questions of production were incidental because there were other competent instructors in farming: the campesinos themselves, the owners, and, after the reparto, the Ejidal Bank. More important, there were facilities and inputs to make increased production a real possibility. To this region, as to the right bank of the Yaqui River, Cárdenas provided water, credit, seeds, and marketing on a scale unheard of in Puebla in the late 1930s. It was not an exorbitant amount, but the Yaqui Valley was one of only a few selected agricultural projects to receive significant state support. The ejidatarios of the Yaqui Valley did not disappoint Cárdenas. Despite consistent predictions of the failure of agriculture under collective management, the ejidos were producing abundant harvests of wheat and rice by the 1940s. In the first years, they did not depend on modern technology. They did not need artificial fertilizers because before the dams began to store the river water upstream, the water itself contained natural nitrogen. Nor did they depend much on tractors or gas-driven machinery. Rather, they turned out their harvests using human muscle and thousands of mules. Twenty to thirty mules hauled their harrows. A single ejido had from five thousand to eight thousand mules purchased from the Sierra de Chihuahua with credit from the Ejidal Bank or with the proceeds of the harvest.[50]

As in Puebla, the teacher was less a technician than a negotiator. Once the ejidatarios received land and began to interact with public and private agencies in production and marketing, teachers acted as advisors and intermediaries. They did so especially in agricultural camps whose leadership was less experienced than that in established communities like Pueblo Yaqui. As in the case of Puebla but more readily, ejidatarios conferred upon teachers "the power of speech." They confirmed teachers' roles as referees in conflicts between ejido members and as protectors of ejido interests in dealings with the Ejidal Bank agents to whom the farmers sold their harvest. These were the kinds of negotiating roles the SEP wanted teachers to play. The SEP did not want teachers to practice politics at the expense of training local leaders or fulfilling their classroom duties. In fact, several teachers left teaching to become ejidal leaders and major politicians. The most prominent among them was Ramón Danzos Palomino, who went on to become a major figure in the national left campesino movement. To graduate from teaching to politics was a long-standing Sonoran custom: it had produced two national presidents and many regional leaders. For the most part, however, those who remained teachers began to lose their role as critical advisors to ejidatarios in the 1940s, as the latter acquired the experience and maturity to negotiate their own affairs.[51]

The role of political advisor was a masculine one. One consequence of the agrarian reform in the Yaqui Valley—and more generally of the consolidation of official political organizations—was the marginalization of women. When Lina Saldívar asked her uncle Saturnino if she could help out with ejidal affairs, he and his buddies shooed her away. It hurt her; the reparto had raised her hopes and horizons. It had changed her life. Cárdenas "gave us pride of knowing that we were equal in work," she said. She and other revolutionary women found themselves relegated to the classroom, hygiene crusades, and cultural festivals. Her political aspirations, excited by the events around her and by her reading of European history, had to be shelved.[52]

With the reparto, ejidatarios asked for more schools and for the federalization of those that existed in recognition of the fact that "the rural school is our most effective collaborator in struggle." Schools were one of the first investments of ejidatario families in the Yaqui Valley. They built new, ample, cement structures with adequate ventilation and light. In Pueblo Yaqui, the ejidatarios put in two hours every afternoon after work until they completed their new school, which they named Lázaro Cárdenas: it had six full grades, compared with four years offered by the old school. On October 31, 1941, the fourth anniversary of the reparto, ejidatario families of Campo 47 Ejido Progreso inaugurated their new school, also named for Lázaro Cárdenas: they had invested thirteen thousand pesos in it. For agricultural camps and colonies that became incorporated towns, building the school was an integral part of community construction, as was planting and harvesting the parcela escolar and serving on the Comités de Educación. As in Puebla, the comités purchased glass for windows, chalk, desks, and benches. Compared with those of Puebla, they were better able to afford such purchases.[53]

The reparto enabled families to send children to school. Before the reparto, remembered Lina Saldívar, valley people were nomads, wandering from camp to camp. Now they had permanent homes and could build communities. They had more income to sustain them in school. As the teacher Manuel del Cid recalled: "It was no longer a question of battling to meet basic needs. Now they harvested and reaped. The children could finally get proper clothing, purchase supplies, and come to school with full stomachs."[54]

Between 1930 and 1940, youth literacy rose sharply on the left bank of the Yaqui River, despite technical and pedagogical deficiencies in the schools. Most male teachers were more engaged in politics than they were in teaching. Women picked up the slack, as they had since the nineteenth century. Sonoran schools had historically been short of textbooks, and these schools continued to be so into the 1940s. As elsewhere, *Simiente* was studied and used by teachers. However, often only the teachers had textbooks: they dictated the text, and children studied from the notes they had taken. Children created their alternative didactic materials, such as billboards and murals attacking alcoholism and promoting cleanliness.[55]

Despite their limitations, these Yaqui Valley schools were the most democratic of the schools examined in this study. They were so not because children practiced the prescriptions of the Cardenista text *Simiente* to challenge abusive authority—although such prescriptions undoubtedly sparked interest and may have been followed. They were democratic because of the open-ness of the ambience—an openness that had always defined the frontier and that especially characterized the valley in its revolutionary moment when power and wealth were redistributed in favor of the poor. The schools were democratic because the parents willed it and had the chance to practice it. Arturo Saldívar recalled what this moment meant to the male ejidatario: "Before he had been a peon; now he was a farmer. As a peon if he had not been abused, he had been indifferently treated by the owner. When he be-came an ejidatario, he was an individual who had to be noticed, taken into account. Possibly, his economic situation had not changed much but his moral situation had. He got his first share of the profits and his dreams were fulfilled. He worked harder with more *sabor*. He was off and running." That openness did not mean that ejidatarios automatically trusted teachers. As the ejidatarios acquired more power and self-assurance, they became more vigi-lant and discriminating. Comités de Educación functioned here, as they did in Puebla, not simply to support the school but to regulate the teacher's be-havior—to ensure against any physical punishment of children or any abuse of funds or the proceeds of the school's harvest.[56]

At the end of the 1930s, children still spent only a short time in school. At the age of ten or eleven, they went to work. Of the fifty children who finished primary school with Arturo Saldívar in Pueblo Yaqui in the early 1940s, only eight went on to secondary school. It was difficult to do so because one had to go to the city, and that required resources and family connections. An ide-ology of advancement and upward mobility through postprimary education began to take hold toward the end of the 1940s and especially in the 1950s. When it did, it had in many cases been vigorously instilled by the teachers themselves.

As in Puebla, what counted in the school's work beyond imparting basic literacy skills was the cultural construction it undertook with children, fam-ilies, and communities. In the Yaqui Valley and in most of Sonora, the con-struction of a national identity and citizenship was much less attached to the past than it was pegged to the future. To be sure, children here learned Mex-ican history as they did in Puebla and as they had since the nineteenth cen-tury, through stories of the patriotic heroes, memorization of important dates, and fiestas and parades.[57] However, schools here were more likely to have a portrait of Rodolfo Elías Calles on their walls prior to 1936 than to dis-play one of Juárez, Hidalgo, or Morelos. The SEP and Rodolfo Elías Calles worked consciously in the early 1930s to integrate Mexican historical iconog-raphy into Sonoran schools; but even then, it was more a learning-by-doing,

present-focused exercise than one grounded in the past. The school of
Rosario Tapia was typical in its homespun iconography fixed on the present
and the future. Placards illustrating the abuses of alcohol decorated the
school walls in Pueblo Yaqui and were taken out during civic festivals and
paraded up and down the dusty paths that passed for streets. They also
served as props in theatrical presentations. In the Yaqui Valley, male teachers
were more engaged in obtaining land and union contracts—and women, in
hygiene and temperance issues—than in retrieving historical, native cultural
traditions. It was easier to import the nationalist folkloric repertoire disseminated by the SEP. The Guadalajara dance of the jarabe, the agrarista hymn,
and the Yaqui Deer Dance, repackaged through Mexico City, became staples
of cultural festival here as elsewhere.

On the left bank of the Yaqui River, the national identity consciously and
unconsciously promoted by the federal school was bound up with the revolution and the future. A key holiday became that of the reparto itself: October 31—All Souls' Day to the majority of Mexicans but a celebration of the
living for the ejidatarios of the valley agricultural camps. The reparto made
for an intense identification with Cárdenas. Cárdenas, asserted Lina Saldívar,
was "un dios grandísimo para todos nosotros" (a great god to all of us). Logically, the ejidatarios mobilized fervently around the oil expropriation, which
followed on the heels of their own receipt of land. With the teachers, the
Comisariados Ejidales staged barbecues and kermises and contributed their
own fresh and initial profits to fortify "national independence."[58] This nationalist identification, articulated through the valley ejidatarios and workers, contrasted with the regionalist populist project of Rodolfo Elías Calles
and clashed mightily with the regional insularity actively promoted by Governor Román Yocupicio. Valley ejidatarios and small-scale settlers regarded
the central government in Mexico City as a source for redress, justice, and
amelioration. Without the central government, they would never have acquired the recognition and dignity, the economic and political power they
achieved through the reparto. The SEP was critical to their movement and to
their construction of class, community, individual, and national identity.

HEGEMONY, RESISTANCE, AND SCHOOLING AFTER 1940

The Yaqui Valley reparto came late in the Cárdenas presidency at a moment of conservative ascendance. Resources available to ejidatarios were
limited by the effects of the oil expropriation; the tide turned in favor of
Yocupicio, Jesús Gutiérrez Cázares, and representatives of the Sonoran agro-

bourgeoisie. As detailed in chapter 3, Yocupicio used Cárdenas's March 1938 cession of powers to the governors to remove the agraristas' supporters in the central government: the agrarian reform delegate, the director of the Ejidal Bank, and the radical SEP director. On the advice of Cárdenas's Secretary of War, Manuel Avila Camacho, the worker-friendly military zone commander was transferred and replaced by Gutiérrez Cázares.

These departures enabled Yocupicio to accelerate his campaign against the southern valley agraristas and their teacher allies. He encouraged splits and violent confrontations among organized agraristas and workers in order to move people out of the CTM and into his own organizations, the CTS and the Sonoran branch of the CNC. He sponsored the emergence of CNC ejidatarios known as "individualistas" and pitted them against the CTM "colectivistas." Although this campaign was waged most intensely in Yocupicio's home territory of the Mayo Valley, he registered a major victory in the Yaqui when the veteran agrarista leader Pascual Ayón went over to the individualists and the CNC.[59]

During the presidency of Manuel Avila Camacho and the governorship of Yocupicio's successor, Anselmo Macías, Sonora's agro-bourgeoisie moved to reestablish power. They took the lion's share of new water and lands opened by the Angostura Dam. Through the Unión de Crédito Agrícola del Valle del Yaqui, created in 1942, they bid for increased public funds. They got permits to import technology and became regional distributors of trucks and automobiles, agricultural machinery, and agro-chemicals. Rodolfo Elías Calles returned to his hacienda of Santa Barbara and invited Norman Borlaug, a University of Minnesota plant geneticist, to found the CIANO, the Centro de Investigaciones Agrícolas del Noroeste. Financed by the Rockefeller Foundation, the World Bank, and the Mexican government, the CIANO produced new hybrid, pest-resistant seeds. The Yaqui Valley became the first site and exporter of the green revolution. Befitting the technification of valley life, the SEP moved the Escuela Rural Normal from Ures to Ciudad Obregón and began to replace existing teachers with normal school graduates. Officially the purpose was to enhance competence, but the move was also designed to weaken the teachers' union and interfere with its radical politics.[60]

Still, in the first half of the 1940s, the radicals survived. Governor Anselmo Macías had to come to terms with the CTM. Despite conservative trends in the SEP, Heriberto Salazar, veteran of militant struggles, was SEP zone inspector in 1941 and became the mayor of Ciudad Obregón in 1943. Saturnino Saldívar became a federal congressional deputy, as did other members of the FOCSS. The collective ejidatarios thrived. They had to fight for credit and favorable marketing arrangements, but they got them. The ejidos became financially solvent: in 1943, out of fourteen collectives in the valley, only three were in debt to the bank. Collective productivity achieved parity with that of private owners in major cash crops such as rice and wheat. In 1940, 90 percent of the ejidatarios had been obliged to work part-time outside their own lands to support their families. By 1950, only 6 percent did so. Between 1943 and 1950, ejidatario income more than doubled, from 1,559 pesos a year to 4,500. They could begin to enjoy some of the treasures from the store windows. In terms of production and productivity, they proved their naysayers wrong. Hundreds of them learned to read in the adult literacy campaigns of the Avila Camacho government.[61]

Then, in 1946, the tide turned decisively against the collectivists. From 1946 to 1952, President Miguel Alemán, with strong support from the valley agro-bourgeoisie, parceled the collective ejidos. In response to the increasing conservatism of the PRI, Jacinto López, Saturnino Saldívar, Machi López, and other CTM leaders in the valley joined with Vicente Lombardo Toledano in leaving the PRI and the CTM and forming the Partido Popular (PP) and the Unión General de Obreros y Campesinos de Mexico (UGOCM). In 1948, encouraged by the Agrarian Department authorities and the CNC, individualists challenged the UGOCM collectivists in violent confrontations. In July 1949, when Jacinto López won gubernatorial elections in Sonora on a PP ticket, President Alemán sent federal troops to impose the PRI candidate and to break up the collective ejidos. The remaining UGOCM collectivists lost their access to credit, which flowed instead to CNC members. In 1953, when the UGOCM tried to renew its defense of landless campesinos, the revered leader Machi López was murdered in his home.[62]

When the collective ejidos disintegrated, many ejidatarios blamed themselves and their leaders. They had been insufficiently educated to handle the machinery, accounts, and organization; they had wasted water. They lacked the foresight and discipline necessary for profit making. They had squandered the payoffs from the first "liquis" (liquidations of accounts) on long barbecues, roasting fine Sonoran beef, on billiards and in bars, and on the purchase of longed-for consumer goods: a coveted Fordsito, a store-bought gown. Most of all, they blamed their leaders for mismanaging accounts, favoring friends and relatives, and substituting political rhetoric and mobilization for good business sense. They blamed the government for hooking them into corrupt dependency: selling them defective machinery at inflated prices, taking bribes and cuts at every corner. The collective ejido—"el sueño cardenista" (the Cardenista dream)—ended in "una epidemia de corruptela" (an epidemic of corruption).[63] There was truth to their explanation, and support among the ejidatarios for parcelization. Arturo Saldívar explained the process with some measure of objectivity. The pre-reparto peones, he said,

> were timid people who did not know how to get things [no sabían como prosperar]. They needed a push. The entire experience of the collective ejido changed their mentality. They learned how to defend themselves. Now they were no longer a herd of sheep pushed around by the patron and pity them if they objected! Those who had benefited the most from the collective ejido were the leaders. Now, the rest matured and sought something else. Things change and become obsolete. But everything had its roots in the reparto and the collective ejido.[64]

He might have added that the ejidatarios' mature perceptions had developed within a hegemonic context of shifting power. They bought into a bourgeois discourse that belittled them and satanized the left.[65] Among the most vociferous were farmers who had done well and who regarded their own ejido leaders as greater enemies than the private owners. This decline in class identity and solidarity had its explanation not only in ejido politics and individual fortunes, but in the behavior of the agro-bourgeoisie itself. The latter no longer functioned as landlords and bosses. Instead, they serviced the ejidatarios with their agribusiness supplies and, like the ejidatarios, were farmers interested in increasing production.

The radical movement of the 1930s had been a regional one, empowered by its association with the central government and with national political associations tied to the official party. When it lost these connections, the movement did not disintegrate. The legacy of the 1930s did not die with Machi López in 1953. It could not, in a region whose wealth continued to attract newcomers in search of well-being and justice. The radical legacy waxed again in 1957, in land invasions throughout the state led by the PP and the UGOCM. It surged in 1975 at San Ignacio Río Muerto in the Yaqui Valley and in the campesino takeover of Block 407 in 1976. In both instances, the Mexican state and the PRI responded with important concessions while jealously protecting their political dominion.[66]

Significantly, the leader of the land invasion at San Ignacio Río Muerto in 1975 was a schoolteacher, Juan de Dios Terán, who was shot and killed by federal troops. Political teaching traditions do not easily die. On the other hand, the school in the Yaqui Valley probably exercised its resistance function after 1940 more in the creation of a civil society than in the mobilization of grassroots political movements. The collapse of the socialist dream was by no means the collapse of the fantasy of modernity: socialism had been one option on a full menu. The 1940s and 1950s were years of rapid growth and prosperity in the Yaqui, confirming and realizing fantasies, disappointing and impoverishing some, but for the most part filling the tortillas of faith with fine Sonoran beef—or, at least, with opportunity. In this world of laboratory-bred wheat seeds, DDT, and factory-made fertilizers, schooling became ever more important. People embraced the ideology of schooling as social mobility because it converged with real conditions and possibilities. Lina Saldívar became a schoolteacher. Abandoned by her husband, she worked to put her seven children through professional and university education. She was one of many who secured their children's mobility.

"Lo técnico" had a meaning in the Yaqui Valley that was only vaguely and mystically alluded to in most of Tecamachalco and Zacapoaxtla: it was part of daily life in a wealthy region that seemed to run on its own internally generated fuel rather than that of the state. Such a notion was illusory—state funds paid for water, supplied credit, and provided the legal and infrastructural framework for marketing. Nonetheless, valley life fostered a sense of modernity independent of the Mexican state—a sense of modernity that schooling helped to encourage.

8

CONCLUSION
THE SCHOOL, HEGEMONY, AND CIVIL SOCIETY

In Gramscian terms, the state is a cultural, educative institution bound to adapt the morality and behavior of the masses to the needs of the productive apparatus. Educational pressure must be applied to subjects in such a way that they consent to collaborate: state necessity and coercion become transformed in the subject's mind into "freedom" (Gramsci 1971:247). From the perspective of the embryonic state arising from the Mexican conflagration of 1910, a rebellious, heterogeneous, and far-flung population had to be brought to order and mobilized for purposes of national development and survival in the context of an increasingly competitive global order. Educational policy focused most intensely on the peasants, understood to be the runt of the race. They were decadent and diseased. They were unhinged from modernity by centuries of oppression at the hands of backward social classes: the landlords and the clergy. In view of the modernizing mandate assumed by the Mexican state, the peasantry was but a "millstone round the nation's neck."[1] Schools had to nationalize and modernize peasants, turning superstitious, locally oriented pariahs into patriotic, scientifically informed, commercial producers wired to national markets, political associations, and informational networks.

When it was established in 1921, the Secretaría de Educación Pública was led by a handful of Mexico City intellectuals for whom the peasant was no more than an imagined, miserable construction. It was not until the 1930s that the SEP acquired the size, jurisdiction, and experienced talent to conduct meaningful dialogue with the peasantry. By then the SEP had articulated with state and municipal primary school systems; it pulled personnel from them, absorbed them in some instances, and collaborated with them in

189

others. By that decade as well, the SEP had devised cheap and imaginative mechanisms for teacher training, for reaching children who attended school briefly and irregularly, and for proselytizing through festival in the broader rural community.

In the 1930s, bolstered by international events and national conditions, the central government's confidence in its educative role grew enormously. At a global level, massive market collapse in the Western world gave rise to unprecedented state intervention in economy and society. At the national level, the Mexican central government's fledgling political party, the PNR, had to develop from a loose association of political leaders, army officers, and phantom parties into a mass party with a base in the working, peasant, and middle classes. It had to do so at a time when workers were mobilizing independently from the central state, and when thousands of peasants were disaffected because of the government's failure to provide land, infuriated by its antireligious policies, or under the tutelage of semiautonomous regional cacicazgos. The situation favored the PNR's left wing. The left had the political discourse appropriate to the moment and had accumulated experience organizing peasants and workers at the regional level. Leftists advocated labor and land reform and state intervention to promote nationalist economic restructuring. They championed the state's cultural, educative mission. Repackaged as socialist education, that mission now acquired the imprint of the revolutionary left, a relatively small group brought to power by extraordinary circumstances and wielding particular strength and influence among federal teachers.

Socialist education was militantly antireligious in its zeal to create a secular society. It advocated collective forms for learning modern productivist and nationalist behavior: producer and consumer cooperatives, sports teams, cultural performance, anti-alcohol and sanitation campaigns. A new curriculum promoted an inclusive, populist, national culture based upon Mexico's multiethnicity and hallowing workers and peasants as the makers and beneficiaries of the revolution of 1910. Concepts of rebellion, struggle, and the right to social justice were etched into the core of the Mexican cultural nation. The Constitution of 1917—with its clauses providing for land reform, worker rights, and nationalization of natural resources—became the scripture that underwrote claims to democracy, justice, and national development.

In the 1930s the SEP told the federal teachers to organize peasants and workers to press for the implementation of federal agrarian and labor laws that would effect a redistribution of property and wealth. President Cárdenas hailed teachers as the vanguard in his massive land reform program and looked to them to inspire workers to assert their class rights. Cárdenas called upon teachers to assist in the formation of national peasant and trade union confederations. These would constitute new, horizontal linkages that would break the peasantry's dependence upon regional landlords, merchants, and religious mentors and open them to participation in a secular, national society and its expanding marketplace. In 1938, Cárdenas integrated these associations as the CNC and the CTM into the official state party as its national, popular base. The PNR became the Partido de la Revolución Mexicana, renamed the PRI in 1946.

In carrying out their cultural revolution, teachers were handicapped by factors residing in the state itself. On the one hand, they lacked the training and resources necessary to effect the transformation assigned to them. Poorly paid, most of them depended on communities for such basics as food and lodging. In rare cases, they were able to join forces with other state agencies in providing the material and infrastructural base necessary to bring about the behavioral transformation they advocated. But often, state agencies worked at cross-purposes with one another and promoted practices that did not correspond to the models of citizenship articulated by the SEP. Most notably, state political associations and economic agencies often sanctioned a machista, patron–clientelist politics at odds with the SEP's hopes for democratizing family and political culture. Patron–clientelist politics proved to be far more powerful than the SEP's cultivation of democratically administered cooperative production and organization. In fact, clientelism absorbed collective organization to become the dominant practice within it.

Teachers were also dependent upon state governors for resources, support, and political space. A friendly governor with resources could facilitate their work; a friendly governor without resources was less useful. Unfriendly governors were formidable obstacles. It is a bitter irony that precisely at the moment that Lázaro Cárdenas established control as the revolution's first radical president, populist, social-democratic movements came to an end in the states of Sonora and Puebla. Conservative governors took advantage of popular hostility to the antireligious aspects of socialist education to marginalize teachers as agents of resource redistribution and democratization. Because these governors represented a considerable force within the state coalition, their role in thwarting the central state's articulated educative mission must not be underestimated. Even in his period of radical ascendance (1936–1938), Cárdenas was careful to balance popular pleas for social justice against conservative interests in his own coalition for the sake of state consolidation. After the oil expropriation of March 1938, Cárdenas faced a mushrooming debt, mounting pressures from international and national business and financial circles, and the possibility of a Fascist movement against his government. He moved to the right. He conceded to governors powers over education and agrarian reform that had served him in promoting radical projects between 1936 and 1938. By 1939, socialist education ended in fact. Its goal of securing mass allegiance to the party and state had been accomplished with the formation of the PRM. Its commitment to behavioral transformation could be sacrificed, or at least postponed. Effective political control over the people was more important in the short run than their ability to learn modern, rational behavior.

Thus, even before the state's cultural project got contested and reworked by peasant societies at the local level during the 1930s, it was handicapped by the politics of the state itself, or by what Gramsci calls the political society—the governing apparatus with its power of coercion and regulation. State incapacity—technical and material, moral and political—enhanced the peasantry's capacity to resist the educators' project and increased its ability to select from the project those aspects amenable to its own efforts to reconstruct power at the local level. Because the peasantry was essential to the state in its constitution of hegemony, peasant demands and claims had to be heard, acknowledged, and met even when this entailed sacrificing the full realization of the state makers' imagined social subject. This dynamic was not unfamiliar in Mexican history: it happened in the aftermath of conquest in the sixteenth century and during the long period of civil wars and foreign invasion in the nineteenth century. Elite weakness never canceled peasant subordination, and elite infighting shaped and deformed peasant options in unanticipated ways. But the absence of unity within the "political society" nonetheless opened space that peasants creatively occupied and struggled to maintain once the elites had reconsolidated.

In order to understand how local cultures negotiated the state's curriculum, this study has examined four societies selected for their distinct ethnic and social composition, their prior histories of schooling and literacy, their relations to land and markets, and their participation in the revolution of 1910. Although located in the states of Sonora and Puebla, they are broadly representative of peasant societies in the Mexican Revolution. Each story speaks eloquently of the importance of history to cultural nation-building. Over historical time preceding the revolution, the educative state had preached different curricula—formal and informal—to these distinct regional societies. In so doing, it had created in them a residue of knowledge, attitude, behavior, and expectations that local people brought to their encounter with the new school of the postrevolutionary state. Each society had experienced state formation over a long period in distinct ways. Correspondingly, they had differentially appropriated or rejected a liberal, patriotic secular culture and its handmaiden, the public primary school. That the Yaqui Indians of Sonora could have nothing to do with the formal curriculum of the revolution's school stemmed from their bitter nineteenth-century war for ethnic and territorial survival against the Mexican state: their Mexican school had been but a barrage of bullets. The Nahuas of central and northern Zacapoaxtla had been only minimally exposed to liberal, secular culture in the nineteenth century and had instead secured relative autonomy in alliance with Catholic elites. Although racist, exploitive, and hierarchical, this relationship nonetheless had been forged in struggle and had entailed some accommodation by the elites to Indian demands. In the 1930s, the Nahuas were best able to protect their cultural integrity from the revolutionary state's transformative curriculum by reaffirming their prerevolutionary ties to local elites.

By contrast, the mestizo societies of Tecamachalco and the left bank of the Yaqui River and the Indian communities on the southern tier of Zacapoaxtla had experienced the liberal, patriotic civic culture of the nineteenth century as exclusionary but promissory. In the revolution, they clamored for inclusion. They appropriated the school, albeit on their own terms and at their own pace. In joining the liberal, patriotic civic culture in the 1930s, they not only endowed it with new local meaning, they contributed to its alteration at the national level: they made it more inclusive, more democratic, and more multicultural. They supplemented its emphasis on individual rights with a commitment to collective rights. They did so with the help of the Secretaría de Educación Pública, which provided the necessary ideological and cultural materials.

Each local society selected from the state's project according to its own power configurations that had been dynamized by the revolutionary process. In several instances, the cultural projects supported by local powerholders were far more important than material resources as determinants in local selection. The Yaquis were given the material wherewithal to become modern, commercial producers and scientific, patriotic subjects. Instead, they chose to use the state's material concessions to re-create an ethnically separate society dedicated to work for ritual rather than profit. "The Yaquis" must be de-essentialized. This option prevailed because the Yaqui governors and organic intellectuals mobilized their forces to promote it. They won because their competitors were disorganized and because they themselves enjoyed broad support in Yaqui society. And most decisively, they were favored by Cárdenas and the central government.

The primacy of culture over material issues was evident all over Mexico when the association of socialist education with antireligiosity provoked pervasive, active, and fervent protest. The entire project foundered on its attack on religion, which sullied and obfuscated the SEP's other messages, diminished its mobilizing capacity, and invited conservative nonpeasant elites both within and outside the state to reassert control. Religion was not the abstraction envisioned by the SEP. It could not be surgically removed and replaced with a scientific, secular implant. Religion was most often part of a local configuration of power entrenched in the practices of daily life. When it was attacked, its power was reconfirmed, often at the expense of progressive change. This was true not only in relations between peasants and elites, as events in Zacapoaxtla showed, but among agraristas. In Tecamachalco, for instance, agrarianism destroyed the exploitive hacienda regime. However, the revolution's cultural politics reinforced the social conservatism of patriarchal ejidatario families. Religious or not, male ejidatarios were going to adopt scientific approaches to farming and participate in secular political associations. However, the attack on religion exacerbated women's isolation from the state's project. It incurred women's ire and opposition, and justified communities' limiting their exposure to a project that men rightly feared would expand female space and freedom.

Material endowment was another important variable influencing local selection from the state's project. Beneficiaries of agrarian reform on the left bank of the Yaqui River embraced the SEP's behavioral paradigm because they were provided with the land, water, credit, marketing arrangements, and health and hygienic facilities that made such behavior possible. Agraristas in Tecamachalco, on the other hand, resisted experimentation with scientific approaches to production and reproduction because they lacked those resources. Poverty reconfirmed the value of the old ways in production, curing, healing, diet, dress, and home construction.

However, in both instances, the cultural and political processing of material resources was as important as their availability in determining attitudes and behavior. Immigrants in the agricultural camps of the Yaqui Valley spun material dreams from the scenery and messages around them: the new machinery that plowed the fields, the fashions and gadgets in the store windows, the cars and motorbikes. They were inundated by the messengers of modernity: the victrola, the radio, and the Hollywood screen. The social organization of community and family life was open and flexible enough to encourage them to embrace the fantasies of modernity and transform their behavior. In Tecamachalco, these artifacts were less available, the messages less audible, and the organization of family and community life more tightly girded. These conditions, together with the state's material parsimony, reconfirmed the wisdom and logic of local customs and traditions. A censoring prism was constructed in the 1930s through which subsequently appearing goods and procedures would be filtered, appropriated, or discarded. No vignette better represents this outcome of revolutionary cultural politics than a scene in Luis Buñuel's 1951 film *Mexican Bus Ride* (Subida al cielo). When the bus gets stuck in a river, a state politician aboard the vehicle hails a nearby farmer on his tractor to pull it out. The state politician is, of course, the bombastic champion of modernity. However, the tractor itself gets stuck in the river mud. A team of oxen, hooked by a wooden yoke and hauled by a young girl, pulls both the bus and the tractor from the river. Everyone cheers and heartily relishes the joke. The humor of this affirmation of tradition and mocking of modernity would resonate anywhere in Mexico—but its social authors were the Tecamachalqueños.

The case studies demonstrate that each society, in its encounter with the state's project in the 1930s, forged new linkages, identities, and associations. These constructions permit us to speak of the formation of a mutual language for consent and dissent, an institutional apparatus for making demands and processing grievances, and a cultural nation within which language and institutions functioned and identities were mutually affirmed, created, and manipulated by state and society. In other words, the encounter helped to forge hegemony and to construct civil society.

In each case, new institutional and informal linkages, identities, and associations differed in their relationship to the central state and its cultural project. With the collapse of the hacienda system and the demise of provisioning by the private sector, Tecamachalco agraristas came to depend on state-provided resources and infrastructural support for agriculture. They became members of the CNC and the official party. Through the school and festival, they could assume identities—tactically or essentially—that made them makers of Mexican history, prototypes of the new national hero, Emiliano Zapata, and beneficiaries of the revolution they had made. For the Nahua communities of central and northern Zacapoaxtla, linkages to the central state remained weak. Local elites maintained their prerevolutionary status as intermediaries between the indigenous peoples and the outside world. Cultural festival celebrated regional autonomy. Regional autonomy absorbed nationalism. On the other hand, federal schoolteachers became the local progressive opposition, empowered by their linkages to the central state through the SEP and through the teachers' union. Nahua communities came to look to them as allies as they strove to improve their conditions and expand their space vis-à-vis the dominating elites, and for assistance in their efforts to pace modernity's entry and determine its content.

The Yaquis of southern Sonora had little use for the assimilative Mexican school in the 1930s. On the other hand, their linkages with the central government were critical to their securing relative autonomy from the voracious, modernizing society around them. They recognized their entitlement not only as indigenous peoples denied their rights but as participants in the Mexican nation's struggle for redemption. This dual citizenship, guaranteed by the central government, was essential to their survival as a people. As for their neighbors, the agraristas of the left bank of the Yaqui River, they owed the realization of their fantasies of modernity to the central government, its educative agency, the SEP, and its worker association, the CTM. They became actors in the incorporation of the aloof and distant state of Sonora into the cultural nation. At the same time, like the Yaquis, they fiercely guarded a regional identity and sense of autonomy.

In the negotiation of cultural politics through schooling in the 1930s, a shared language for dissent and consent was forged. It was not a language imposed by a state elite or the bourgeoisie; it was a language mutually constructed through negotiation between a fledgling, fragmented state and a highly mobilized, fragmented society. It incorporated subaltern demands, concepts, and claims in order to secure consent for the state's modernization project. This shared language was organized around three concepts: the rights of collective groups to social justice; to inclusion in modernity; and to membership in a multicultural society.

In the 1930s, through schooling and politics, the social provisions of the Constitution of 1917—guaranteeing collective rights and national control over development—melded in the forging of the cultural nation. Articles 27 and 123 spoke directly to the rights of peasants to land and of workers to organization and protection. Broadly, the Constitution endorsed collective rights to justice and well-being. This constitutional language was learned and made in communities as they struggled with state agencies and the society around them to restructure themselves. It was strongly articulated by the SEP as teachers enshrined the Constitution in cultural festival and assisted popular movements in implementing central state legislation; and it came to have different meanings in local societies where its appropriation was based upon distinct historical precedent.

For the agraristas of Tecamachalco, group rights recalled the rights of peasant villages to subsistence in an ancient moral economy once dominated by landlords and kings. For the Nahuas of the Sierra Norte, south of Zaca-poaxtla, collective rights blended indigenous communal autonomy with the liberal notions of yeoman freedom and citizenship forged through participation in the nineteenth-century civil wars. For their Nahua neighbors to the north, the rights of indigenous communities were best negotiated locally, with less adherence to external notions of law and justice. For the Yaquis, collective rights meant tribal rights to autonomy based upon a divine claim invented in the late nineteenth century in the midst of war with the Mexicans. For their left-bank neighbors, collective rights were class rights, specified on paper in constitutional Articles 27 and 123 and in subsequent agrarian and labor legislation. They had no precedent prior to the revolution of 1910. In each case, the social concepts of the Constitution became the language of consent when collective rights were honored, and the language of resistance when they were not.

Although much has been made of the Mexican Revolution as a struggle waged against modernity to preserve a rustic peasant utopia, cultural negotiations of the 1930s point toward an acceptance of modernity, not as an avalanche of consumer goods or a parade of technology but as an enabler of human life. Modernity was a goal to work for, not a steamroller flattening tradition and dignity. Modernity was a process to be judged, assessed, and selected. What was left unsaid but remained implicit was that shifting relations of power in communities and families affected those judgments and selections. In some cases, as with the Nahuas, the power relations that solidified in the 1930s acted as a filter that kept modernity distant and preserved the supremacy of male elders for some time. In the most modern of the four societies in the 1930s, women and youth were most free to make decisions and least afraid of modernity. In the other societies, they waited longer to become major decision makers.

The notion of the cultural nation as a multiethnic one made up of a multiplicity of local cultures and their artistic expression was the work of the SEP as it negotiated with peasants. The browning of Mexican culture begun by the muralists Rivera and Orozco in the 1920s was not something desired by the Mexican elites. Still today they shun it as much as possible in their private practices. The browning of the cultural nation was a political necessity, a sine qua non for the creation of a national civil society and for its relatively harmonious modernization. The broad canvas displaying such diverse folkloric expression was the monumental work of schoolteachers. Hundreds of them gathered up local aesthetic expressions and placed them one by one into a patchwork synthesis. They honored the integrity of local culture while crafting an empowering national culture. This notion of the cultural nation was immediately available to all through the celebration of festival, and after 1940, through the movies, comic books, radio, and television. It was a profoundly democratizing and inclusive achievement of the postrevolutionary Mexican state. In a revolution that most indigenous people shunned because of its aggressively assimilative pretension, this notion of the multicultural nation provided an outlet for legitimate resistance and self-preservation.

If this shared language facilitated consent within the structures of the consolidated state, it was also the language of resistance. The language of resistance was not simply the autonomous voice of the subaltern, nor was it the product of central state cunning and manipulation. The forging and employment of the language of resistance had much to do with schoolteachers and the negotiations they undertook with communities in the 1930s. In this encounter, the teachers (with the exception of the primary school teachers among the Yaquis) lost their condescension toward the peasantry as sick, poor, profligate, and savage. They came to see themselves as collaborators with the peasantry in mutual liberation and national development. They helped to provide the peasantry with a nationally grounded oppositional ideology of class and oppression, potentially useful in overcoming internecine and intercommunity factionalism and winning extralocal visibility and support for political causes. They helped to universalize local struggle at the discursive and pragmatic levels. Even when teachers were not leaders of subaltern battles, they worked, as the case of Puebla demonstrates, to understand rural people in order to represent their interests. In many instances, it became more important for teachers to hear and represent the peasantry than to exhort them to modernize their behavior. Teachers' critical perspective on the emerging Mexican state and its potential for abusing the peasantry stemmed from the discrimination they themselves suffered at the hands of other state agencies and state-affiliated actors, and from the ideology they imbibed from the SEP in the 1930s. They were empowered to practice a critical politics through their membership in a federal agency, in the largest trade union in the Western Hemisphere, and in many instances, in opposition political parties. Like the peasants, teachers came to practice a clientelist politics, but such political behavior was not incompatible with resistance and opposition. Like the organized peasantry, their organizational structures and political culture made them susceptible to becoming caciques, bureaucrats, and petty exploiters. Some succumbed. However, teachers' potential for principled protest remained. And it was practiced, as the case of Zacapoaxtla demonstrates.[2]

In Gramsci's view, hegemony is achieved when political society (the governmental apparatus of coercion) fuses with the civil society or when the latter, as a set of voluntary associations independent of the state, becomes infused with ruling-class ideology. Such a definition is unsuitable to the case of Mexico, where the state and its official party achieved hegemony by incorporating subaltern claims, demands, and concepts in order to move forward with a bourgeois project. The formation of the Mexican postrevolutionary state hardly resulted in an unadulterated bourgeois project. It redistributed wealth and power. It refashioned social policy. It spoke a language of inclusion and social justice, not of individual competition in a marketplace unfettered by a regulatory state. That language had to be forged because of popular participation in state formation and the traditions and practices it brought to the table. One does not rule a modern society for any period of time without harnessing the energies of a majority of citizens, and to do that requires accommodation and compromise.

More appropriate to the Mexican experience is Gramsci's notion of statolatry, a condition in which the state acts as tutor to a weak and incipient civil society in order to prepare it for a higher stage of complexity and maturity suitable to the state's development project (Gramsci 1971:268–69). One can argue that modern Mexican civil society was created in large part by the state by way of its interaction with social groups in the 1930s. Prior to 1934, national government was a weak, disarticulated, and largely unsuccessful association of disparate generals and civilian politicians, increasingly alienated from each other and from society. Cárdenas created the national apparatus for economic development and for the processing of political and social demands and grievances from a multiplicity of social classes and groups. The state created or promoted the emergence of political parties, class and professional associations, economic cooperatives, credit societies and banks, and the communication system through which all of them articulated.

At the same time, the state in the 1930s created the social and cultural parameters for civil society—parameters that encouraged the growth and deepening of civil society. To begin with, the church won its right to continue as a major power in Mexican society and politics. Formally, the government did not recognize the Catholic church, but in practice it fully acknowledged and interacted with it. The church at least curbed its zeal for establishing its own hegemony and agreed to negotiate. Second, the cultural parameters set by the state encouraged the development of a multicultural,

multiethnic nation. For instance, without support from the central government, the Yaqui Indians would never have survived in twentieth-century
Sonoran society. Without central state protection, SEP proselytism on the
subject of multiethnicity, and government promotion of political association, mutual tolerance between Yaquis and Yoris would not have developed—or would have emerged more painfully, fitfully, and violently. Third,
the civil society had to recognize the rights of the subaltern classes to material well-being and justice. Class identity and association may have facilitated
the state's capacity to dominate the subaltern, but it also empowered the latter in forging solidarity with extralocal groups for the purpose of resistance.
At the same time, the civil society had to accept the peaceful coexistence of
social classes and so submitted, not always willingly, to a long period of social development, differentiation, and maturation. Fourth, the state promoted the notion of a civil society open to the expanding participation of
women. No state agency did more to promote women than the SEP.

The state's ideological construct legitimized challenges to discriminatory,
exclusive, and unjust practices (for example, the teachers' movement of 1958,
the railroad workers' strike of 1958–59, the Catholic protest against SEP textbooks in 1960, the student mobilization of 1968, and the Zapatista uprising
of 1994). It helped to accelerate change. In its dynamic, inclusive parameters,
the Mexican state was unique in Latin America. It permitted the development of an increasingly complex and articulated civil society under conditions of relative harmony and persistent civilian rule. The state sponsored
the development of civil society by promoting economic growth, a pluralis-
tic and relatively autonomous mass print and electronic media, and an increasingly complex and extensive system of public education. The school
played its most important role in resistance by developing the skills of modern social subjects. It provided tools for contesting state policies and helped
to create the civil society that would eventually render obsolete the political
monopoly of a single-party state.

Hegemony is ephemeral. It is a contentiously negotiated acceptance of
domination. Its life span depends upon the dominators' capacity to meet social demands and to satisfactorily process grievances. To understand its life
cycle in Mexico I must bring in an actor barely visible in the stories I have
told: international politics. Most accounts argue—and future regional research is likely to conclude—that the official party lost the elections of 1940
to the opposition candidate. It was the government's decision to support the
United States and the Allied cause in World War II that altered internal relations of power at the highest levels of Mexican politics and solidified

PRI/state hegemony. Through this wartime alliance, the party/state seized the moral high ground at the expense of the religious right and the socialist left. The organized Catholic movement lost face through its associations—tenuous or not—with Fascism. At the same time, the government's commitment to the war effort elicited concessions from the left and later, under the aegis of Cold War discourse, justified its marginalization from the party and state. Finally, government collaboration with the United States in the war effort brought the capital, markets, and technology necessary to sustain a long period of economic growth and thereby to deliver on the promises of modernity to millions of Mexicans—even when these benefits came in the smallest of packages—a can of sardines for a peasant family who otherwise subsisted on tortillas and beans; an antibiotic to stop a baby's diarrhea; a deepwater well to irrigate the fields; a movie with Cantinflas or María Félix; a bouncing bus that at least got a woman from Hueyapán to Atlixco where she could sell her vegetables. As is well known, the particular partnership between the Mexican government and the United States also came to limit the possibilities for ongoing economic growth and equitable distribution of its goods while at the same time shoring up a party/government increasingly distant from the needs and deaf to the claims of its civil society.[3]

In fact, the state was much more successful in promoting the development of a complex civil society than it was in meeting the proliferating demands of that civil society. The hegemonic contract began to break down. It became increasingly clear to citizens that the state had substituted political association and relations for the rule of law. In its monopoly of political power and expression, it had nurtured its own culture based upon unaccountability to society, private appropriation of public wealth, and a megalomaniac obsession with suppressing and absorbing oppositional expression. Overcommitted to subsidizing the economic well-being of multiple social groups, it increasingly lacked the resources to do so. It could not tax its own entrepreneurs, could not harness the resources of foreign investors, and had failed to build a technological base capable of amplifying Mexican options and bargaining chips in the global marketplace. Its guiding principles were manipulation, self-preservation, and self-enrichment. None of these sat well with an increasingly mature civil society no longer in need of tutelage but much in need of a new pact for expressing consent and resistance.

For purposes of economy and out of respect for the reader, I have tried to keep notes to a minimum. The bibliography lists the archival sources consulted and the works cited. It begins with a list of the archives and their abbreviations; only the abbreviations are used here. Secondary works are cited in the notes rather than in the text when they provide general reference to a topic, require explanation, or are part of a large citation with archival materials. Unpublished archival materials, periodicals, and interviews are cited in the notes. In the case of archival sources, when a file (*expediente*) contains more than one relevant document, I have indicated only the expediente. When the expediente contains only one pertinent document, I have listed the expediente and the document.

Chapter 1
The Cultural Politics of the Mexican Revolution

1. On the Cárdenas presidency, see, among others, Knight 1994a:73–107; Anguiano 1975; Hamilton 1982; Medin 1972; Córdova 1974a.

2. For treatments critical of socialist education, see Britton 1976; Lerner 1979a, 1979b; Vázquez 1969; Mora Forero 1970, 1976. For favorable treatment, see Raby 1976; Córdova 1974b. Alan Knight earlier argued (1990b) that rural society resisted the SEP's prescriptions and began to alter behaviors only under market pressure in the 1940s. In his most recent essay, based on extensive use of SEP archives, he argues that some aspects of socialist education "took" in certain settings (Knight 1994b).

3. Raby (1976) examined teachers in Michoacán and Campeche. Regional studies of socialist education are now being published, e.g., Bantjes 1994; Camacho Sandoval 1991; Vaughan 1987, 1990b, 1992b, 1994a, 1994b, 1994c; Yankelevich 1985. Marjorie Becker's work on Cardenismo in Michoacán (1987, 1994, 1995) includes but is not confined to an examination of socialist education.

4. In the *Dictionary of Human Geography* (Johnson 1994:388), modernity is defined as "a particular constellation of power, knowledge, and social practices which first emerged in Europe in the sixteenth and seventeenth centuries, and the forms and structures of which changed over time and extended themselves over space until, by the middle of the twentieth century, they constituted the dominant social order of the planet. . . . Common to virtually all Post-Enlightenment discussions of modernity is an emphasis on novelty, change, and 'progress.'" I argue that major Mexican state makers and educational policy makers thought and acted upon this set of assumptions and used surrogate words to define it, such as "improvement," "civilization," or the "struggle for survival." I argue that peasant societies through the revolution gained some capacity to manipulate and shape modernity as a concept and as practice. For a rich discussion of the term, see Harvey 1990:10–138.

5. Among revisionist studies are essays in Brading 1982; Córdova 1972, 1974a; J. Meyer 1973. For analysis of revisionism, see Knight 1990c:193–210.

6. Impressive recent works have opened new conceptual and methodological approaches to the question. See introduction and essays in Joseph and Nugent (1994). The essays engage the works of Philip Corrigan and Derek Sayer (1985) and James C. Scott (1976, 1985, 1990). See also Nugent 1993; Alonso 1995; Becker 1995; essays in Beezley, Martin, and French 1994; Fowler-Salamini and Vaughan 1994.

7. De Grazia's work is one among many to examine the intersection between politics, professional notions of reform, and regulation in mass society in the first half of the twentieth century. I refer to her work because of her comparative and gendered approach.

8. Eric Wolf (1969:xiv) defines peasants as primarily subsistence cultivators (owner-operators, tenants, or sharecroppers) subject to the dictates of a state. I understand peasants to function as household units of production. I expand upon Wolf's definition to include landless laborers because they were part of the modernization process affecting peasants in the late nineteenth and twentieth centuries and because they played a critical role in land reform politics in the 1930s.

9. Elsie Rockwell and her colleagues at the Departamento de Investigaciones Educativas in Mexico City were the first Mexican scholars of education to contest the revisionist emphasis on education as social engineering and to examine the school as a place of empowerment as well as domination. Elsie Rockwell's approach to the school as a social construction and a generator of civil society has inspired my reading of education in the revolution. See Ezpeleta and Rockwell 1983; Rockwell 1994.

10. On local institutional control over schools and teachers in communities, see Rockwell 1994:7–25; Vaughan 1994b:114–15. On teachers' extraschool functions, see Lira González 1982:545–600; Starr 1895:260; Knight 1992a; Vaughan 1990a:42–55; 1994a:216–21; Thomson 1989a; Galván 1988:200–22.

11. While not yielding on the primacy of antagonism and resistance, Becker's

subsequent work (1994, 1995) suggests some negotiation between teachers and communities.

12. For historicity as a component of subaltern agendas, see Steve Stern 1987:12–15.

13. Equally useful is Florencia Mallon's gendered construction of community as contested space (Mallon 1994a; 1995:63–88).

14. For classic articulations of this theme, see Luis Buñuel's 1951 film *Mexican Bus Ride* (Subida al cielo) and Laura Esquivel's *Like Water for Chocolate* (1992).

15. Gramsci's notions of hegemony, fragmentary and interspersed in his writings (1971:206–69), have given rise to an expanded, theoretical literature, e.g., Adamson 1980: 169–99; Boggs 1984; Mouffe 1979:108–27; Lears 1985:65–91; LaClau and Mouffe 1986:65–91.

16. I borrow the quip from Alan Knight (1994a:100).

17. On schools and civil society, see Ezpeleta and Rockwell 1983:70–80; Rockwell 1994:199–208.

Chapter 2
The Secretaría de Educación Pública

1. *Boletín de Educación* 1, no. 2 (1915): 252.

2. AHSEP-DGEP, "Datos que deben rendir los Directores de las Escuelas Rurales Federales," 1938.

3. *Boletín de la SEP* 3, nos. 5–6 (1924): 598–606.

4. On SEP prescriptions, program, and Ramírez, *El Maestro Rural* (hereafter, MR) 1, no. 1 (March 1, 1932): 10–11; 1, no. 2 (March 15, 1932):7; 3, no. 2 (July 1, 1933): 25; 3, no. 4 (July 15, 1933): 9, 17, 24.

5. On the cultural movement, see José Clemente Orozco 1962; Vaughan 1982:239–66; Monsiváis 1981:33–44; Carr 1994:342–45.

6. On the formation of the PRI, see Garrido 1982. On the cristero rebellion, Bailey 1974; Jrade 1980; J. Meyer 1973; Olivera Sedano 1966. On politics from 1928 to 1934, L. Meyer 1978.

7. On SEP radicalization, see Raby 1976:22–24, 32–39; *Boletín de la SEP* 9, nos.9–10 (Sept.–Oct. 1930): 78–81; Castillo 1965:337–42; SEP 1933a:52–58; Bremauntz 1943:160–61.

8. Bassols 1964:49–52, 116–18; Britton 1976, vol. 1: 22–56; MR 1, no. 3 (April 1, 1932): 8–9; 2, no. 8 (Feb. 1933): 8, 33; L. Meyer 1978:221, 236–38.

9. On *El Maestro Rural*, see, among others, MR 3, no. 4 (July 15, 1933): 24; 3, no. 5 (Aug. 1, 1933): 12–13; 3, no. 6 (Aug. 15, 1933): 26–27; 3, no. 9 (Oct. 1, 1933): 29–31; 3, no. 12 (Nov. 15, 1933): 10.

10. There were 1,285 Article 123 schools in 1934 (SEP 1934b:10–27). For an overview, see Loyo 1991.

11. On the genesis of socialist education, see Bremauntz 1943; Meneses Morales 1988: 28–71; Britton 1976, vol. 2: 12, 17, 33; L. Meyer 1978:317, L. Meyer, Lajous, and Segovia 1978: 180–83; Lerner 1979b:11–82; Guevara Niebla 1985:37–94.

12. See text in Meneses Morales 1988:38.

13. For texts in the 1920s, see Vaughan 1982:214–38; for comparison of 1920s and 1930s texts, Vaughan 1992b; Loyo and Torres Septien 1992; Loyo 1988. For textbooks in the nineteenth and twentieth centuries, see Vázquez 1970.

14. Vaughan 1982:239–66; *El Universal,* June 26, 1924; *Excelsior,* July 10, 1924; Salvador Novo, *El Universal Ilustrado,* March 5, 1925; Wolfe 1939:155–233; Rivera 1924:175–76; AEC, Ezequiel Chávez to SEP, May 8, 1924; Orozco 1962:166.

15. *MR* 2, no. 3 (March 15, 1932): 20–24; 2, no. 4 (April 1, 1932): 8–9; 3, no. 9 (Oct. 1, 1933): 36–38.

16. Velázquez Andrade [1929] 1986; *MR* 1, no. 2 (March 15, 1932): 7; 3, no. 3 (July 1, 1933): 10; 3, no. 5 (Aug. 1, 1933): 9.

17. *MR* 3, no. 5 (Aug. 1, 1933): 40.

18. *MR* 3, no. 4 (July 15, 1933): 24; 3, no. 5 (Aug. 1, 1933): 12–13, 22; 3, no. 6 (Aug. 15, 1933): 26–29; 3, no. 14 (Dec. 15, 1933): 28–29.

19. *MR* 1, no. 1 (March 1, 1932): 10–11; 3, no. 5 (Aug. 1, 1933): 6; 3, no. 10 (Oct. 15, 1933): 16–17.

20. *MR* 3, no. 3 (July 1, 1933): 27; 3, no. 5 (Aug. 1, 1933): 31.

21. *MR* 3, no. 3 (July 1, 1933): 13–15, 36–38; 3, no. 4 (July 15, 1933): 15; Lucio 1935a:129–39; 1935b:23–24, 35, 40, 63–64.

22. On the aesthetic thinking of Vasconcelos, see Vaughan 1982:238–66; Fell 1989; Blanco 1977.

23. *MR* 1, no. 3 (April 1, 1932): 10–11; 3, no. 10 (Oct. 15, 1933): 35; 3, no. 5 (Aug. 1, 1933): 23; García Téllez 1935:140–44.

24. *MR* 3, no. 13 (Dec. 1, 1933): 12.

25. In 1937, the new Departamento de Educación Indígena (later Asuntos Indígenas) supported the idea of bilingual teaching. Under the leadership of Luis Chávez Orozco in 1939–40, it showed greater sensitivity toward indigenous languages and cultures (Meneses Morales 1988:70–72).

26. On teachers and oil expropriation, see Vaughan 1992a:904; Knight 1992b:105–13; Camacho Sandoval 1988.

CHAPTER 3
THE MOBILIZATION OF FEDERAL TEACHERS

1. Literacy figures, taken from the censuses (Secretaría de la Economía 1934, 1943), are suspect for Puebla because the 1940 category of illiterates ages 10–14 is almost twice as large as it was in 1930. Even allowing for an undercount in 1930, the size of this category in 1940 does not match the state's demographic profile. Enrollment statistics are from Secretaría de la Economía 1930, 192–200; 1942, 340–50.

2. On Juan Crisóstomo Bonilla, see Morales Jiménez 1986:199–202; Carol 1979:110–32; Thomson 1989a:31–68; 1989b:65–74.

3. For archival sources, see chapters 4 and 5.

4. For analysis of school distribution, enrollments, expenditures, and literacy across Puebla's districts, see Vaughan 1990b:70–88.

5. Interview with Porfirio Cordero, Puebla, July 14, 1987.

6. On the origins of the desert society and the nomadic character of Sonora's rural population, see Radding 1990:129–56; 1992:551–78. On nineteenth-century development, see Voss 1982; Ruiz 1988; Tinker Salas 1989.

7. AES-Instrucción Pública, vol. 1569, exp. 4, Sept. 13 and Nov. 5, 1900; vol. 1578, exp. 163, June 15 and Oct. 17, 1900; 1576, exp. 140, Sept. 14, 1900; vols. 3064 and 3066, "Cuestionarios," May 11, 1916, Hermosillo; vol. 1569, exp. 4, Sept. 19, 1900; vol. 1574, exp. 116, Jan. 20 and March 16, 1899.

8. AES-Instrucción Pública, vol. 1564, exp. 4, Aug. 8, 1900; vol. 1572, Jan. 3, 1900. For a good analysis of nonindigenous identities in relation to the indigenous peoples of Sonora, see Tinker Salas 1989:102–74.

9. In addition, on Sonoran teachers in revolution, AES-IP, vols. 3064/6, "Cuestionarios," re. Ignacio Munguía, Manuel C. Ortega, Francisco R. Almada, Manuel Paredes, A. González Ramírez, Manuel M. Elías, Antonio Rivera, L. Domínguez. On Puebla teachers, interview with Gilberto Bosques, Mexico City, May 15, 1987; Cabrera Oropeza 1972:11–12; Candañedo 1971:8–9; del Castillo 1953:201–27.

10. By 1932, 689,308 hectares of land had been definitively distributed to 97,490 ejidatarios in Puebla: the largest amount of land and second-largest number of ejidatarios among central Mexico's ten states. Puebla's ejidatarios made up 20 percent of all ejidatarios in central Mexico and had received 24 percent of land allocated in that region (Secretaría de la Economía 1937:21, 81). On Puebla's revolution, see LaFrance 1989; Glockner 1982; Márquez Carrillo 1983; Pansters 1990; Sánchez López 1992.

11. The blending of spiritism and liberalism among the middle class of northern Mexico is currently being studied by Raquel Rubio Goldsmith. On this blending in a Sonoran teacher, see, for example, AES-Instrucción Pública, vol. 3064, "Cuestionario," L. Domínguez.

12. AES-IP, vols. 3064 and 3066, "Cuestionarios."

13. Interview with Elvira Figueroa, Hermosillo, May 8, 1987.

14. On Calles's politics, see Estado de Sonora 1932:2–10; 1933:2–10; 1934:16–37; Corbalá 1970:107–72; Ramírez 1988b:135–50; Vaughan 1987; Bantjes 1991. On the expulsion of the Chinese, Hu-DeHart 1982:1–128; Trueba Lara 1990. For expulsion of Chinese and taxing foreigners, see USSD 812.00/1098, Nogales, Sept. 1, 1931; /1121, Feb. 29, 1932; /1127, April 30, 1932; /1138, Guaymas, Aug. 1, 1932. On Sonoran cattle ranchers as targets for Calles Jr., see AAGES, multiple correspondence in exp. 411.12"32"/193 re. Tubutama and 411.14/91"33" re. La Reforma, Altar. On effects of the depression, USSD 812.00/1070, Nogales, May 1, 1931; /1079, Agua Prieta, May 19, 1931; /1120, Feb. 7, 1932; /1166, April 29, 1933.

15. AHSEP-DER, Elpidio López (hereafter, EL), director (hereafter, dir.), SEP Sonora, "Informe," Hermosillo, Nov.–Dec. 1932.

16. AHSEP-DER, EL, "Informes," Sept. and Nov. 1932; Feb., March, and Nov. 1933; Ramón Bonfil, dir., SEP Sonora, Memorandum, Feb. 3, 1932; Ocampo Bolaños (hereafter, OB), "El Buen Lider Social," Oct. 30, 1933.

17. AHSEP-DER, Lamberto Moreno (hereafter, LM), inspector (hereafter, insp.), Alamos, "Informes," June–July 1933, Magdalena, "Informe," Jan. 1934; José Bernal Rodríguez (hereafter, JBR), insp., Sahuaripa, "Informes," Jan., July, and April 1933; Mario Aguilera (hereafter, MA), insp., Cumpas, "Informe," Nov. 1933.

18. AHSEP-DER, MA, insp., Cumpas, "Informes," March, April, and Nov. 1933; LM, insp., Alamos, "Informe," Aug. 2, 1933.

19. AHSEP-DER, EL, dir., SEP Sonora, "Informe," Sept. 25, 1933.

20. AHSEP-DER, LM, insp., Alamos, "Informes," Feb., March, and April 1933; Magdalena, "Informes," Oct., Nov., and Dec. 1933; EL, dir., SEP Sonora, "Informe," July 17, 1933; MA, insp., Cumpas, to MP, Moctezuma, Nov. 10, 1933; "Informes," Oct. and Nov. 1933, "Plan de Trabajo . . . 1933–34"; JBR, insp., Sahuaripa, "Informes," Oct., Nov., and Dec. 1934; OB, insp., Ures, "Informes," Feb., June, and July 1933.

21. AHSEP-DER, EL, dir., SEP Sonora, "Informe," April 15, 1933; MA, insp., Cumpas, Nov. 10, 1933; OB, insp., Ures, "Informes," Nov. 1932 and June 1933.

22. AHSEP-DER, EL, dir., SEP Sonora, "Informe," March 1933; OB, insp., Ures, "Informe," Feb. 1933; LM, insp., Magdalena, "Informe," Nov. 8, 1933.

23. AHSEP-DER, LM, insp., Alamos, "Informes," March 4 and Dec. 17, 1933; Magdalena, "Informes," Jan. 1934; JBR, insp., Sahuaripa, "Informes," Jan., April, July, and Nov. 1933; OB, insp., Ures, "Informes," April, June, Sept., and Oct. 1933; AHSEP-DGEP, exp. 319.3, Juan Oropeza (hereafter, JO), insp., Arizpe, "Informe," March 1936; El Intruso, Cananea, vol. 42, March 23, 28, 1935.

24. AHSEP-DGEP, exp. 319.3, JO, insp., Arizpe, "Informe," March 1936; AHSEP-DER,

LM, insp., Alamos, "Informe," March 1933; Magdalena, "Informe," Jan. 1934; *El Intruso,* vol. 45, Feb. 5, 1935.

25. AHSEP-DER, OB, insp., Ures, "Informe," June 1933; LM, insp., Alamos, "Informe," June 17, 1933; Magdalena, "Informe," April 19, 1934; Ramón Reyes, insp., Alamos, "Informe," Nov. 1933.

26. AHSEP-DER, OB, insp., Ures, "Informes," May and June 1933; LM, insp., Magdalena, "Informe," Jan. 1934.

27. AHSEP-DER, LM, insp., Alamos, "Informes," April and June 1933; interview, Manuel Ferra Martínez, Hermosillo, May 7, 1987.

28. AHSEP-DER, MA, insp., Cumpas, "Informes," April and May 1933; LM, insp., Magdalena, "Informes," Dec. 1933 and Jan. 1934; JBR, insp., Sahuaripa, "Informes," Jan. and April 1933.

29. On the Papagos (Tohono O'odham), AHSEP-DER, EL, dir., SEP Sonora, "Informe," March 25, 1933. On the Mayos, SEP Sonora, "Relación de las Escuelas Rurales Primarias," Dec. 1932; Constantino Magdaleno, insp., Navojoa, "Informes," Nov. and Dec. 1933, Jan. 1934; LM, insp., Alamos, "Informe," June 1933.

30. AHSEP-DER, OB, insp., Ures, "Informe," June 1933; "A los Maestros y Campesinos . . . ," Feb. 1, 1934; LM, insp., Magdalena, "Informe," Dec. 1933; EL, dir., SEP Sonora, "Informe," Sept. 1933. On Calles's anticlericalism, Bantjes 1991:33–58; on the Mayos, 97–110; Crumrine 1977:21–26, 82, 120–51; Guadarrama 1988b:178–81.

31. AHSEP-DER, JO, insp., Cumpas, "Informes," Nov. and Dec. 1934, Jan. and Feb. 1935; JBR, insp., Sahuaripa, "Informe," Dec. 1934; USSD 812.00/1233, Guaymas, Jan. 2, 1935; /1236, Jan. 31, 1935. On popular hostility to the anticlerical campaign, Bantjes 1991:71–79, 96.

32. AHSEP-DGEP, exp. 329.13, Laura Paredes et al., Hermosillo, to SEP, June 4, 1935; AHSEP-DER, exp. 249.7, LM, dir., SEP Sonora, "Informes," Jan.–Feb., May 12, and Nov.–Dec. 1935; Circulars, Feb. 25 and April 17, 1935; Calles, "Informe," 1934, 2–5; AHSEP-ERN, exp. 366.8, Alma Sonorense Federación de Agrupaciones de Maestros Federales de Sonora, No. 2, May 2, 1934; Aspiraciones Escuela Rural Normal, Ures, No. 24, May 1934; AHSEP-DER, exp. 249.4, Bloque Revolucionario de Obreros y Campesinos de Magdalena to Cárdenas, Feb. 1, 1935. On iconoclasm, Bantjes 1994:261–84.

33. AHSEP-DER, EL, dir., SEP Sonora, "Informes," June and July 1933; AHSEP-DGEP, exp. 249.20, F. Ximello (hereafter FX), dir., SEP Sonora, "Informe Año Escolar, 1935–36." For a range of Ramos supporters among organized workers and campesinos, see AGN-AP-LCR, exp. 559.3/25, summer–fall 1935. On the revolt, exp. 559.3/25, Oct. 1935; AAGES, exp. 251"35"/1–35; exp. 411.14/91"33," Altar, Nov.–Dec. 1935; USSD 812.00/1270 to 1293, Oct.–Nov. 1935; USWD 2657 G 605/374, Oct. 15, 1935; 2657 G 657 167, Oct. 17, 1935; 2657 G 605/381, Nov. 12, 1935. See also Bantjes 1991:66–171; Encinas Blanco 1985:445–46; Guadarrama 1988b:189; Chávez Camacho 1983; Acuña Cruz 1985; interview with Padre López Yescas, Hermosillo, May 12, 1989.

34. Various state PNR groups said the rebels were anti-Callista Cardenistas and accused commanding general Zertuche of being sympathetic to them. See AGN-AP-LCR, exp. 559.3/35, Alberto Ruiz, secretario general (hereafter, sec. gen.), Sindicato de Obreros Mártires de 1906, Cananea, to Cárdenas, Nov. 2, 1935; PM, Moctezuma, to Cárdenas, Oct. 30, 1935; F. Frías to Rubén Mejía, Oct. 18, 1935; USSD 812/00/1291, Guaymas, Oct. 22, 1935. On the deposition of Ramos, ibid., 812.00/1314, Nogales, Dec. 17, 1935.

35. AHSEP-DER, J. C. Fuentes, insp., Teziutlán, "Informes," May and Dec. 1933; Chalchicomula, "Informes," March, April, and Nov. 1932; G. Vega (hereafter, GV), insp., Chalchicomula, "Informes," April, June, Aug., and Nov. 1933.

36. AHSEP-DER, Manuel Quiroz (hereafter, MQ), insp., Cholula, "Informe," March 1933.

37. In addition to chapters 4 and 5, see AHSEP-DER, Neri, insp., Tlacuilotepec, "Informes," Feb. and March 1933; Modesto Lezama (hereafter ML), insp., Matamoros, "Informe," Jan. 1934; MQ, insp., Cholula, "Informes," April and Dec. 1933.

38. In urbanized areas around Puebla and Atlixco, inspectors claimed to have Sociedades de Madres participating in anti-alcohol campaigns. Here the number of women teachers was also higher than in other regions. See AHSEP-DER, MQ, insp., Cholula, "Informes," April and Dec. 1933; ML, insp., Matamoros, "Informe," Jan. 1933.

39. AHSEP-DER, GV, insp., Chalchicomula, "Informes," July, Aug., Oct., and Nov. 1933; chapters 4 and 5. On the Catholic movement, Márquez Carrillo 1983:64–85, 108–50.

40. See chapters 4 and 5. On school desertion, see, among many others, AHSEP-DER, exp. 242.30, exp. 206.2, and exp. 206.5, 1935.

41. AHSEP-DGEP, exp. 249.20, FX, dir., SEP Sonora, "Informe . . . 1935–36," "Informes," Jan.–Feb. and July 1936; FX to SEP, April 14, 1936; exp. 249.7, FX to SEP, Nov. 28, 1935.

42. AHSEP-DER, exp. 249.20, LM, dir., SEP Sonora, to SEP, Jan. 23, 1935; "Informe," Sept.–Oct. 1935; exp. 308.1, F. Corzo, insp. regional, "Informe," Nov. 1935; AHSEP-DGEP, exp. 319.5, Gilberto Valenzuela, insp., Huatabampo, "Informes," Jan.–Feb. and March–April 1936; exp. 319.12, Daniel Domínguez Duarte, insp., Navojoa, "Informe," March–April 1936; "Informe Anual 1936"; exp. 319.11, Leonardo Magaña (hereafter, LeM), insp., Empalme, "Informes," Dec.–Jan., Feb.–March, and April–May 1936.

43. On the struggle between Ximello and teachers, AHSEP-DGEP, exp. 339.4, 1936. On the CNTE–CMM struggle, see Sindicato Nacional de Trabajadores de la Educación 1969: 18–19; Raby 1976:72–78; Britton 1979:674–90.

44. Multiple correspondence in AGN-AP-LCR, exp. 534.1/8, May 1937; AAGES, exp. 243.3/"36" "Conflictos"; Dabdoub 1964:344–53; Guadarrama 1988c:238–42. On Yocupicio, Bantjes 1991:219–395.

45. See chapters 6 and 7. For land allocations, Guadarrama 1988c:252. In the Yaqui and

Mayo Valleys, Cárdenas allotted additional pastureland to ejidatarios, which was later converted to cropland.

46. AAGES, exp. 411.12"37"/2; exp. 234."39," "Informe," CTS, 1938–39; *El Popular,* July 7, 1938; Estado de Sonora 1938:21–28; Guadarrama 1988c:263; Bantjes 1991:352–88.

47. See AGN-AP-LCR, exp. 534.1/8, 1937–38; exp. 404.1/6774.22, July–Oct. 1938; exp. 404.1/7, Yocupicio to Cárdenas, May 17 and 30, 1938; *El Popular,* June 6 and 7, 1938.

48. On campesino protests, see AGN-AP-LCR, exp. 404.1/7, April–May 1938. On press denunciations, *El Imparcial,* Jan. 4 and 19, March 1 and 4, and April 6, 1939.

49. AGN-AP-LCR, exp. 404.1/6774.22, 1938; exp. 534.1/8, Oct.–Nov. 1938; AAGES, exp. 411.12"37"/2; *El Imparcial,* Jan. 12–15, 1939.

50. On religious opposition, AHSEP-DER, exp. 242.9, SEP Puebla, Aug.–Nov. 1935; printed propaganda of the Unión Nacional de Padres de Familia, republished by the Puebla branch of the Liga Defensora de la Libertad in AEEP, Puebla, Baja de Maestros, exp. 121/1, Victor Sosa. On teacher deaths and persecution, AGN-AP-LCR, exp. 545.2/2, Federación de Agrupaciones Magisteriales Federales del Estado de Puebla to Cárdenas, Sept. 1935 and March 26, 1936; exp. 433/74, Rogelio Coria, Federación de Maestros de Puebla, to SEP, Sept. 6, 1936. On Odilón Vega's cristeros, see AHSEP-DGEP, exp. 315.8, fall 1936; exp. 338.1, fall 1936; AGN-AP-LCR, exp. 545.2/2, Sept.–April 1936–37; exp. 559.1/15, Jan.–Feb. 1939; exp. 556.63/165, Nov. 1938. On El Tallarín in southern Puebla, AHSEP-DER, exp. 242.9, Fausto Molina Betancourt (hereafter cited as FMB) to Cárdenas, Oct. 17, 1935; AHSEP-DGEP, exp. 315.5, J. Cuanalo, insp., Acatlán, Oct. 5, 1936; exp. 316.10, Miguel Angel Godínez, insp., Matamoros, "Informe," Feb.–March 1936; AGN-AP-LCR, exp. 559.1/15, 1935–38.

51. On Maximino's platform, see *El Diario de Puebla,* Jan. 8, 10, 15, 19, 20, 29, 30, and 31, Feb. 1, 1936; Márquez Carrillo 1983:11, 29–51; Pansters 1990:69–71; Glockner 1982:31–45. On the FROC, *El Diario de Puebla,* April 2 and 3, 1935; Malpica 1980:152–54. On land invasions and repression, AGN-AP-LCR, exps. 4041/1889 and 403/478; *La Opinión,* Puebla, April 8, 13, and 15, May 30, and June 18, 1935. Cárdenas's major intervention in Puebla affairs was his division in January 1936 of the Sumerville estate in northwestern Chignahuapan. The estate was not of vital interest to the Avila Camachos. However, Maximino protected important portions of American William Jenkins's holdings at Atencingo in southern Puebla, and Cárdenas acquiesced (Ronfeldt 1973:16–32; Pansters 1990:62–63, 185).

52. Figures from Comité Directivo Estatal—PRI 1974:480.

53. On the city teachers' strike, see AEEP, Puebla, Bajas de Maestros, exp. 121/1, Victor Sosa; AHSEP-DGEP, exp. 338.1, Enrique León Uribe, Federación de Agrupaciones Magisteriales Federales del Estado de Puebla, Jan. 25, 1936; *La Opinión,* Sept. 13, 1935; *El Diario de Puebla,* Jan. 30 and 31, Feb. 1, March 7 and 26, 1936. On teacher unionism in Puebla, see multiple correspondence in AGN-AP-LCR, exp. 433/11; 433.74, AHSEP-DGEP, exp. 338.1, 1935–36.

54. Interview with Socorro Rivera, Puebla, May 16, 1984.

55. AHSEP-DGEP, exp. 316.5, Salomón Pérez, insp., Chalchicomula, "Plan de Trabajo, 1936"; exp. 316.4, Miguel Villa, insp., Texmelucan, "Informes," April–May 1936.

56. On the role of patriotic festival in party formation, see *Diario de Puebla*, Jan, 4, 1935, Jan., 19, 30, March 21, 1936, June 14, Dec. 30, 1938; *La Opinión*, Feb. 1 and Dec. 30, 1937.

57. Interview with Socorro Rivera, Puebla, May 21, 1984.

Chapter 4
Campesino Duels with Schools in Tecamachalco

1. In 1900, Tecamachalco was a district of eight municipalities with a population of 48,000. The Constitution of 1917 abolished the district to recognize "free" municipalities. A new municipality, Felipe Angeles, was created after the revolution from villages formerly belonging to the municipality of Quecholac. In 1930, the ex-district of Tecamachalco consisted of nine municipalities with a population of 52,123. The percentage of ejidatarios in 1930 is calculated from the census (Secretaría de la Economía 1943) and indicated by municipality in table 1.

2. Tecamachalco numbers for 1940 indicate an unrealistic growth in the population ages 10–14 in relation to other groups between 1930 and 1940. Thus, the fall in literacy was probably not as severe or perhaps was nonexistent. On the other hand, the numbers would not suggest much of an increase. I use statistics between 1900 and 1950 because, despite flaws, they indicate trends within and between municipalities over time.

3. AMT, Gobierno, legajo 70, año 1889–90, "Actas de exámenes de escuelas," Xochitlán, Dec. 9 and 15, 1890. On collective labor in building and maintaining schools, see Estado de Puebla 1908:256–57; 1910:18, 41, 69.

4. AMT, Gobernación, "Datos sobre Instrucción Pública," 1909; AEEP-Puebla, "Nombramiento de Maestros," exp. 89, 1918.

5. In estimating the percentage of property owners, I understand the census term *agricultor* to mean owner, as opposed to the terms *peon* and *jornalero*.

6. In 1930, in Tochtepec, 48 percent of marriages were sanctioned by church and state, while in Quecholac and Felipe Angeles, 77 percent of marriages were sanctioned only by the church (Secretaría de la Economía 1943). I have correlated literacy in Tecamachalco municipalities with property ownership, peonage, town size, religious marriages, agrarian reform, and female-headed households in Vaughan 1994c:110–11. On campesino skepticism about schooling, see Redfield 1950:137–38; Furet and Ozouf 1983:243; Weber 1976:318–23.

7. For data on enrollments and correlation with economic and social variables, see Vaughan 1990b:106; 1994c:109–10.

8. On the pedagogy of space and ritual, see Ozouf 1988:126–27, 147. On Tecamachalco, Vaughan 1994a:213–45.

9. AMT, Gobierno, caja 129, exp. 58, "Relativo a la manera de solemnizar en el distrito el 40 aniversario del triunfo que tuvieron las armas nacionales el 5 de mayo de 1862," March 4, April 29, May 2 and 3, 1902; caja 266, exp. 13, " . . . 5 de mayo," April 29, 1909.

10. AMT, Gobierno, caja 129, "Actas de Cabildo," May 3, 1901.

11. On festival and intervillage competition, see Dennis 1987:29, 151–56; Gibson 1989:378.

12. Estado de Puebla 1908:256–57; AMT, Gobierno, caja 299, año 1909, "Sesión pública ordinaria, Ayuntamiento," March 3 and Aug. 4, 1909.

13. ARA-P, exp. 174, Tecamachalco; exp. 291, Tochtepec, exp., 23/36, Tenango; AGN-AP-OC, exp. 818-T-183, 1924–25; exp. 818-5-101, 1922–23.

14. ARA-P, exp. 225, San Bartolo Tepetlacaltecho, "Informe," Vicente Santiago Páez, CNA, Dec. 12, 1929.

15. González's (hereafter, JHG) ideology runs through his monthly reports in AHSEP-DER, caja 905, 1932; caja 969, 1933; AHSEP-DGEP, exp. 207.1, 1935; exp. 316.1, 1936.

16. AMT, Gobierno, legajo 68, año 1936, Dolores Navarro, San Antonio La Portilla, to PM, May 2, 1936; AHSEP-DER, caja 969, JHG, insp., "Informe," March 1933; AHSEP-AP-ERF, Palmarito, "Informes," April and Sept. 1931, April 1932.

17. AHSEP-DGEP, exp. 316.1, JHG, insp., "Plan de Trabajo, 1936"; AHSEP-DER, caja 905, "Informes," Aug. and Nov. 1932; caja 969, "Informe," June 1933; "Informe Anual," Dec. 1933; AGN-AP-LCR, exp. 564.1/2091, O. Luna, Comisariado Ejidal, San Mateo Tlaixpan, to Cárdenas, Jan. 18, 1940; AMT, Presidencia, caja 65, año 1935, Celso Campos, PM, to Secretaría de Agricultura, Jan. 30, 1935.

18. AHSEP-DER, caja 905, JHG, "Informe," May 1932; caja 969, JHG, insp., "Informe Anual, 1933"; AHSEP-DGEP, exp. 316.1, JHG, "Plan de Trabajo, 1936"; AHSEP-AP-ERF, Caltenco, Hermila Bañuelos Bravo to insp., April 16, 1934, and Aug. 15, 1935.

19. AHSEP-DER, caja 905, JHG, "Informes," March, Aug. 1932; caja 969, "Informes," May, Aug. 1933; AHSEP-DGEP, exp. 316.1, "Informe," Aug.–Sept. 1936; AHSEP-AP-ERF, Caltenco, H. Bañuelos Bravo to SEP, Aug. 15, 1935; Santa Rosa, "Informes," March 11, 1932, and March 14, 1933; Alseseca, JHG to SEP, Oct. 3, 1931; "Informe," May 24, 1932. On the importance of the school as community space, see Rockwell 1994:200; 1996: 301–24.

20. AHSEP-DER, caja 969, JHG, "Informes," May–Sept., 1933; interviews with Horacio Caro, Puebla, July 6, 1991, and Manuel Bravo Bañuelos, Tecamachalco, July 25, 1989.

21. On the Avilacamachista assault on Almazanistas in elections, see AHSEP-DER, caja 969, JHG, "Informe," May 1933; AGN-AP-LCR, exps. 544.5/625, 544.4/314/544.5/97,

1935–36. On the alliance between Avila Camacho, landowners, and Defensas Rurales, AGN-AP-LCR, exp. 541/88/404.1/1235/404.1/632, Dec. 1936–Sept. 1937.

22. On struggles between agraristas and landowners, municipal councils, and the governor over idle lands, see, among others, ibid., exps. 403.812, Feb. 1936; 404.1/2670, March 1938; AMT, Presidencia, año 1938, caja 74, March–June 1938.

23. On peasant opposition to established agraristas, see, among others, AGN-AP-LCR, exp. 404.1/3166, Sept. 1936; exp. 402.4/6828, May 1937; on struggles between FROC-backed campesinos and established leaders, see AMT, Presidencia, año 1935, legajo 65, Gustavo Ariza, sec. gen. de gobierno, to PM, April 5, 1935; AGN-AP-LCR, exp. 542.1/1515, Fernando Amilpa, CGOCM, to Cárdenas, Nov. 6, 1935; exp. 541/88, Rafael Aranda, sec. gen., Unión de Ejidatarios Flores Magón, San Antonio Portezuelo, Jan. 9, 1937. On intervillage disputes, exp. 403/716, Antonio Rosas, Comisariado Ejidal, La Compañia, to Cárdenas, n.d.; AMT, Presidencia, año 1938, caja 74, Jan.–Aug. 1938.

24. AHSEP-DER, exp. 206.5, JHG, "Informe," Aug.–Sept., 1935; AHSEP-AP-ERF, Chipiltepec, Sara Robles Jiménez, "Indicadores de actividades," Jan. 1936; "Datos," Nov. 1938; interview with Reyna Manzano, Puebla, July 5, 1991. For a more extensive treatment of the SEP and Tecamachalco women, see Vaughan 1994c:106–24. For an excellent portrait of the social meaning of gender hierarchies and the reproductive sphere in rural communities, see Mallon 1994a:3–26. On the spiritual meaning and social organization of health practices in contemporary Mexican rural communities, see essays by Galante, Sesia-Lewis, and Alejandre; Feyermuth Enciso; and Guadarrama and Piedrasanta Herrero in Aranda Bezaury 1988.

25. AHSEP-DER, caja 905, JHG, "Informe," Nov. 1932; caja 969, "Informe Anual," Dec. 1935; AMT, Gobierno, año 1936, Clemente Guevara to PM, Jan. 2, 1936; F. Juárez, pres. auxiliar, San Mateo Tlaixpan, to PM, Jan. 3, 1936; interview with anonymous federal teacher, Puebla, March 6, 1984.

26. On violence and its effects on women's relations with schools, AHSEP-DER, caja 905, JHG, "Informes," April and June 1932; caja 969, "Informe," March 1933, "Informe Anual," Dec. 1933. On crimes against women, AMT, Presidencia, año 1935, caja 65, Carlos Maldonado to Ministerio Público, Aug. 6, 1935; Arnulfo Maldonado, Santiago Alseseca, to PM, April 11, 1935; caja 74, Carlos Fuentes Miramón, Comandante de la Sección Palmarito-Tochapan, to Gen. Comandante del Sector Militar, Tehuacán, Sept. 13, 1938. On women's opposition to socialist education, AHSEP-DER, exp. 206.7, JHG, "Informe Anual," 1935.

27. AHSEP-DER, caja 905, JHG, "Informe," May 1932, "Informe Anual," Dec. 1932.

28. AHSEP-DER, caja 969, JHG, "Informe," June 1933; "Informe Anual," 1933; AEEP, Puebla, Bajas de Maestros, exp. 121/1, pamphlet of Unión Nacional de Padres de Familia, Mexico City, July 2, 1935, published by Liga Defensora de la Libertad, Puebla.

29. Ibid.; AHSEP-DER, exp. 206.7, JHG, "Informe," Feb.–March 1935; *La Opinión,* Nov.

7, 9, and 10, 1935; AMT, Presidencia, año 1935, legajo 65, C. Campos, PM, to sec. gen. de gobierno, Puebla, Jan. 17 and 27, 1935; José Montes, Palmar, to PM, Jan. 28, 1935.

30. Ibid., caja 74, Juan Amador et al., La Portilla, to PM, June 20, 1938; interview with Manuel Bravo Bañuelos, Tecamachalco, July 1, 1991.

31. AGN-AP-LCR, exp. 403/716, Sebastián Paredes, pres., Comité del PNR, Quecholac, to Cárdenas, June 13, 1935; AMT, Presidencia, año 1935, legajo 65, March–June 1935; legajo 74, año 1938, Carlos Ortiz et al., La Compañia, to PM, April 18, 1938.

32. AMT, Presidencia, año 1935, legajo 65, Ariza, Puebla, to Comandancia de la Gendarmería Montada, March 1, 1935; La Opinión, Dec. 5, 1936. On the Defensas Rurales, José Martínez Castro, and Luis Ibáñez, see AGN-AP-LCR, exp. 541/88, Jan. 1937; exp. 404.1/1235, Eligio Avelino, Comisariado Ejidal, Purísima Hidalgo, to Cárdenas, Dec. 28, 1936; exp. 404.1/2687, Sotero G. Jiménez, sec. gen., Unión Ejidatarios Camerino Mendoza, Felipe Angeles, to Cárdenas, Jan. 5, 1937. On the FROC in Tochtepec and Tecamachalco, exp. 404.1/1889, Rubén Ortiz, senador, Puebla, to Cárdenas, April 7, 1935; exp. 562.4/263, Vicente Lombardo Toledano (hereafter cited as VLT), CTM, to Cárdenas, Dec. 30, 1936.

33. AHSEP-AP-ERF, Alseseca, FMB, dir., SEP Puebla, to SEP, March 13, 1936; El Diario de Puebla, Feb. 15, 1936; interview with Manuel Bravo Bañuelos.

34. AHSEP-DGEP, exp. 206.7, JHG, "Informes," Feb.–March, "Informe Anual," 1935; AHSEP-DGEP, exp. 316.1, "Informes," Feb.–Sept. 1936.

35. AHSEP-DER, exp. 316.1, JHG, "Informe," Aug.–Sept. 1936.

36. On festivals, schools, and community reconstruction, see, among others, AHSEP-DER, caja 905, JHG, "Informes," July and Sept. 1932; caja 969, "Informes," May and July 1933; AHSEP-DGEP, exp. 316.1, "Informe," Oct.–Nov. 1936; interviews with Manuel Bravo Bañuelos, July 25, 1989, Horacio Caro, Puebla, July 6, 1991. For towns using SEP schools to free themselves from dominant headtowns, see also Rockwell 1994:188.

37. AHSEP-DGEP, exp. 316.1, "Informes," April–Sept., 1936; AMT, Presidencia, año 1938, legajo 74. Miguel Navarro, Comisariado Ejidal, La Portilla, to PM, July 19, 1938.

38. Interview with Horacio Caro, Puebla, July 6, 1991; interview with Reyna Manzano, Puebla, March 15, 1987; AHSEP-AP-ERF, Colonia Francisco I. Madero, "Datos," Nov. 28, 1938, San Nicolás el Viejo, "Datos," Nov. 30, 1938.

39. AHSEP-DER, caja 905, JHG, "Informes," Feb.–June 1932; "Informe Anual," Dec. 1932; caja 969, "Informe," July 1933; AHSEP-DGEP, exp. 206.7, JHG, "Informes," Oct.–Nov. 1935; "Informe Anual," Dec. 1935; exp. 316.7, "Informes," May–Sept. 1936; "Plan de Trabajo, 1936"; Redfield 1950:15, 136.

40. Interviews with Horacio Caro and Agustina Barrojas, Puebla, July 6, 1991; Victor Alva, Puebla, July 2, 1991.

41. AHSEP-DER, caja 905, JHG, "Informes," July, Sept., and Oct. 1932; caja 969, "Informe," March 1933; AHSEP-DGEP, exp. 206.7, "Informe," Oct.–Nov., "Informe Anual," 1935; exp. 316.1, "Informes," Feb.–Sept. 1936, "Plan de Trabajo, 1936"; AHSEP-AP-ERF, Santa Rosa, "Informes," Sept. and June 1932, June 1933; San Nicolás el Viejo, "Datos," Nov. 1938; Pericotepec, "Datos," Nov. 1938; Palmarito, "Informes," May and July 1933; Chipiltepec, "Informes," Aug. 1932 and Aug. 1933.

42. AHSEP-DER, caja 905, JHG, "Informe," May 1932; interview with Victor Alva, Puebla, July 2, 1991; Vaughan 1994c:120.

43. The description is drawn from Inspector González's reports in AHSEP-DER, caja 905, 1932; caja 969, 1933; AHSEP-DGEP, exp. 206.7, 1935; exp. 316.1, 1936; interviews with teachers Horacio Caro, Victor Alva, Reyna Manzano, Manuel Bravo Bañuelos; school archives (AHSEP-AP-ERF) in San Martín Caltenco, Santa Rosa, Chipiltepec, Palmarito, Alseseca, San Nicolás el Viejo, Pericotepec, Colonia Francisco I. Madero, and Nazareño. The latter include scattered monthly reports on school attendance, curriculum, schedules, methods, learning, inventories of books and furnishings, and community relations between 1931 and 1945.

44. On schools and gender in this period, see Vaughan 1990c:143–68; 1994c:117–21; Lewis 1951:323, 327, 342, 389–98; Redfield 1950:39–42, 134–45, 159–60; Rockwell 1994:204; interviews with Reyna Manzano.

45. On the imposition of ejido officers and subsequent negotiations, see, among others, multiple correspondence in AGN-AP-LCR, exps. 404.1/632; 404.2/430, 1937; on use of violence against agraristas, exp. 404.1/632, Sept. 1937; AGN-AP-MAC, exp. 541/610, 1942–45; exp. 541/892, 1943. On suppression of Almazanista votes in 1940 elections, see AGN-AP-LCR, exp. 544.1/20, 1939–40; AMT, Presidencia, año 1940, legajo 81, "Elecciones"; AGN-AP-MAC, exp. 703.4/178, José María Sánchez, Tlacotepec, to Manuel Avila Camacho, Oct. 18, 1941.

46. For example, two survivors who had consistently backed the agrarista cause were Eligio Avelino of La Purísima, Palmar, and Encarnación Alducín of Cuesta Blanca, Palmar.

47. On the state as provider, see multiple correspondence in AGN-AP-MAC, exps. 151.3/125; 151.3/163, 1941; exp. 507.1/191, 1946; AMT, Presidencia, año 1940, legajo 81, July 13, 1940. On provision of water, see ibid., Presidencia, año 1938, legajo 74; AGN-AP-MAC, exp. 508.1/351, 1944; exp. 515.1/467, 1946.

48. AHSEP-AP-ERF, Chipiltepec, Horacio Caro Castillo to SEP, March 1, 1940, "Acuerdo, Comité de Educación, Comité de Administración de la Parcela Escolar, Inspector, Director de Escuela," July 17, 1945; Nazareño, "Entrega del Inventario," Feb. 8, 1937; Caltenco, "Entrega del Inventario," March 27, 1939; interviews with Reyna Manzano.

49. AGN-AP-MAC, exp. 404.2/55, Aniceto Meza, Vicente Alducín, et al., Cuesta Blanca, to Maximino Avila Camacho, Feb. 20, 1941.

50. AHSEP-DGEP, exp. 316.1, JHG, "Plan de Trabajo, 1936"; AHSEP-AP-ERF, San Antonio, Ubaldo Macías Marín, director escuela, Cirilio Rodríguez, Comisariado Ejidal, et al. to Banco de Crédito Ejidal, July 17, 1945.

51. Interviews with Horacio Caro, Victor Alva, and Reyna Manzano, Puebla. Re. corruption, caciques often offered teachers subsidies to clientelize them. Tips were normal fare. Reyna Manzano and her husband received tips from Comisariado Ejidal officers in Tochtepec in the mid-1940s. Corruption depended upon the amount given, the consistency of the contribution, and the degree of compliance exhibited.

52. On boys and buses, AHSEP-DER, caja 905, JHG, "Informe," Aug. 1932.

53. On sports and travel, interview with Victor Alva, Puebla, July 22, 1989.

54. On government mobilization of traditional curers to facilitate the use of modern medicine, interview with Reyna Manzano, Puebla, July 12–15, 1989; Friedlander 1994:137. On infant mortality, Ayala and Schaffer Vázquez 1991:126–27.

CHAPTER 5
SOCIALIST EDUCATION IN ZACAPOAXTLA

1. In 1900, the district of Zacapoaxtla, with a population of 32,853, consisted of four municipalities (Zacapoaxtla, Cuetzalan, Xochitlán, and Nauzontla). The municipality of Xochiapulco (population 2,302 in 1900) seceded from Zacapoaxtla in 1870 to join the district of Tetela. It is included in this story because of its proximity to and influence within the Zacapoaxtla region. The 1917 Constitution dissolved the district of Zacapoaxtla.

2. My understanding of these strategies is based upon my interpretation of the work of Guy P. C. Thomson and Florencia Mallon. See Thomson with LaFrance manuscript (hereafter Thomson w/LA ms) 1996; Thomson and LaFrance 1987:1–13; Thomson 1989b:59–78; 1989a:31–68; 1991a:259–87; 1991b:205–68; Mallon 1991:107–29; 1994a:3–26; 1995:23–136, 276–309.

3. On Xochiapulco's ideals, see also Mallon 1995:63–133; 276–309.

4. Thomson 1991a:283; AMTO, Gobierno, año 1883, caja 440, exp. 6, "Lista de premios," Xochiapulco, Dec. 27, 1884.

5. AMTO, Gobierno, caja 75, año 1883, exp. 54, "Relativo a . . . los fondos de instrucción primaria," Feb. 1, 1882; ARA-P, exp. 187, Atzalan, "Informe de Visita," Eduardo Unda, March 15, 1932.

6. On teachers as local intellectuals, see Mallon 1995:279–80; Pozos 1991, 49–53; on Protestantism and teachers, Bastian 1989:73–85, 105–45, 225. On Pozos as an inspiration to teachers, interviews with Eduardo Ramírez Díaz, Puebla, March 18, 1987; Porfirio Cordero (hereafter, PC), Puebla, July 14, 1987.

7. Beaucage 1973b:121–22; Sosa n.d.:107–31; Thomson 1991b:250–51; AMZ, Fondo

Común Auxiliar, "Fábricas de Aguardiente," 1916–17, "Pasajeros que entraron ayer, Mesón de la Aurora, Posada de Ignacio Soto," various months, 1905; Sánchez Flores 1984:223–41; *Boletín Estadística del Estado de Puebla* 3, no. 1 (March 1902): 16–17; Caballero 1891:198–99.

8. Fabila 1949:83–86, 137–39, 150; Sáenz 1927:81; on property ceded as collateral on loans, see AMZ, Notario Público to Recaudador de Rentas, Jan. 27, 1930; on labor demands for public works, Thomson 1991b:255.

9. Sánchez Flores 1984:230–33; Thomson 1991a:275; 1991b 215–16; 1989b:69, 74. *Boletín Estadística del Estado de Puebla* 3, no. 1 (March 1902): 16–17, listed fifteen Nahua sugar processors among the district's entrepreneurs in 1902. On indigenous government, see Nutini and Isaac 1974:157, 169, 175, 325–26; Durand 1986:43–93; Mallon 1995:63–84; Montoya Briones 1964:106–9; Torres Trueba 1970:157–60.

10. For description of religion and life in indigenous Sierra towns at the turn of the century, see Starr 1895:242–86. On contemporary Nahuatl religious philosophy, see Taggart 1983; on beliefs and practices, Nutini and Isaac 1974:151–203; Torres Trueba 1970:118–29; on patriarchy and family organization, Fabila 1949:147–49; Arizpe 1989:118–22; 199–208; Mallon 1994a:3–26; Taggart 1976:137–53; Montoya Briones 1964:85–122.

11. AMZ, Instrucción Pública (hereafter, IP), Feb. 1988; no exp., "Listas escolares," 1904; exp. 65, July 17, 1909; Tesorería Municipal, exp. 51, March and April 1899, March 1902; exp. 15, Jan.–March 1905; AMX, "Actas de Cabildo, Sesión pública," Jan. 7, Feb. 4 and 18, March 20, and April 17, 1907; Sáenz 1927:81–83; interview with Ebundio Carreón, Comaltepec, March 1, 1993.

12. AMZ, IP, no exp., "Exámenes," Dec. 1, 1905. Prepared for the 1890 census, "padrones de sección" indicated practically no indigenous literacy, AMZ, s.e., 1888. On Cuetzalan, Estado de Puebla 1910, 266.

13. AMX, Sección de Gobernación, "Sobre inventario de enseres pertenecientes a la Junta Auxiliar de Huahuaxtla," Feb. 2, 1907; AMZ, IP, exp. 22, Sept. 1901; Estado de Puebla 1910, 262–67; interviews with Ebundio Carreón, Comaltepec, March 1, 1993 and Francisco Toral, Zacapoaxtla, Feb. 28, 1993.

14. On festival in Zacapoaxtla, AMZ, Gobernación, exp. 68, "Festividades Nacionales: Programa Independencia Nacional," Sept. 11, 1909; exp. 67, "Festividades Nacionales," "5 de Mayo y 15–16 Sept., 1910"; interview with Carreón.

15. AMZ, IP, exp. 22, Sept. 1901.

16. ARA-P, exp. 187, Atzalan; Paré 1978:47, 55–60.

17. AHSEP-DECI, Rafael Molina Betancourt (hereafter, RMB), "Informes," Jan. 7 and 25, April 26, and July 20, 1923; Sáenz 1927:81–85. On teachers and Nahuatl, interview with Ebundio Carreón. On opposition to SEP crusade, Sáenz 1927:72, 80; AMZ, IP, exp. 4,

Miguel Martínez, Maestro Rural Federal, Xalacapan, to PM, May 4, 1932; exp. 3, FMB, insp., SEP, Zacapoaxtla, to PM, March 2, 1932; AHSEP-AP-ERF, Xochitepec, "Informe," FMB, insp., May 1931; interview with Carreón.

18. AHSEP-DER, exp. 48.80, 1922–23.

19. AHSEP-ERN, exp. 362.14, Escuela Rural Normal, Tlatlauqui, "Informes," Aug.–Nov. 1934; exp. 482, "Junta Patriótica," Sept. 16, 1934, Zaragoza, M. Martínez, dir., to SEP, Sept. 10 and Nov. 14, 1934; exp. 360.1, Silverio Arena, PM, Xochiapulco to SEP, June 5, 1934.

20. On Burgos, interviews with PC, Eduardo Ramírez Díaz, and Faustino Hernández, Puebla, March 20, 1987; Juan Cuamatzin, Tetela, April 17, 1984; Filadelfo Vázquez, Zacapoaxtla, March 2, 1993.

21. Interviews cited in previous note; on teacher radicalism, Fabila 1949:185–86.

22. ARA-P, exp. 867, Jilotepec; exp. 935, Las Lomas; exp. 1026, Xalticpac; AGN-AP-LCR, exp. 403/190, 1937. On use of the CCEZ, AMZ, Presidencia, Manuel Molina to CCEZ, April 25, 1931; Gobernación to PM, Dec. 16, 1930.

23. Interviews with Francisco Toral, Ebundio Carreón, Rafael Alcántara Cárcamo, Zacapoaxtla, Feb.–March 1993.

24. AMZ, "Sección de Trabajo y Previsión Social," 1935; Crescencio Tamañiz, Comité Agrario, Ramosco, Ahuacatlán, to PM, June 8 and 12, 1931; Eliseo Tejeda et al., Tatoxcac, to PM, Nov. 8, 1932; PM to sec. gen. de gobierno, April 25, 1932; Hacienda, Joaquín Hacquet to same, July 5, 1935; ARA-P, exp. 1026, Xalticpac; exp. 1022, Tahitic; interview with Faustino Hernández.

25. Interviews with PC, July 14, 1987; León Ramírez, Puebla, March 17, 1987; Eduardo Ramírez Díaz; Ebundio Carreón; ARA-P, exp. 187, Atzalan; exp. 1026, Xalticpac, Eliseo Bonilla, to Comisión Agraria Mixta, Sept. 3, 1935; AMX, "Actas de Cabildo," Jan. 20, 1932; AMZ, Gobernación, exp. 10, Manuel Molina, PM, to CCEZ, Feb. 26, 1931; s.e., "Acta de Jueces," Emilio de Jesús et al., Xaltetela, to PM, Nov. 8, 1935; Eliseo Tejeda et al., Tatoxcac, to PM, Nov. 8, 1932; Paré 1978:47–48, 55–56.

26. In 1935, the SEP employed thirty male and fifteen female teachers. Female attendance improved in the headtowns with women teachers (AHSEP-AP-ERF, Zaragoza, "Informe," July 30, 1927; Nauzontla, "Informes," Aug. and Oct. 1933). On low female attendance, see AHSEP-AP-ERF, Ahuacatlán, "Informes," May 31, 1931 (20 boys, 4 girls); Oct. 10, 1931 (31 boys, 5 girls); Feb. 12, 1932 (no girls); Aug. 1932 (24 boys, 8 girls); Feb. 1933 (10 boys, no girls); Xochitepec, "Informes," July–Sept. 1931 (no girls); Sept. 2, 1932 (56 boys, 13 girls in preparatory class). On the Nauzontla revolt against coeducation, ibid., Nauzontla, Jacinto Maldonado, dir., SEP Puebla, to SEP, Sept. 13, 1934. On "original sin" and women, AHSEP-DER, exp. 296.4, PC, insp., Zacapoaxtla, "Informe," Jan. 4, 1936.

27. On reaction to moving the cemetery, AHSEP-AP-ERF, Ahuacatlán, "Informe," Oct. 17, 1932. On the meaning and use of alcohol, Nutini and Isaac 1974:157, 356–57; Fabila 1949:120–21, 174; Montoya Briones 1964:72–76, 92, 110, 125–27.

28. Interviews with Ebundio Carreón, Atalo de Santillán Aldana, Puebla, July 11, 1987; Eduardo Ramírez Díaz, Puebla, March 18, 1987; AMZ, FMB, dir., SEP Puebla, to PM, Feb. 6, April 19, 1935; José N. Molina, Zacapexpan, to PM, March 7, 1935; Guadalupe Martínez, to PM, Aug. 7, 1935; Joaquín Hacquet, Circular to Jueces de Paz, May 1, 1935; AHSEP-DER, exp. 206.4, PC, "Informes," Jan. 24, May 29, 1936; AGN-AP-LCR, exp. 151.31/1181, RMB to Cárdenas, Feb. 1, 1939.

29. Interviews with Atalo de Santillán, Eduardo Ramírez Díaz, Faustino Hernández, Ebundio Carreón; AHSEP-DER, exp. 338.1, FMB, dir., SEP Puebla, Nov. 25, 1935; AMZ, Presidencia, Domingo Organo, juez de paz, Comaltepec, to PM, Aug. 13, 1935; AGN-AP-LCR, exp. 541/711, Raul Isidro Burgos, dir., Normal Rural, to Cárdenas, Nov. 15, 1935; exp. 545.2/2, Mariano Franco, Confederación Mexicana de Maestros, to Cárdenas, May 16, 1936.

30. On outrage at the state PNR's recognition of the Lobato slate and dismantling of Almazanismo, see AGN-AP-LCR, exps. 544.5/270; 544.5/673, 544.6/550, Nov. 1935–Feb. 1936. On disputes over land between communities, see ARA-P, exp. 935, Las Lomas; exp. 867, Jilotepec, exp. 1926, Xalticpac, exp. 2211, El Molino, exp. 2198, Nexticapan, exp. 1008, Atacpan; AGN-AP-LCR, exps. 404.1/4759, Oct. 1936; exp. 403/190, Sept. 1937.

31. AHSEP-DGEP, exp. 316.7, PC, "Informes," May–Oct. 1936; interviews with Eduardo Ramírez Díaz, Faustino Hernández; AGN-AP-LCR, exp. 151.3/1181, RMB to Cárdenas, Feb. 1, 1939.

32. AMZ, Hervila Morales, Las Lomas, to PM, March 29, 1935; Carlos Vázquez, Comisariado Ejidal, Jilotepec, to PM, Jan. 8, 1935. On support from Zaragoza, AHSEP-DER, exp. 242.9, Padres de Familia y Campesinos, Oyameles, Las Trancas, Huitzilzila-pam, Tenextatiloyan, to SEP and Confederación Mexicana de Maestros, 1935, n.d. On Xochiapulco and surrounding schools, AHSEP-ERN, exp. 360.1, Escuela Normal Rural, Tlatlauqui, Silverio Arenas, PM, Xochiapulco, to SEP, June 5, 1934; AHSEP-AP-ERF, Cuauximaloyan, Moisés Gil Galicia, March 14, 1940, and Nov. 21, 1941; La Manzanilla, "Datos," Nov. 1938; Francisco Alejo, José Tiburcio to SEP, May 12, 1936; AHSEP-DER, exp. 206.7, PM, "Informe," Jan. 4, 1936; AGN-AP-LCR, exp. 151.3/1744, "Frente Unico Popular Regional Xochiapulco," to Cárdenas, May 31, 1940.

33. Lyrics and anecdotes from Ebundio Carreón.

34. The Lobato campaign was carefully coordinated with the Avila Camacho brothers, Maximino and Rafael. See correspondence in AMZ, Presidencia, 1937, especially Maximino Avila Camacho to Lobato, Feb. 24, 1937; Joaquín Varela to Rafael Avila Camacho, Feb. 26, 1937. On Lobato, see Paré 1978:47–48, 55–56. The only land grants in the Zacapoaxtla region between 1930 and 1950 went to southern-tier towns (Atacpan, Las Lomas, Jilotepec). Several villages in the municipality of Zaragoza received land from Macip properties (Estado de Puebla 1984:19–23). Atacpan received its land at the expense

of the Zaragoza ejidos, centers of Almazanista strength (ARA-P, exp. 1008, Atacpan, Ejecución de Dotación, Dec. 13, 1945). For RMB memorandum, AGN-AP-LCR, exp. 151.3/1181. For a different experience of Cardenismo in a similar indigenous region, see Rus 1994:265–300; Benjamin 1989:202–4; 210–24; Wasserstrom 1983:169.

35. The following description of schools is derived from these sources: AHSEP-DER, exp. 206.4, PC, insp., Zacapoaxtla, 1935; AHSEP-DGEP, exp. 316.7, 1936; exp. 2989, PC, "Plan de Trabajo," Jan. 17, 1939; AHSEP-AP-ERF, Ahuacatlán, Las Trancas, Tahitic, Cuaximaloyan, La Manzanilla, Xalacapan, Xochitepec, Atioyan, Zaragoza, 1931–1946; AHSEP-ERN, exp. 482, Escuela Rural Normal, Tlatlauqui, 1934; Fabila 1949:10, 33; interviews with Eduardo Ramírez Díaz, PC, Atalo de Santillán.

Youth literacy statistics for 1930 and 1940 in Table 2 make sense except for Nauzontla and Cuetzalan. Both areas were hardhit by cristero attacks. Still, overall figures for Nauzontla are erratic. The youth literacy decline in Cuetzalan is exaggerated because the 10–14-year-old population identified as illiterate is inordinately large in relation to other age groups and longitudinal trends.

36. Mimeographed lyrics, n.d., Biblioteca Pública, Zacapoaxtla.

37. Rivera 1991, 35; also in mimeographed tribute to Burgos provided by PC, Puebla, July 14, 1987.

38. Mimeographed lyrics in Biblioteca Pública, Zacapoaxtla.

39. AMZ, Presidencia, "Manifiesto al Pueblo del Décimo Distrito Electoral Federal del Estado de Puebla," Julio Lobato, Feb. 1937; AHSEP-AP-ERF, Tahitic, Emilio Angeles, Comité de Educación, to SEP, May 11, 1945.

40. Interview with Natalia Molina, Jan. 20, 1986.

41. On cacique support, AHSEP-DEEP, exp. 316.7, PC, "Informes," June–Oct. 1936. On relations with caciques, interviews with Faustino Hernández, PC, León Ramírez.

42. Interviews, Eduardo Ramírez Díaz, Francisco Toral, Rafael Alcántara Cárcamo; Paré 1978:47–48, 55–59; Torres Trueba 1970:43–44, 177–92.

43. Interviews with Toral and Alcántara Cárcamo. This form of caciquismo differs from other cases in the Sierra where elites utilized agrarismo during the revolution simply to expand their personal interests at the expense of another elite group (see Durand 1986:220–23). On the good patriarch in this region of the Sierra, see Thomson w/LF ms 1996:18, 34, 173; Mallon 1995:72–84; 1994a:12–17. For a darker view of Toral, see Paré 1978:47–48.

44. On teachers as allies in struggles for barrio political and economic independence, see Torres Trueba 1970:160–66, 177–92; interviews with Eduardo Ramírez Díaz, PC, Faustino Hernández. On Tosepan Titataniske, interviews with Filadelfo Vázquez, Rafael Alcántara Cárcamo.

45. Interview with Faustino Hernández.

46. I thank Miguel Felix Mirón and Moisés Chávez Rosario of San Miguel for sharing this story with me. They participated with their fathers in building the school and today are community elders. I visited San Miguel in July 1993 and August 1994 and thank the village council for having received me and facilitated my visit.

47. There are several claims to the ashes of Burgos. Filadelfo Vázquez, SEP official in Zacapoaxtla and former Burgos student, related to me that before Burgos died in 1971 he asked that his ashes be scattered to the four winds near the Laurel de India trees he had planted at the Normal Rural in Tixtla, Guerrero, in the "casco" of an expropriated hacienda. Teachers came from all over Mexico in a caravan of buses to take part in the ceremony. The Cortés brothers of the Titataniske cooperative did a yearly homage to Burgos in Totula in the Sierra. When he was municipal president of Zacapoaxtla, Samuel Cárcamo named a new normal school after him. Streets and schools throughout the Sierra bear his name.

CHAPTER 6
THE YAQUIS OF SONORA, THE SCHOOL, AND THE STATE

1. It is impossible to get accurate literacy figures for the Yaquis before or after the revolution. In 1895 and 1900, when the first national censuses were taken, the Yaquis were at war with the Mexicans. In 1910, their number in the valley had been greatly reduced by war and deportation. In the 1930 and 1940 censuses, one cannot distinguish the Yaquis from other citizens in the municipalities of Guaymas and Bacum.

On the impact of the Jesuits, see Spicer 1980:5–57; Hu-DeHart 1981:22–57; Radding 1989:336–37; on Jesuits and literacy, Spicer 1954:26; ASM-ESFN, Potam, Feb. 22, 1942; on maestros' notebooks, Spicer 1980:326; Painter Series, Arizona State Museum Archives MS 18 SG 4 S4 F4, "Notebooks of Maestro Ignacio Alvarez," Pascua Village, Tucson, April 13, 1923; ASM-ESP, archive A-466, "Arizona's Indian Refugees," 29. On Catholic instruction, Párroco de la Diócesis de León, *Manual completo de sacristanes: Maestros de instrucción primaria y personas piadosas que acostumbran acompañar y ayudar a los señores párrocos para oficiar las funciones de iglesia en los pueblos en que hay escasez de clérigos* (5th ed., Valladolid, 1892) in ASM-ESFN, Feb. 12 and March 19, 1942.

2. The notion of a restricted, religious literacy is taken from Goody 1968:11–14; see also Street 1984:132–57. On Yaqui maestros taking books into the hills, ASM-ESFN, Juan Valenzuela, Potam, March 18, 1942.

3. On educational experiences in the United States, see ASM-ESFN, Juan Basolihte-mea, March 3, 1942, Cruz Valenzuela Castillo, Vicam, June 5 and 25, 1947; ASM-WWP, Lucas Alvarez, life history, 4–5; J. Cupis, life history, tape 1; ASM, archive A-469a/b, Rosalio Chávez, life history, 14–18 (the basis for Moisés, Kelley, and Holden 1971); ASM-ESP, archive A-384, Roanna H. Winsor, "Some Findings on Richey School," May 1954. On letter writing, Spicer 1954:17; Moisés, 45.

4. Fabila 1940:90; ASM-ESFN, Cenobio Valenzuela, June 6, 1947; J. Ujllolimea, Jan. 29,

1942; Ambrosio Castro, Feb. 21, 1942; ASM-ESP, archive A-466, "The Yaqui Problem," 1942, 2, 4, 8. For more on Yaqui origin myth and history, Spicer 1980:164–76; Radding 1989:335–36.

5. ASM-WWP, Lucas Chávez, life history, 10–11; ASM-ESFN, Ambrosio Castro, Feb. 1942; ASM-WWP, "Peace at Pitahaya," Juan Valenzuela, Rahum, 1947.

6. ASM-WWP, Lucas Chávez, life history, 10–16; J. Cupis, tape 1, 20–28; Tomás Alvarez Gitta, life history, tape 18, n.p.; archive A-469a/b, Rosalio Moisés, 2–11. Historians have also pointed out that haciendas could be institutions of protection for the Yaquis (Radding 1989:341; Spicer 1980:149–50; Hu-DeHart 1984:127–29.)

7. ASM-ESFN, Potam, Feb. 4, March 11, 1942; ASM-ESP, "The Yaqui Problem," 1942, 22.

8. AGRA, Dotación Ejidos, exp. 23/8519, Bacum, vol. 1, "Informe," Olivier Ortiz, April 18, 1932.

9. AGN-AP-ALR, exp. 514.1/2-83, Luciano Jécari et al., Yaqui gobernadores, Bacum, to Rodríguez, June 12, 1933; ASM-ESP, archive A-466, "Sonora's Fighting Farmers," 9.

10. William C. Holden (1936:10) estimated 2,600 Yaquis in five villages in the early 1930s. Using the 1930 census, Fabila (1940:110) estimated 8,548 in 1935.

11. I have paraphrased and rearranged the descriptive prose of Edward Spicer because he says it so well. ASM-ESP, "Sonora's Fighting Farmers," 8, 15–17.

12. Based upon his study of Potam, Spicer identified two broad groups of conservatives and progressives (ASM-ESP, "The Yaqui Problem," 15–18; also Holden 1936:10). I have chosen to call the conservatives Restorationists. Figueroa Valenzuela (1992:143–44) sees the division between "civilistas," seeking Yaqui autonomy from the Mexicans, and "militaristas," soldiers who had been with the Mexicans and wanted modernization of production and government aid. Dabdoub (1964:235–37) makes the same distinction.

13. ASM, archive A-469a/b, Moisés, 18, 41–43, 54, 60, 252–53, 275, 289, 305–7; ASM-ESFN, Jesús Alvarez, Potam, June 17, 1947; Juan Aguilar, Cuesta Alta, Feb. 18, 1942.

14. Spicer 1954:35–38; ASM-ESFN, Potam, Jan. 2 and 16, Feb. 4 and 13, A. Castro, Feb. 24, P. Valenzuela, March 5, B. Valenzuela, March 5 and 20, 1942; ASM-ESP, archive A-466, "The Yaqui Problem," 15–17.

15. On Yaqui political organization, see Spicer 1980:178–223; Fabila 1940:159–73; Holden 1936:11–19; McGuire 1986:22–74. On the intellectuals, ASM-ESFN, Potam, Jan. 29, Feb 12, 21, and 25, March 2 and 26, 1942; June 6, 1947.

16. ASM, archive A-469a/b, Moisés, 2–9.

17. Fabila 1940:57; ASM-ESP, archive A-466, "Sonora's Fighting Farmers," 8; "The Yaqui Problem," 18–19; ASM-ESFN, Potam, Jan. 17, Feb. 4 and 17, 1942; June 29, 1947; Tonichi, Sept. 9, 1947; AGN-AP-LCR, exp. 533.11/1, Gutiérrez Cázares to Cárdenas, Sept.

28, 1940; ASM-ESP, archive A-384, C. E. Duarte, "Mexican and Yaqui Relations during the Revolution," 1961; on imminent rebellions, *El Heraldo del Yaqui,* April 12, 1942; USSD 812.00/1182, Guaymas, Aug. 31, 1933; /1220, Aug. 31, 1934; /1221, Aug. 31, 1934; USWD, G-2 Reports, 2657-G-605/373, Aug. 27, 1935.

18. AGN-AP-ALR, exp. 514.1/2-83, Luciano Jécari and Juan María Valenzuela, goberna-dores, Bacum, to Rodríguez, June 12, 1933; exp.106/2, Calles to Rodríguez, Sept. 7, 1933.

19. Interview with Celia Ruedeflores, Hermosillo, April 6, 1989. On Mexican authorities' corruption, AGN-AP-ALR, exp. 106/2, Jécari and Valenzuela, Bacum, to Rodríguez, April 19, 1933; exp. 514.1/2-83, Jécari and Valenzuela, Bacum, to Rodríguez, June 12, 1933; AHSEP-DER, exp. 249.7, FX, dir., SEP Sonora, "Informe," Nov. 28, 1935; F. Corzo, insp. regional, "Informe," Nov. 8, 1935; ADN, José F. Botello, XI/III/1-249, on army pillaging and extortion, Juan Ramírez, Empalme, to Sec. de Guerra, Jan. 22, 1936; Jesús Gámez, "Denuncia," Empalme, Dec. 22, 1937; José Peralta, Empalme, to Sec. de Guerra, May 6, 1936; Fabila 1940:18, 49, 129–30, 149–50.

20. ASM-ESFN, Potam, J. Valenzuela, March 18, 1942; ASM, archive A-469a/b, Moisés, 55.

21. ASM-ESFN, April 4–5, 1947; Spicer 1954:88–93; 1980:70–88. For a more contempo-rary interpretation of Yaqui ceremony, see McGuire 1986:68–78 and 1989:159–78.

22. ASM-ESFN, Potam, Feb. 2, 16, 21, 22, March 17, April 4, 5, 1942; Barrio Libre, June 24, 1947; ASM, archive A-469a/b, Moisés, 267–68; Bartell 1965:97–98.

23. For an excellent description of fluctuating household membership and linkage to religion and coparenthood, see Moisés, Kelley, and Holden 1971:xl, xli–xlv; Kelley 1978: 30–50, 94; on limited religious experience on sisal plantations and in revolutionary armies, 136–39, 160–64, 167–69, 183.

24. AGN-AP-LCR, exp. 425.5/117, Gutiérrez Cázares to Cárdenas, June 28, 1938, Sept. 28, 1940; exp. 533.11/1, Gutiérrez Cázares to Cárdenas, May 12, 1939; March 28 and Oct. 10, 1940; Santiago Betemea et al. to Cárdenas, May 20, 1939; ADN, exp. xi/iii/1-675, Gutiérrez Cázares; AHSEP-DER, exp. 249.7, F. Corzo, "Informe," Nov. 8, 1935.

25. ADN, matrícula 2755505, Gen. Juventino Espinosa Sánchez, xi/iii/1-471, Espinosa to Sec. de Guerra, Feb. 11, 1930; Fabila 1940:49–53.

26. AGN-AP-LCR, exp. 533.11/1, 1937–40; exp. 425.5/117, 1938; Fabila 1940:28–29, 33–36, 52–53, 103.

27. On Cárdenas's materialist notions, see AGN-AP-LCR, exp. 533.11/1, Cárdenas to Guillermo de la Garza, Vicam, June 6, 1939; "Cárdenas a la Jefatura," June 10, 1939; Cárdenas 1940:296, 357, 426–28; Figueroa Valenzuela 1992:75, 287. On government providing space for relative autonomy and ceremonial options, see Erasmus 1978:30; Spicer 1954:44–45; Bartell 1965:206–7.

28. AHSEP-DGEP, exp. 319.11, LeM, insp., Empalme, "Informe," March 1936.

29. AHSEP-DER, exp. 208.1.1, LeM, "Informe," Nov. 1935; AHSEP-DGEP, exp. 319.11, "Informe," May 1936.

30. Ibid.; AHSEP-DGEP, exp. 391.11, "Informes," Jan. and March 1936.

31. Fabila 1940:262–64; ASM-ESFN, Potam, Jan. 22 and 23, Feb. 3 and 4, 1942, June 7, 1947; AHSEP-DER, exp. 249.7, LM, dir., SEP Sonora, "Informe," Jan.–Feb., 1935; exp. 249.23, July 1, 1935; AHSEP-DER, exp. 208.1.1, LeM, "Informe," Nov. 1935; AHSEP-DGEP, exp. 319.1, LeM, "Informes," Jan.–May 1936.

32. AHSEP-DGEP, LeM, "Informe," March 1936; Kelley 1978:183–85.

33. AGN-AP-LCR, exp. 533/11.1, Dept. Agrario to SEP, Sept. 2, 1939, reporting on assessment of schools by Procurador de Comunidades Indígenas; ASM-ESFN, Potam, Jan. 22 and 23, Feb. 3, 1942; Fabila 1940:145–46, 283.

34. Fabila 1940:145, 167; *El Heraldo del Yaqui,* Feb. 26, 1942; Spicer 1954:159–60; AHSEP-DER, exp. 249.23, Promotor de Educación Física, Sonora, to SEP, July 1, 1935; ASM-ESFN, Potam, June 24 and 25, 1947.

35. ASM-ESFN, Feb. 24, 1942.

36. Fabila 1940:262–63; AHSEP-DGEP, exp. 319.1, LeM, "Informes," March and May 1936.

37. ASM-ESFN, Cuesta Alta, Feb. 18, 1942.

38. AGN-AP-LCR, exp. 533.11/1, Cárdenas to Yocupicio, June 12, 1939; AHSEP-DER, exp. 249.7, LM, dir., SEP Sonora, "Informe," Jan.–Feb. 1935, F. Corzo, "Informe," Nov. 8, 1935; FX, dir., SEP Sonora, to SEP, Oct. 21, 1935; exp. 249.13, SEP to LM, April 25, 1935; exp. 240.23, LM, dir., SEP Sonora, July 1, 1935; AHSEP-DGEP, exp. 319.1, LeM, "Informe," May 1936; Fabila 1940:276.

39. Fabila 1940:145–46, 267; AGN-AP-LCR, exp. 533.11/1, 1938–39.

40. Fabila 1940:288; ASM-ESP, "Sonora's Fighting Farmers," 19; AGN-AP-LCR, exp. 533.11/1, Maestros de la Zona Yaqui to Cárdenas, June 22, 1939, Rafael Castro, Dept. de Asuntos Indígenas, to Cárdenas, Oct. 30, 1939, Gob. Santiago Betemea, Vicam, to Cárdenas, Jan. 3, 1940; exp. 559.3/25, Lt. Col. Francisco Salcedo Casilla to Gutiérrez Cázares, May 7, 1940. Interview with Celia Ruedeflores.

41. AGN-AP-LCR, exp. 533.11/1, 1939; Exp 559.3/25, 1938–40; exp. 534.3.28, Cárdenas to SEP, June 10, 1938.

42. See multiple complaints of governors against military trafficking in timber, private rental of government machinery to Yaquis and Yoris, investments in local stores and concessions, and protection of Yori land invasions in ADN, José F. Botello Borrego, 0652, folder XI/III/1-249, no. 5, Miguel Valencia to Avila Camacho, Dec. 25, 1941; AGN-AP-MAC, exp. 501.2/20, Gob. Miguel Valencia et al., Vicam, to Avila Camacho, May 2, July 1 and Aug. 4, 1941; exp. 703.4/315, Francisco Pluma Blanca et al. to Avila Camacho, Nov.

13, 1942; exp. 151.3/240, Gen. Miguel Guerrero Verduzco to Avila Camacho, Oct. 23, 1946. Gutiérrez Cázares still had his private ranch on Yaqui lands at Aguacaliente in 1943 (exp. 135.2/234, Gen. Alatorre Blanco to Avila Camacho, April 3, 1943).

43. Fabila 1940:273–78; AGN-AP-MAC, exp. 534.6/325, Isidro Candia, Dept. de Asuntos Indígenas, to Avila Camacho, Sept. 8, 1942; Gen. Alatorre Blanco to Avila Camacho, Aug. 28, 1942; LCR, exp. 533.11/1, Col. I. Beteta, Vicam, to Sec. de Guerra, Aug. 19, 1938.

44. AGN-AP-MAC, exp. 482.1/18, Prof. Alberto Terán, dir. gen. de enseñanza primaria, to SEP, Nov. 18, 1942; "Memorandum," Dept. de Asuntos Indígenas, Dec. 15, 1942; exp. 151.3/540, Gen. Alatorre Blanco, Vicam, to Avila Camacho, April 12, 1943; 151.3/240, "Acta que se levanta en el poblado de Bataconcica del Municipio de Guaymas, Sonora, para exponer ante la Presidencia de la República los problemas de las Colonias Yaquis y de los Miembros de las Tribus," March 14, 1946.

45. AGN-AP-MAC, exp. 501.2/20, Miguel Valencia to Avila Camacho, Aug. 4, 1941. Cárdenas personally corresponded with the governors and sent them trucks, mules, and tools. See multiple correspondence in AGN-AP-LCR, exp. 533.11/1, 1939–40. Like many Mexicans, the Yaquis called him "Tata Cárdenas," and are said to have viewed his accord with them as a Magna Carta for their nation (interview with Celia Ruedeflores).

46. AGN-AP-LCR, exp. 533.11/1, Gobs. José M. Buitemea, A. Rodríguez, et al. to Cárdenas, June 5, 1939; AGN-AP-MAC, exp. 501.2/20, Miguel Valencia et al. to Avila Camacho, Aug. 4, 1941; ADN, José F. Botello Borrego, XI/III/1-129, Miguel Valencia to Avila Camacho. On the question of Yaqui identity and participation in the revolution, see also Figueroa Valenzuela 1992:347–56.

47. On military abuses and governors' complaints, multiple correspondence in AGN-AP-MAC, exps. 703.4/315; 151.3/540; 703.1/722, 1943; exp. 135.2/234, Feb.1945; exp. 151.3/240, March 1946. On the Ejidal Bank, Erasmus 1978:26-32; Figueroa Valenzuela 1992:82–87; Hewitt Alcántara 1978:248–61.

48. On government agencies, Fabila 1940:28, 31; AGN-AP-LCR, exp. 425.4/117, Gutiérrez Cázares to Cárdenas, May 12, 1939; AGN-AP-MAC, exp. 151.3/540, Gen. Alatorre Blanco to Avila Camacho, April 28 and June 8, 1943. Each agency complained about the other and each military commander claimed he would clean up the problems created by his predecessors. On Yaqui society and economy in the 1950s and 1960s, Nolasco de Armas 1969:312; Figueroa Valenzuela 1992:82–87; Hewitt Alcántara 1978:248–61; Erasmus 1978:21–71.

49. Erasmus 1978:26–32; AGN-AP-LCR, exp. 533.11/1, Fabila to Cárdenas, Aug. 3, 1938; exp. 550.3/25, Santiago Betemea to Cárdenas, Jan. 3, 1940; AGN-AP-MAC, exp. 501.2/20, Sec. de Agricultura, "Informe," Mexico City, May 2, 1941.

50. For McGuire's critique of Spicer's argument for the centrality of religion, see McGuire 1989:159–78. He supports his argument with Anya Peterson Royce's criteria for ethnic identity: shared language, moral values, and political organization (Royce 1982). On the fishermen's cooperative, McGuire 1986:56, 66, 123–24, 139–47.

Chapter 7
The Cultural Politics of Schooling

1. The phrase "tortillas filled with faith" I have borrowed from Cornejo 1977:72, 85.

2. Interview with Marcelina Saldívar de Murrieta, Hermosillo, April 7, 1989; Marcelina Saldívar in Mayo Murrieta and María Eugenia Graf (hereafter, MG) 1992:85. Here, I make extensive use of this ably retrieved and engagingly edited collection of oral histories.

3. Figures for the municipalities of Cajeme (Ciudad Obregón) and Bacum are from Secretaría de la Economía 1934, 1943.

4. The 1940 census counted 6,198 persons in Bacum and 27,519 in Cajeme.

5. Descriptions based on reading of MG 1992:5–6, 32, 72; Cornejo 1977:74–76, 81–83; on Yori settlement, see Radding 1989:346–47; Hu-DeHart 1984:161–62.

6. Interview with Marcelina Saldívar; Marcelina Saldívar in MG 1992:84–85.

7. Interview with Arturo Saldívar, Ciudad Obregón, April 8, 1989; Viviano Alatorre Valenzuela, MG 1992:77. In federal schools in Campos 36, 35, and El Castillo in 1935, two years of study were offered and in Campo 7, three years (AHSEP-DER, exp. 249.23, Roberto Sánchez Lima, promotor de educación física, "Informe," July 1, 1935).

8. The notion of a society homogeneous by virtue of its commitment to conquering nature and savagery is the thesis of MG 1992:vii–xii, and Cornejo 1977:76–77. On McGriffith, Francisco Vega Carrizoza in MG 1992:32–33; on Domingo Pérez, Alfonso Encinas García in MG 1992:5; on Obregón, Alfonso Encinas García, 8; José García Santana, 30; Francisco Vega Carrizoza, 31; Francisco Schwarsbeck Ramírez, 225–27 (all in MG 1992); on entrepreneurs as role models, interview with Arturo Saldívar.

9. On gas and oil, Francisco Vega Carrizoza in MG 1992:33; Alejandro Méndez, 148–49; on Fordsitos, Reyes Anaya Zamorano, 18, Francisco Coronado Limón, 199.

10. Aurora Ayala de Ayón in MG 1992:54–55; Viviano Alatorre Valenzuela, 76–77; Marcelina Saldívar, 87, 90; Cornejo 1977:66–74, 93.

11. On women and the use of remedies and tools, Manuel Cano Valenzuela, MG 1992:41–42; Aurora Ayala de Ayón, 55; Viviano Alatorre Valenzuela, 76; on valley militants and agricultural machinery manuals, Reyes Anaya Zamorano, 14. On life in the sierra, Manuela Cano Valenzuela, 42; Cornejo 1977:1–15, 95–97.

12. On Hollywood, in MG 1992, Viviano Alatorre Valenzuela, 74–75; Marcelina Saldívar, 87, 90–91; Alejandro Méndez Limón, 134; see also Cornejo 1977:88–89. On Tom Mix, Marcelina Saldívar, MG 1992:87.

13. Manuela Cano Valenzuela in MG 1992:38.

14. On bands, MG 1992:39, Alejandro Méndez Limón, 134; Francisco Vega Carrizoza, 33; on religious women, Manuela Cano Valenzuela, 75, Marcelina Saldívar, 87; on frocks, 86.

15. Women workers in the canneries and packing plants of the Río Mayo towns and Cajeme were active in unionization.

16. Marcelina Saldívar in MG 1992:86–88; interview with Marcelina Saldívar.

17. According to the censuses of 1930 and 1940, 30 percent of households in Cajeme and 22 to 25 percent of those in Bacum were female-headed.

18. On the bawdy side of valley life, MG 1992:85; Viviano Alatorre Valenzuela, 73–74. On raising money for schools, Aurora Ayala de Ayón, 55.

19. Marcelina Saldívar in MG 1992:85; interview with Marcelina Saldívar.

20. On religion and valley life, interview with Manuel Ferra Martínez, Hermosillo, May 7, 1987; interview with Arturo Saldívar. On reaction to antireligious policies in Ciudad Obregón, USSD 812.00/1212, Guaymas, June 1, 1934; /1216, July 31, 1934.

21. MG 1992:vii; Alfonso Encinas García, 3–5; Aurora Ayala de Ayón, 53; AGN-AP-OC, exp. 101-V-2, Francisco Elías, gobernador, to Obregón, Aug. 15, 1921; "Vecinos de los varios pueblos y congregaciones de la región del Río Yaqui," Bacum to Obregón, May 31, 1922; exp. 101-Y-5, multiple correspondence asking for indemnization against Yaqui destruction of private property, 1923. On imagining Yaqui witches, Cornejo 1977:86.

22. AGRA, exp.23/8519, Dotación e Ejidos, vol. 1, Bacum, "Informe del Ing. A. Hernández," Sonora, Oct. 18, 1934; Ramón I. Monroy to Dept. Agrario, Nov. 9, 1934; Aurora Ayala de Ayón in MG 1992:55–59.

23. AGRA, exp. 23/8519, vol. 1, Bacum, Arturo Orci to Comisión Nacional Agraria, Oct. 19, 1934; Vallescillo, Comité Particular Ejecutivo, Bacum, to same, Sept. 1, 1932; Corbalá 1970:165. On the Richardson, see also Radding 1989:345–48.

24. Aurora Ayala de Ayón in MG 1992:60.

25. SEP inspector Leonardo Magaña estimated that approximately five thousand "men" worked in the Yaqui agricultural camps in 1936 (AHSEP-DGEP, exp. 319.11, LeM, "Informe," May 1936). The population of Cajeme and Bacum grew by 17 percent in the decade of the 1930s, from 27,799 to 33,717. On unrest in the valley, Reyes Anaya Zamorano in MG 1992:19; AGRA, exp. 23/8510, vol. 1, Bacum, Vallescillo, Comité Particular Ejecutivo, to Comisión Nacional Agraria, Sept. 1, 1932. On organizing, interview with Elvira Figueroa, Hermosillo, May 8, 1987, interviews with Arturo Saldívar and Manuel del Cid, teacher, Ciudad Obregón, April 8–9, 1989; Vicente Padilla Hernández in MG 1992:110–11.

26. Vicente Padilla Hernández in MG 1992:110–11.

27. Corbalá 1970:114, 121, 164–68; Estado de Sonora 1932:8; 1933:6–10; 1934:6, 16, 35–37.

28. Estado de Sonora 1932:8–10; Corbalá 1970:141–42; Ramírez 1988b:141; Guadarrama 1988a:166–72.

29. AGRA, exp. 23/8519, vol. 1, Bacum, Confederación de Asociaciones Agrícolas del Estado to Comisión Nacional Agraria (hereafter, CNA), Oct. 9, 1934; L. G. Antillón, Jesús Antonio Parada, A. Astiazarán, W. A. Ryan, et al. to Cárdenas, Oct. 13, 1934.

30. Ibid., and Arturo Orci, on behalf of Jesús Antonio Parada, to CNA, Oct. 19, 1934; Aguilar to Dept. Agrario, Jan. 12, 1935; J. Pérez et al., Comité Particular Ejecutivo, Campo 60, Bacum, to CNA, June 26, 1935; AGN-AP-LCR, exp. 404.1/964, Feliciano Mora Villalobos, Comité Particular Ejecutivo, Bacum, to Cárdenas, Jan. 17, June 22, 1935; E. Corella, gobernador interino, to Cárdenas, July 22, 1935.

31. The largest U.S. owners were B. F. and Asa J. Brunk, W. A. and J. J. Ryan, Z. O. Stocker, O. Herold, and Fred C. Hetschel. Others included Cornelius Whitney and W. R. Grace and Company. See USSD, 812.52/2036, Mexico City, Oct. 19, 1936; /2037, Oct. 26, 1936; /2063, Dec. 7, 1936; /2012, Guaymas, Oct. 5, 1936. On owner apprehension, 812.52/1975, March 19, 1936; /1938, Dec. 1935; also *El Pueblo*, Hermosillo, Feb. 26, 1936.

32. USSD, 812.52/2107, Guaymas, Jan. 29, 1937; Aurora Ayala de Ayón in MG 1992:64.

33. USSD, 812.52/2000, Mexico City, Sept. 25; /2051, Nov. 19;/2952, Nov. 17, 1936; /2063, Dec. 7, 1936; /2012, Guaymas, Oct. 5, 1936; /2024, Oct. 14, 1936; /2028, Oct. 15, 1936; /2034, Washington, D.C., Oct. 31, 1936. On Mexican owners, AGN-AP-LCR, exp. 404.2/41, Rafael G. Esquer et al. to Sec. de Agricultura, May 1937.

34. USSD, 812.52/2106, Guaymas, Jan. 29, 1936; /1379, March 1; /1382, March 31, 1937; AAGES, exp. 243.4/"1936," Conflictos, Yocupicio to Procurador de la Defensa del Trabajo, Feb. 5, 1937; *Excelsior*, Feb. 4, 1937; AGN-AP-LCR, exp. 534.1/8, multiple correspondence from unions supporting López and those supporting Yocupicio, 1937. On these struggles between unions, federal teachers always supported the CTM. See, for example, ibid., Gabriel González, Unión de Maestros Federales, Magdalena, to Cárdenas, May 21, 1937; Sixto Duarte, Comisariado Ejidal, Pitiquito, Altar, March 3, 1937. On repression of teachers, all correspondence in exps. 423.6/873, 542.2/859, AAGES, exp. 411.12"37"/2.

35. Ibid., exp. 534.1/8, multiple correspondence, June–July 1937; USSD, 812.52/1356, Guaymas, May 5, 1937; Vicente Padilla in MG 1992:112.

36. AGN-AP-LCR, exp. 534.1/8, VLT to Ignacio García Téllez, Sept. 27, 1937; exp. 533.11/1, "Acuerdo . . . para resolver el problema agrario en la región Yaqui," Oct. 21, 1937; Hewitt Alcántara 1978:125, 165; USSD, 812.52/1410, Guaymas, Nov. 29, 1937; Guadarrama 1988c:252.

37. Vicente Padilla in MG 1992:114–15.

38. AHSEP-DER, exp. 249.20, LM, dir., SEP Sonora, Jan. 23, 1935; exp. 249.7, LM, Circular, Feb. 25, 1935, "Informe," Jan.-Feb. 1935; exp. 209.7, LM, "Informe," Nov. 1935; AGN-AP-LCR, exp. 534.1/8, multiple correspondence, 1937–38; exp. 534.6/873, March 1938. On repression of teachers, see also exps. 423.6/873, 542.2/859; AAGES, exp. 411.12"37"/2.

39. AHSEP-DER, exp. 249.7, F. Corzo, insp. regional, "Informe," Nov. 1935; exp. 208.1.2, LeM, insp., Nov. 1935; exp. 249.7, "Eventos atléticos . . . Empalme," Bloque Juvenil Revolu-

cionario, Félix Sánchez Corral, Feb. 1935; exp. 249.23, Roberto Sánchez Lima, promotor de educación física, Sonora, "Informes," April 30 and July 1, 1935.

40. AHSEP-DER, exp. 208.1.1, LeM, "Informe," Nov. 1935; exp. 249.29, LM, dir., SEP Sonora, to SEP, Jan. 23 and July 23, 1935; exp. 249.7, SEP, Circular to Art. 123 schools, July 27, 1935.

41. AHSEP-DGEP, exp. 319.11, LeM, "Informe," Jan. 29, 1936; interview with Manuel del Cid.

42. AHSEP-DER, exp. 208.1.2, LeM, "Informe," Nov. 1935.

43. AHSEP-DGEP, exp. 319.11, LeM, "Informes," Jan., March, May 1936; interview with Manuel del Cid.

44. AHSEP-DGEP, exp. 319.11, LeM, "Informes," Jan., March, May 1936.

45. Ibid., AHSEP-DER, exp. 208.1.2, LeM, "Informe," Nov. 1935.

46. AGRA, exp. 23/8519, vol. 1, Bacum, Mora Villalobos, Comité Particular Ejecutivo, Sept. 15, 1934.

47. AHSEP-DGEP, exp. 319.1, LeM, "Informe," July 1936.

48. AGRA, exp.23/8519, vol. 1, Bacum, Mora Villalobos and A. Vallescillo, Comité Particular Ejecutivo, Sept. 15, 1934.

49. Information in this paragraph comes from Magaña's reports, interviews with Manuel del Cid, teacher, Arturo Saldívar, student in this period, and Marcelina Saldívar, also a student; AHSEP-DER, exp. 249.23, Roberto Sánchez Lima, promotor de educación física, Sonora, "Informe," July 1935.

50. On teachers and agriculture, interview with Manuel del Cid. Of 183,768,000 pesos of credit provided by the Banco Nacional de Crédito Ejidal between 1938 and 1940, 7,613,327 or 4 percent went to the Yaqui Valley ejidos. The major beneficiaries of credit in those years were the collective ejidos of La Laguna, Yucatán, Nueva Italia, Mexicali, and the Yaqui Valley (Sanderson 1981:121.) One of the strongest naysayers about the prospects for the ejido was U.S. consul Yepis in Guaymas (see USSD 812.52/3102, Aug. 10, 1938, 49). On reliance on animals, nature, and human power in the first years, interviews with Arturo Saldívar and Manuel del Cid.

51. On teachers and political leadership in ejidos, interviews with Arturo Saldívar and Manuel del Cid. On teachers, politics, and neglect of duties, AHSEP, exp. 15-26-200, Inspección Escolar Federal, Sonora, "Planes y programas de estudios," LeM, insp., Magdalena, Oct. 2, 1939. Magaña wanted teachers to be effective negotiators between communities and the state.

52. Interview with Marcelina Saldívar; and Marcelina Saldívar in MG 1992:89, 93.

53. Interviews with Arturo Saldívar and Manuel del Cid; AGN-AP-LCR, exp. 151.3/890,

multiple correspondence, 1938–1943. Among the settlements becoming incorporated towns, Colonia Irrigación became Villa Juárez. Cornejo notes in *La sierra y el viento* that the first thing people did when they "made a pueblo," was to lay out the sports field and build the school (104).

54. Interviews with Manuel del Cid and Arturo Saldívar.

55. Interviews with Manuel del Cid, Arturo Saldívar, and Marcelina Saldívar; AHSEP-DGEP, exp. 319.1, LeM, "Informe," Jan. 1936; AHSEP, exp. 15-26-200, Inspección Escolar Federal, Sonora, "Planes y programas de estudios," LeM, Magdalena, Oct.2, 1939. On the pillorying of teachers for doing politics rather than teaching, *El Imparcial*, Hermosillo, Jan. 19 and June 21, 1939.

56. Interviews with Arturo Saldívar and Marcelina Saldívar.

57. Interview with Marcelina Saldívar.

58. See, for example, Aurora Ayala de Ayón in MG 1992:67; Marcelina Saldívar, 87; interview with Marcelina Saldívar.

59. See chapter 3; *El Imparcial*, Jan. 13, 1939; multiple correspondence in AGN-AP-LCR, exp. 404.1/6774.22, 1938; exp. 404.1/7, 1937–38; *El Popular*, June 6 and 7, 1938; Aurora Ayala de Ayón in MG 1992:66–67.

60. Hewitt Alcántara 1978:166, 173; Francisco Schwarsbeck Ramírez in MG 1992:229–33; interviews with Arturo Saldívar and Manuel del Cid, Ciudad Obregón; interview with Norman Borlaug, Stillwater, Oklahoma, May 6, 1992. On Normalistas replacing other teachers, interview with Manuel del Cid and AHSEP, exp.IV/130(IV-5) (421.5), Marcial Ruiz Vargas, sec. XXVI, STERM, Hermosillo, to SEP, March 11, 1939.

61. Information from AGN-AP-MAC, exp. 151.3/82, Ruben Morales and Luis León to Secretaría de Hacienda, Jan. 15, 1942; Fidel Velásquez, Francisco J. Macín, CTM, to Avila Camacho, Oct. 13, 1942; Saturnino A. Saldívar, diputado federal, to Avila Camacho, Jan. 19, 1945; Hewitt Alcántara 1978:168–72; Sanderson 1981:145–46.

62. MG 1992:115–19; Sanderson 1981:139–42; Hewitt Alcántara 1978:174–200.

63. On critique of the reparto by participants and observers, see MG 1992:11–13, 19, 21–23, 34–35, 157–59; interviews with Arturo Saldívar and Manuel del Cid. Hewitt Alcántara (1978:166–75) analyzes how problems integral to the ejidal structure gave rise to corruption, inequities, and discontent.

64. Interview with Arturo Saldívar.

65. On politicians blaming the left ("los comunistas"), see Hewitt Alcántara 1978:173–74.

66. On the 1975 agrarian movement, see, among others, Sanderson 1981:157–202; McGuire 1986:79–107.

CHAPTER 8
THE SCHOOL, HEGEMONY, AND CIVIL SOCIETY

1. *Boletín de la SEP* 1, no. 3 (1923): 256.

2. The question of teacher resistance to or enforcement of the state's order is an excellent topic for research, especially in relation to the period between 1940 and 1970. For teachers as agents of the state in Chiapas, see Wasserstrom 1983; for teachers in opposition politics, see Loyo Brambila 1979; Carr 1994:326–52; Foweraker 1993; and Street 1992.

3. On U.S.–Mexican relations during World War II and its aftermath, see Niblo 1995.

BIBLIOGRAPHY

ARCHIVAL SOURCES

MEXICO CITY

AND	Archivo de la Defensa Nacional
AEC	Archivo de Ezequiel Chávez
AGN	Archivo General de la Nación
AGN-AP-OC	Acervos Presidentes, Fondo Obregón Calles
AGN-AP-EPG	Acervos Presidentes, Fondo Emilio Portes Gil
AGN-AP-OR	Acervos Presidentes, Fondo Ortiz Rubio
AGN-AP-ALR	Acervos Presidentes, Fondo Abelardo Rodríguez
AGN-AP-LCR	Acervos Presidentes, Fondo Lázaro Cárdenas del Río
AGN-AP-MAC	Acervos Presidentes, Fondo Manuel Avila Camacho
AGN-G	Gobernación
AHSEP	Archivo Histórico de la Secretaría de Educación Pública
AHSEP-DECI	Departamento de Educación y Cultura Indígena
AHSEP-DE	Departamento Escolar
AHSER-DER	Departamento de Escuelas Rurales
AHSEP-DGEP	Dirección General de Educación Primaria Urbana y Rural en los Estados y Territorios
AHSEP-AP-ERF	Archivos Particulares—Escuelas Rurales Federales
AHSEP-ERN	Escuelas Rurales Normales
AGRA	Archivo General de la Reforma Agraria

PUEBLA

AEEP	Archivo Estatal de Educación Pública, Puebla
ARA-P	Archivo de la Reforma Agraria—Puebla
AMT	Archivo Municipal de Tecamachalco
AMTO	Archivo Municipal de Tetela de Ocampo

AMX   Archivo Municipal de Xochitlán
AMZ   Archivo Municipal de Zacapoaxtla

SONORA

AES   Archivo del Estado de Sonora
AAGES   Archivo Administrativo General del Estado de Sonora

TUCSON, ARIZONA

ASM   Arizona State Museum Archives
ASM-ESFN   Edward Spicer Field Notes (Potam, Valle Yaqui)
ASM-ESP   Edward Spicer Papers
ASM-WWP   William Willard Papers

WASHINGTON, D.C.

USSD   U.S. State Department Records relating to the Internal Affairs of
              Mexico, 1930–40
USWD   U.S. War Department Military Intelligence G-2 Reports

PERIODICALS

Alma Sonorense. Federación de Agrupaciones de Maestros Federales de Sonora.
Aspiraciones. Escuela Rural Normal, Ures.
Boletín de Educación. Veracruz, Mexico City.
Boletín Estadística del Estado de Puebla. Puebla.
Boletín de la SEP. Mexico City.
El Diario de Puebla. Puebla.
Excelsior. Mexico City.
La Fogata. Puebla.
El Heraldo del Yaqui. Ciudad Obregón.
El Imparcial. Hermosillo.
El Intruso. Cananea.
El Maestro Rural. Mexico City.
El Popular. Mexico City.
El Pueblo. Hermosillo.
La Opinión. Puebla.
Reforma Escolar. Maestros de Magdalena, Sonora.
Revista Futuro. Mexico City.
El Universal. Mexico City.
El Universal Ilustrado. Mexico City.

INTERVIEWS

Rafael Alcántara Cárcamo. Zacapoaxtla, Feb. 28–March 6, 1993.
Victor Alva. Puebla, July 22, 1989, and July 2, 1991.

Agustina Barrojas de Caro. Puebla, July 6, 1991.

Norman Borlaug. Stillwater, Oklahoma, May 6, 1992.

Gilberto Bosques. Mexico City, May 15, 1987.

Manuel Bravo Bañuelos. Tecamachalco, July 25, 1989, and July 1, 1991.

Horacio Caro. Puebla, July 6, 1991.

Ebundio Carreón. Comaltepec, March 1, 1993.

Moisés Chávez Rosario. San Miguel Tzinacapan, July 1993.

Porfirio Cordero. Puebla, July 14, 1987.

Juan Cuamatzin. Tetela, April 17, 1984.

Manuel del Cid. Ciudad Obregón, April 8–9, 1989.

Manuel Ferra Martínez. Hermosillo, May 7, 1987.

Elvira Figueroa. Hermosillo, May 8, 1987.

Faustino Hernández. Puebla, March 20, 1987.

Padre López Yescas. Hermosillo, May 12, 1989.

Reyna Manzano. Puebla, March 15, 1987, July 12–15, 1989, and July 5, 1991.

Natalia Molina. Zacapoaxtla, Jan. 20, 1986.

Leon Ramírez. Puebla, March 17, 1987.

Eduardo Ramírez Díaz. Puebla, March 18, 1987.

Donna Rivera. Xochiapulco, Feb. 26, 1993.

Socorro Rivera. Puebla, May 16, 21, 1984.

Celia Ruedeflores. Hermosillo, April 6, 1989.

Marcelina Saldívar de Murrieta. Hermosillo, April 7, 1989.

Arturo Saldívar. Ciudad Obregón, April 8, 1989.

Rafael Santa Cruz Reyes. Hermosillo, May 3, 1987.

Atalo de Santillán Aldana. Puebla, July 11, 1987.

Rosamund Spicer. Tucson, May 21, 1993.

Francisco Toral. Zacapoaxtla, Feb. 28, 1993.

Filadelfo Vázquez. Zacapoaxtla, March 2, 1993.

WORKS CITED

Acuña Cruz, C. 1985. *Juan Navarrete: Medio siglo de historia sonorense.* Hermosillo.

Adamson, Walter L. 1980. *Hegemony and Revolution: A Study of Antonio Gramsci's Political and Cultural Theory.* Berkeley: University of California Press.

Aguilar Camín, Héctor. 1977. *La frontera nómada: Sonora y la Revolución Mexicana.* Mexico: Siglo Veintiuno.
———. 1982. "The Relevant Tradition: Sonoran Leaders in the Revolution." In Brading, *Caudillo and Peasant.*

Aguirre Cinta, Rafael. 1926. *Historia de México.* Mexico: Sociedad de Ediciones y Librería Franco-Americana, S.A.

Almada, Francisco. 1971. *La Revolución en el Estado de Sonora.* Mexico City: Instituto de Estudios Históricos de la Revolución Mexicana.

Almada Bay, Ignacio. 1992. "Conflictos y contactos del Estado y de la iglesia en Sonora." In Felipe Mora Arellano, ed., *Coloquio sobre las relaciones del Estado*.

Alonso, Ana María. 1995. *Thread of Blood: Colonialism, Revolution, and Gender on Mexico's Northern Frontier*. Tucson: University of Arizona Press.

Althusser, Louis. 1975. *Lenin and Philosophy and Other Essays*. New York: Monthly Review Press.

Alvarado, Salvador. [1916] 1962. *El Primero Congreso Feminista de Yucatán, convocado por el C. Gobernador y Comandante Militar del Estado, Gral. don Salvador Alvarado*. Reprint, Mérida: Talleres Tipográficos del Ateneo Peninsular.
———. 1920. *Problemas de Mexico*. San Antonio, Tex.
———. 1962. "Carta al pueblo de Yucatán publicada en *La Voz de la Revolución*, 5 de mayo de 1916, aniversario de gloria para la patria mexicana." In *La cuestión de la tierra, 1915–1917: Colección de folletos para la historia de la Revolución mexicana, dirigida por Jesús Silva Herzog*. Mexico: Instituto Mexicano de Investigaciones Económicas.

Anderson, Benedict. 1991. *Imagined Communities: Reflections on the Origin and Spread of Nationalism*. Revised edition. London: Verso.

Anguiano, Arturo. 1975. *El estado y la política obrera del cardenismo*. Mexico: Era.

Aranda Bezaury, Josefina, ed. 1988. *Las mujeres en el campo*. Oaxaca: Universidad Autónoma Benito Juárez de Oaxaca.

Arizpe, Lourdes. 1989. *Parentesco y economía en una sociedad nahua: Nican Pehua Zacatipan*. Mexico: Conaculta/Instituto Nacional Indigenista.

Ayala, Raul, and Carlos Schaffer Vázquez. 1991. *Salud y seguridad social: Crisis, ajuste, y grupos vulnerables*. Mexico: Instituto Nacional de Salud Pública.

Bailey, David C. 1974. *Viva Cristo Rey: The Cristero Rebellion and the Church–State Conflict in Mexico*. Austin: University of Texas Press.

Bantjes, Adrian A. 1991. "Politics, Class, and Culture in Post-Revolutionary Mexico: Cardenismo and Sonora, 1929–1940." Ph.D. diss., University of Texas, Austin.
———. 1994. "Burning Saints, Molding Minds: Iconoclasm, Civic Ritual, and the Failed Cultural Revolution." In Beezley, Martin, and French, eds., *Rituals of Rule*.

Bartell, Gilbert D. 1965. "Directed Culture Change among the Sonoran Yaqui." Ph.D. diss., University of Arizona.

Bartra, Roger, ed. 1978. *Caciquismo y poder político en el México rural*. Fourth edition. Mexico: Siglo Veintiuno.

Bassols, Narciso. 1964. *Obras*. Mexico: Fondo de Cultura Económica.

Bastian, Jean Pierre. 1989. *Los disidentes, sociedades protestantes y revolución en México, 1872–1911*. Mexico: Colegio de México.

Bauer, Arnold. 1990. "Millers and Grinders: Technology and Household Economy in Meso-America." *Agricultural History* 64, no. 1:1–17.

Beaucage, Pierre. 1973a. "Antropologie economique des communautés indigenes de la Sierra Norte de Puebla (Mexique) Les villages de basse montagne." *Canadian Review of Sociology and Anthropology* 10, no. 2:114–31.
———. 1973b. "Antropologie economique des communautés indigenes de la Sierra Norte de Puebla (Mexique) 2. Les villages de haute montagne." *Canadian Review of Sociology and Anthropology* 10, no. 4:290–303.

Becker, Marjorie. 1987. "Black and White and Color: Cardenismo and the Search for a Campesino Ideology." *Comparative Studies in Society and History* 29:453–65.
———. 1994. "Torching La Purísima, Dancing at the Altar: The Construction of Revolutionary Hegemony in Michoacán, 1934–1940." In Joseph and Nugent, *Everyday Forms.*
———. 1995. *Setting the Virgin on Fire: Lázaro Cárdenas, Michoacán Campesinos, and the Redemption of the Mexican Revolution.* Berkeley: University of California Press.

Beezley, William H., and Judith Ewell, eds. 1987. *The Human Tradition in Latin America: The Twentieth Century.* Wilmington, Del.: Scholarly Resources.

Beezley, William H., Cheryl English Martin, and William E. French, eds. 1994. *Rituals of Rule, Rituals of Resistance: Public Celebration and Popular Culture in Mexico.* Wilmington, Del.: Scholarly Resources.

Benjamin, Thomas. 1989. *A Rich Land, a Poor People: Politics and Society in Modern Chiapas.* Albuquerque: University of New Mexico Press.

Benjamin, Thomas, and M. Wasserman, eds. 1990. *Provinces of the Revolution: Essays on Regional Mexican History, 1910–1929.* Albuquerque: University of New Mexico Press.

Bethell, Leslie, ed. 1989. *Colonial Spanish America.* Cambridge: Cambridge University Press.

Blanco, José Joaquín. 1977. *Se llamaba Vasconcelos: Una evocación crítica.* Mexico: Fondo de Cultura Económica.

Boggs, Karl. 1984. *The Two Revolutions: Gramsci and the Dilemmas of Western Marxism.* Boston: South End Press.

Bonilla, José María. 1918a. *Derechos civiles.* Mexico: Herrero Hermanos.
———. 1918b. *Derechos individuales.* Mexico: Herrero Hermanos.
———. 1923. *Evolución del pueblo mexicano.* Mexico: Herrero Hermanos.

Brading, David. 1982. *Caudillo and Peasant in the Mexican Revolution.* Cambridge: Cambridge University Press.

Bremauntz, Alberto. 1943. *La educación socialista en Mexico: Antecedentes y fundamentos de la reforma de 1934.* Mexico: Imprenta Rivadeneyra.

Britton, John A. 1976. *Educación y radicalismo en México.* 2 vols. Mexico: SepSetentas.
———. 1979. "Teacher Unionization and the Corporate State in Mexico, 1931–1945." *Hispanic American Historical Review* 59:674–90.
———, ed. 1994. *Molding the Hearts and Minds: Education, Communications, and Social Change in Latin America.* Wilmington, Del.: Scholarly Resources.

Brown, Jonathan C., and Alan Knight, eds. 1992. *The Mexican Petroleum Industry in the Twentieth Century.* Austin: University of Texas Press.

Caballero, Manuel. 1891. *Primer Directorio General del Estado de Puebla.* Puebla.

Cabrera Oropeza, Jenaro. 1972. "Paulina Maraver Cortés." *Bohemia Poblana,* Jan., 8–9.

Cadena, Longinos. 1921. *Elementos de historia general y de historia patria.* 2 vols. Mexico: Herrero Hermanos.

Camacho Sandoval, Salvador. 1988. "Los maestros socialistas y la expropriación petrolera." *El Unicornio, El Sol del Centro,* Aguascalientes, no. 2271 (March 21).
———. 1991. *Controversia educativa entre la ideología y la fe: La educación socialista en la historia de Aguascalientes.* Mexico: Consejo Nacional para la Cultura y las Artes, Serie Regiones.

Camou Healy, Ernesto, Rocío Guadarrama, and José Carlos Ramírez. 1988. *Historia contemporanea de Sonora, 1929–1984.* Second edition. Hermosillo: Colegio de Sonora.

Camp, Roderic A., Charles A. Hale, and Josefina Zoraida Vázquez, eds. 1992. *Los intelectuales y el poder en México.* Mexico and Los Angeles: Colegio de México and UCLA Latin American Studies Center.

Candañedo, Baudelio. 1971. "Professor Roberto Quiroz Martínez." *Bohemia Poblana,* Jan., 8–9.

Cárdenas, Lázaro. 1940. *Obras, Apuntes.* 1913–1940. Vol. 1. Mexico: Departamento de Asuntos Indígenas.

Carol, Valeria. 1979. *La vida fascinante de Juan Crisóstomo Bonilla.* Mexico: Editorial del Magisterio Benito Juárez.

Carr, Barry. 1994. "The Fate of the Vanguard under a Revolutionary State: Marxism's Contribution to the Construction of the Great Arch." In Joseph and Nugent, *Everyday Forms.*

Castillo, Isidro. 1965. *México y su revolución educativa.* Vol. 1. Mexico: Editorial Pax-México, Librería Carlos Cesarman, S.A.

Castro Cancio, Jorge. 1935. *Historia de la patria.* Mexico: Editorial Patria.

Chávez Camacho, Armanedo. 1983. *Juan Navarrete: Un hombre enviado por Dios.* Mexico: Porrua.

Civera, Alicia. 1993. "La educación socialista en la Escuela Regional Campesina de Tenería, Estado de México, 1933–1935." Tesis de maestría, Departamento de Investigaciones Educativas, Mexico.

Cockcroft, James. 1967. "El maestro en la revolución mexicana." *Historia Mexicana* 16:565–87.

Comité Directivo Estatal—P R I. 1974. Centro de Estudios Políticos, Económicos, y Sociales. *Dinámica política, económica y social del estado de Puebla.* Vol 2. Puebla.

Corbalá, Manuel S. 1970. *Rodolfo Elías Calles: Perfiles de un sonorense.* Hermosillo.

Córdova, Arnaldo. 1972. *La ideología de la Revolución Mexicana: La formación del nuevo régimen.* Mexico: Era.
———. 1974a. *La política de masas del cardenismo.* Mexico: Era.
———. 1974b. "Los maestros rurales en el cardenismo." *Cuadernos Políticos* 2:77–92.

Cornejo, Gerardo. 1977. *La sierra y el viento.* Hermosillo: Arte y libros.

Corrigan, Philip, and Derek Sayer. 1985. *The Great Arch: English State Formation as Cultural Revolution.* Oxford: Blackwell.

Crumrine, Ross. 1977. *The Mayo Indians of Sonora: A People That Refuse to Die.* Tucson: University of Arizona Press.

Dabdoub, Claudio. 1964. *Historia del Valle del Yaqui.* Mexico: Editorial Porrua.

De Certeau, Michel. 1992. *The Practice of Everyday Life.* Berkeley: University of California Press.

De Grazia, Victoria. 1992. *How Facism Ruled Women: Italy, 1922–1945.* Berkeley: University of California Press.

Del Castillo, Porfirio. 1953. *Puebla y Tlaxcala en los días de la Revolución.* Mexico: Zavala.

Delgadillo, Daniel. 1920. *Adelante.* Mexico: Herrero Hermanos.

Dennis, Phillip A. 1987. *Intervillage Conflict in Oaxaca: San Andrés Zautla and Santo Tomás Mazaltepec.* New Brunswick, N.J.: Rutgers University Press.

Durand, Pierre. 1986. *Nanacatlán: Sociedad campesina y lucha de clases en México.* Mexico: Fondo de Cultura Económica.

Eisenstadt, S., and R. Lemarchand, eds. 1981. *Political Clientelism, Patronage, and Development.* Beverly Hills, Calif.: Sage, 1981.

Ekloff, Ben. 1986. *Russian Peasant Schools: Officialdom, Village Culture, and Popular Pedagogy, 1861–1914.* Berkeley: University of California Press.
———. 1990. "Peasants and Schools." In Ekloff and Frank, *The World of the Russian Peasant.*

Ekloff, Ben, and Stephen P. Frank, eds. 1990. *The World of the Russian Peasant: Post-Emancipation Culture and Society.* Boston: Unwin Hyman.

Encinas Blanco, Angel. 1985. "El movimiento cristero de Luis Ibarra en Granados." In *Memoria: IX Simposio de Historia de Sonora.* Hermosillo: Instituto de Investigaciones Históricas, Universidad Autónoma de Sonora.

Erasmus, Charles. 1978. "Cultural Change in Northwest Mexico." In Erasmus, Miller, and Faron, *Contemporary Change in Traditional Communities.*

Erasmus, Charles, Solomon Miller, and Louis C. Faron, eds. 1978. *Contemporary Change in Traditional Communities of Mexico and Peru.* Vol. 3. Urbana: University of Illinois Press.

Esquivel, Laura. 1992. *Like Water for Chocolate.* Translated by Carl Christensen and Thomas Christensen. New York: Doubleday.

Estado de Puebla. 1908. *Memoria instructiva y documentada que el Jefe del Departamento Ejecutivo del Estado presenta al XX Congreso.* Puebla.
———. 1910. *Memoria instructiva y documentada que el Jefe del Departamento Ejecutivo del Estado presenta al XXI Congreso.* Puebla.
———. Secretaría de la Reforma Agraria. 1984. *Actualización cartográfica y de recursos para el desarrollo del Estado de Puebla. La tenencia de la tierra: Catálogo de la propiedad definitiva ejidal y comunal.* Puebla.

Estado de Sonora. 1932. *Primer informe rendido por el Gobnerador Constitucional del Estado, Rodolfo Elías Calles, a la XXXI Legislatura de Sonora.* Hermosillo.
———. 1933. *Informe que el C. Rodolfo Elías Calles, Gobernador Constitucional del Estado Libre y Soberano de Sonora rindió ante la Honorable Legislatura del mismo con la fecha 16 de septiembre de 1933.* Mexico City.
———. 1934. *Informe rendido por Rodolfo Elías Calles, Gobernador Constitucional del Estado ante la XXXII Legislatura local.* Hermosillo.
———. 1938. *Informe que rinde el C. Gral. Román Yocupicio, Gobernador Constitucional del Estado de Sonora, al G. Congreso del Estado, sobre la labor administrativa realizada durante el período comprendido de septiembre de 1937 a 16 de septiembre de 1938.* Hermosillo.

Ezpeleta, Justa, and Elsie Rockwell. 1983. "Escuela y clases subalternas." *Cuadernos Políticos* 37:70–80.

Fabila, Alfonso. 1940. *Las tribus yaquis de Sonora. Su cultura y anhelada autodeterminación.* Mexico: Departamento de Asuntos Indígenas.
———. 1949. *Sierra Norte de Puebla: Contribución para su estudio.* Mexico: SEP.

Fell, Claude. 1989. *José Vasconcelos: Los años del águila, 1920–1925: Educación, cultura, Iberoamericanismo en el México pos-revolucionario.* Mexico: UNAM.

Feyermuth Enciso, Graciela. 1988. "Atención del Parto: Modificaciones en las prácticas tradicionales y su impacto en la salud." In Aranda Bezaury, *Las mujeres en el campo.*

Figueroa Valenzuela, Alejandro. 1992. "Identidad étnica y persistencia cultural: Un estudio de la sociedad y de la cultura de los yaquis y de los mayos." Ph.D. diss., Centro de Estudios Históricos, Colegio de México.

Foucault, Michel. 1979. *Discipline and Punish.* Harmondsworth, Eng.: Penguin.
———. 1980. *History of Sexuality.* vol I. New York: Pantheon.

Foweraker, Joe. 1993. *Popular Mobilization in Mexico: The Teachers' Movement, 1977–1987.* Cambridge: Cambridge University Press.

Fowler-Salamini, Heather. 1982. "Revolutionary Caudillos in the 1920s: Francisco Mújica and Adalberto Tejeda." In Brading, *Caudillo and Peasant.*
———. 1990. "Tamaulipas: Land Reform and the State." In Benjamin and Wasserman, *Provinces of the Revolution.*

Fowler-Salamini, Heather, and Mary Kay Vaughan. 1994. *Women of the Mexican Countryside, 1850–1990: Creating Spaces, Shaping Transitions.* Tucson: University of Arizona Press.

Friedlander, Judith. 1975. *Being Indian in Hueyapán: A Study of Forced Identity in Contemporary Mexico.* New York: St. Martin's Press.
———. 1994. "Doña Zeferina Barreto." In Fowler-Salamini and Vaughan, *Women of the Mexican Countryside.*

Furet, François, and Jacques Ozouf. 1983. *Reading and Writing in France: Literacy from Calvin to Jules Ferry.* Cambridge: Cambridge University Press.

Galante, María Cristina, Paola Sesia-Lewis, and Virginia Alejandre. 1988. "Mujeres y parteras: Protagonistas activas en la relación entre medicina moderna y medicina tradicional." In Aranda Bezaury, *Las mujeres en el campo.*

Galván, Luz Elena. 1988. "La soledad compartida: Una historia de maestros, 1908–1910." Ph.D. diss., Universidad Iberoamericana.

García Martínez, Bernardo. 1987. *Los pueblos de la Sierra: El poder y el espacio entre los indios del norte de Puebla hasta 1700.* Mexico: Colegio de México.

García Téllez, Ignacio. 1935. *La socialización de la cultura: Seis meses de acción educativa.* Mexico: La Impresora.

Garrido, Luis Javier. 1982. *El partido de la revolución institucionalizada: La formación del nuevo estado en México (1928–1945).* Mexico: Siglo XXI Editores.

Gibson, Charles. 1989. "Indians under Spanish Rule." In Bethell, *Colonial Spanish America.*

Glockner, Julio. 1982. *La presencia del estado en el medio rural: Puebla (1929–1941).* Puebla: Universidad Autónoma de Puebla, Centro de Investigaciones Filosóficas.

Goody, Jack. 1968. *Literacy in Traditional Societies.* Cambridge: Cambridge University Press.

Gramsci, Antonio. 1971. *Selections from the Prison Notebooks, 1929–35.* Edited and translated by Quintin Hoare and Geoffrey Nowell-Smith. New York: International Publishers.

Gruzinski, Serge. 1989. *Man-gods in the Mexican Highlands: Indian Power and Colonial Society, 1520–1800.* Translated by Eileen Corrigan. Stanford: Stanford University Press.

Guadarrama, María Teresa, and Ruth Piedrasanta Herrero. 1988. "El papel de las mujeres en la medicina popular y tradicional." In Aranda Bezaury, *Las mujeres en el campo.*

Guadarrama, Rocío. 1988a. "La reorganización de la sociedad." In Camou Healy, Guadarrama, and Ramírez, *Historia contemporanea de Sonora.*
———. 1988b. "Los cambios en la política." In Camou Healy, Guadarrama, and Ramírez, *Historia contemporanea de Sonora.*
———. 1988c. "La integración institucional." In Camou Healy, Guadarrama, and Ramírez, *Historia contemporanea de Sonora.*

Guevara Niebla, Gilberto. 1985. *La educación socialista en México.* Mexico: SEP/ Ediciones El Caballito.

Hamilton, Nora. 1982. *The Limits of State Autonomy: Post-Revolutionary Mexico.* Princeton: Princeton University Press.

Harvey, David. 1990. *The Condition of Post-Modernity: An Inquiry into the Origins of Cultural Change.* Oxford: Blackwell.

Hewitt Alcántara, Cynthia. 1978. *La modernización de la agricultura mexicana, 1940–1970.* Mexico: Siglo Veintiuno.

Hobsbawm, Eric. 1983. "Mass Producing Traditions: Europe, 1870–1914." In Hobsbawm and Ranger, eds., *The Invention of Tradition.*

Hobsbawm, Eric, and Terrence Ranger, eds. 1983. *The Invention of Tradition.* Cambridge: Cambridge University Press.

Holden, William C. 1936. "Studies of the Yaqui Indians of Sonora, Mexico." *Texas Technological College Bulletin* 12, no. 1.

Hu-DeHart, Evelyn. 1981. *Missionaries, Miners, and Indians: Spanish Contact with the Yaqui Nation of Northwestern New Spain, 1533–1820.* Tucson: University of Arizona Press.
———. 1982. "Racism and Anti-Chinese Persecution in Sonora, Mexico, 1876–1932." *Amerasia* 9, no. 2:1–28.
———. 1984. *Yaqui Resistance and Survival.* Madison: University of Wisconsin Press.
———. 1988. "Peasant Rebellion in the Northwest: The Yaqui Indians of Sonora, 1740–1976." In Katz, *Riot, Rebellion, and Revolution.*

Johnson, R. J., ed. 1994. *Dictionary of Human Geography.* Cambridge: Cambridge University Press.

Joseph, Gilbert. 1982. "Caciquismo and Revolution: Carrillo Puerto in Yucatán." In Brading, *Caudillo and Peasant*.

Joseph, Gilbert, and Daniel Nugent, eds. 1994. *Everyday Forms of State Formation: Revolution and the Negotiation of Rule in Modern Mexico*. Durham, N.C.: Duke University Press.

Jrade, Ramón. 1980. "Counterrevolution in Mexico: The Cristero Movement in Social and Historical Perspective." Ph.D. diss., Brown University.

Kapferer, Bruce. 1988. *Legends of People, Myths of State: Violence, Intolerance, and Political Culture in Sri Lanka and Australia*. Washington, D.C.: Smithsonian Institution Press.

Katz, Friedrich, ed. 1988. *Riot, Rebellion, and Revolution: Rural Social Conflict in Mexico*. Princeton: Princeton University Press.

Kaufman Purcell, Susan. 1981. "Mexico: Clientelism, Corporatism, and Political Stability." In Eisenstadt and Lemarchand, eds., *Political Clientelism*.

Kelley, Jane Holden. 1978. *Yaqui Women: Contemporary Life Histories*. Lincoln: University of Nebraska Press.

Keremitsis, Dawn. 1983. "Del metate al molino: La mujer mexicana de 1910 a 1940." *Historia Mexicana* 33:285–305.

Knight, Alan. 1985. "The Mexican Revolution: Bourgeois? Nationalist? Or Just a 'Great Rebellion'?" *Bulletin of Latin American Research* 4, no. 2:1–37.
———. 1990a. *The Mexican Revolution*. 2 vols. Lincoln: University of Nebraska Press.
———. 1990b. "Revolutionary Project, Recalcitrant People: Mexico, 1910–1940." In Jaime E. Rodríguez O., *The Revolutionary Process in Mexico*. Los Angeles: UCLA Latin America Center Publications.
———. 1990c. "Interpretaciones recientes de la Revolución Mexicana." *Memorias del Simposio de Historiografía Mexicanista*, 193–210. Mexico: Comité Mexicano de Ciencias Históricas, Gobierno del Estado de Morelos, Instituto de Investigaciones Históricas, UNAM.
———. 1992a. "Intellectuals in the Mexican Revolution." In Camp, Hale, and Vázquez, eds., *Los intelectuales y el poder en México*.
———. 1992b. "The Politics of the Expropriation." In Brown and Knight, eds., *The Mexican Petroleum Industry*.
———. 1994a. "The Cardenismo: Juggernaut or Jalopy?" *Journal of Latin American Studies* 26:73–107.
———. 1994b. "Popular Culture and the Revolutionary State in Mexico, 1910–1940." *Hispanic American Historical Review* 74, no. 3:393–444.

Laclau, Ernesto, and Chantal Mouffe. 1986. *Hegemony and Socialist Strategy: Towards a Radical Democratic Politics*. London: Verso.

LaFrance, David. 1989. *The Mexican Revolution in Puebla, 1908–1913*. Wilmington, Del.: Scholarly Resources.

Lears, Jackson. 1985. "The Concept of Cultural Hegemony: Problems and Possibilities."
American Historical Review 90, no. 3:576–93.

Lerner, Victoria. 1979a. "Historia de la reforma educativa, 1933–1945." *Historia Mexicana*
29:91–132.
———. 1979b. *Historia de la Revolución Mexicana.* Vol. 17, *La educación socialista.*
Mexico: Colegio de México.

Levinson, Bradley, Douglas Foley, and Dorothy Holland, eds. 1996. *The Cultural Production of the Educated Person: Critical Ethnographies of Schooling and Local Practice.*
Albany: State University of New York.

Lewis, Oscar. 1951. *Life in a Mexican Village: Tepoztlán Restudied.* Urbana: University of
Illinois Press.

Lira González, Andrés. 1982. "Indian Communities in Mexico City: The Parcialidades de
Tenochtitlán and Tlatelolco, 1812–1919." Ph.D. diss., State University of New York,
Stony Brook.

Lomnitz Adler, Claudio. 1992. *Exits from the Labyrinth: Culture and Ideology in the Mexican National Space.* Berkeley: University of California Press.

Loyo, Engracia. 1984. "Lectura para el pueblo." *Historia Mexicana* 33, no. 3:298–345.
———. 1988. "La lectura en México, 1920–1940." In *Historia de la lectura en México.*
Seminario de Historia de la Educación en México de El Colegio de México. Mexico:
Colegio de México and Ediciónes de Ermitano.
———. 1991. "Escuelas Rurales Artículo 123 (1917–1940)." *Historia Mexicana* 40, no.
2:299–336.

Loyo, Engracia, and Valentina Torres Septien. 1992. "Radicalización y conservadurismo:
Dos orientaciones en los textos escolares, 1920–1940." In Camp, Hale, and Vázquez,
Los intelectuales y el poder en México.

Loyo Brambila, Aurora. 1979. *El movimiento magisterial de 1958 en México.* Mexico: Era.

Lucio, Gabriel. 1935a. *Simiente: Libro Tercero para Escuelas Rurales.* Mexico: SEP.
———. 1935b. *Libro Cuatro.* Mexico: SEP.

Mallon, Florencia. 1991. "Los héroes anónimos: Xochiapulco ante la historia," and "Cinco
de Mayo: Pugna en la Sierra." In Donna Rivera, ed., *Xochiapulco: Una gloria
olvidada.*
———. 1994a. "Exploring the Origins of Democratic Patriarchy in Mexico: Gender and
Popular Resistance in the Puebla Highlands, 1850–1876." In Fowler-Salamini and
Vaughan, *Women of the Mexican Countryside.*
———. 1994b. "Reflections on the Ruins: Everyday Forms of State Formation in
Nineteenth-Century Mexico." In Joseph and Nugent, *Everyday Forms.*
———. 1995. *Peasant and Nation: The Making of Postcolonial Mexico and Peru.* Berkeley:
University of California Press.

Malpica, Samuel. 1980. "La derrota de la FROC en Atlixco, 1931–1939." In *Memorias del encuentro sobre la historia del movimiento obrero*. Vol. 2. Puebla: Centro de Investigaciones Históricas del Movimiento Obrero de la Universidad Autónoma de Puebla.

Márquez Carrillo, Jesús. 1983. "Los orígenes de Avilacamachismo: Una arqueología de fuerzas en la constitución de un poder regional: El estado de Puebla, 1929–1941." Tesis de licenciatura, Universidad Autónoma de Puebla.

Marroni de Velázquez, Gloria. 1994. "Changes in Rural Society and Domestic Labor in Atlixco, Puebla, 1940–1990." In Fowler-Salamini and Vaughan, *Women of the Mexican Countryside*.

Martin, Joann. 1993. "Contesting Authenticity: Battles over the Representation of History in Morelos, Mexico." *Ethnohistory* 40, no. 3:438–65.

Martínez Assad, Carlos. 1979. *El laboratorio de la Revolución: El Tabasco garridista*. Mexico: Siglo Veintiuno.

McGuire, Thomas. 1986. *Politics and Ethnicity on the Rio Yaqui: Potam Revisited*. Tucson: University of Arizona Press.
———. 1989. "Ritual, Theater, and the Persistence of the Ethnic Group: Interpreting Yaqui Semana Santa." *Journal of the Southwest* 31, no. 2:159–78.

Medin, Tzvi. 1972. *Ideología y praxis política de Lázaro Cárdenas*. Mexico: Siglo Veintiuno.

Mediz Bolio, Antonio. 1968. *Salvador Alvarado*. Mexico: Secretaría de Educación Pública.

Meneses Morales, Ernesto. 1986. *Tendencias educativas oficiales en México, 1911–1934*. Mexico: Centro de Estudios Educativos, Universidad Iberoamericana.
———. 1988. *Tendencias educativas oficiales en México, 1934–1964*. Mexico: Centro de Estudios Educativos, Universidad Iberoamericana.

Meyer, Jean. 1973. *La cristiada*. 3 vols. Mexico: Siglo Veintiuno.

Meyer, Lorenzo. 1978. *Historia de la Revolución Mexicana*. Vol. 13, *Los conflictos sociales y los gobiernos del Maximato*. Mexico: Colegio de México, 1978.

Meyer, Lorenzo, Alejandra Lajous, and Rafael Segovia. 1978. *Historia de la Revolución Mexicana*. Vol. 12, *Los inicios de institucionalización, 1928–1934*. Mexico: Colegio de México.

Ministerio de Fomento. Dirección General de Estadística. 1902. *Censo general de la República mexicana, 1900*. Mexico.

Moisés, Rosalio, Jane Holden Kelley, and William Curry Holden. 1971. *A Yaqui Life: The Personal Chronicle of a Yaqui Indian*. Lincoln: University of Nebraska Press.

Monsiváis, Carlos. 1981. "Notas sobre el Estado, la cultura nacional, y las culturas populares en México." *Cuadernos Políticos* 30:33–44.

Montoya Briones, José de Jesús. 1964. *Atla: Etnografía de un pueblo nahuatl.* Mexico: Instituto Nacional de Antropología e Historia.

Mora Arellano, Felipe, ed. 1992. *Coloquio sobre las relaciones del Estado y las iglesias en Sonora y México: Memoria.* Hermosillo: Colegio de Sonora.

Mora Forero, Jorge. 1970. "Los maestros y la práctica de la educación socialista." *Historia Mexicana* 29:133–62.
————. 1976. *La ideología educativa del régimen cardenista.* Mexico: Colegio de México.

Morales Jiménez, Alberto. 1986. *Maestros de la Revolución Mexicana.* Mexico: Instituto Nacional de Estudios de la Revolución Mexicana.

Mouffe, Chantal. 1979. "Hegemony and Ideology in Gramsci." In Chantal Mouffe, ed., *Gramsci and Marxist Theory.* London: Routledge and Kegan Paul.

Murrieta, Mayo, and María Eugenia Graf. 1992. *Por el milagro de afferrarse: Tierra y vecindad en el Valle del Yaqui.* Hermosillo: Colegio de Sonora, Instituto Tecnológico de Sonora, Instituto Sonorense de Cultura.

Niblo, Stephen R. 1994. *War, Diplomacy, and Development: The U.S. and Mexico, 1938–54.* Wilmington, Del.: Scholarly Resources.

Nolasco de Armas, Margarita. 1969. "La reforma agraria en cuatro situaciones culturales distintas de México." *Anales, Instituto Nacional de Antropología e Historia* 2:312–20.

Nugent, Daniel. 1993. *Spent Cartridges: An Anthropological History of Namiquipa, Chihuahua.* Chicago: University of Chicago Press.

Nugent, Daniel, and Ana María Alonso. 1994. "Multiple Selective Traditions in Agrarian Reform and Agrarian Struggle: Popular Culture and State Formation in the Ejido of Namiquipa, Chihuahua." In Joseph and Nugent, *Everyday Forms.*

Nutini, Hugo G., Pedro Carrasco, and James M. Taggart, eds. 1976. *Essays on Mexican Kinship.* Pittsburgh: University of Pittsburgh Press.

Nutini, Hugo G., and Barry L. Isaac. 1974. *Los pueblos de habla nahuatl de la región de Tlaxcala y Puebla.* Mexico: Instituto Nacional Indigenista.

Olivera Sedano, Alicia. 1966. *Aspectos del conflicto religioso de 1926 a 1929.* Mexico: Instituto Nacional de Antropología e Historia.

Orozco, José Clemente. 1962. *Autobiography.* Translated by Robert C. Stephenson. Austin: University of Texas Press.

Ozouf, Mona. 1988. *Festivals and the French Revolution.* Translated by Alan Sheridan. Cambridge: Harvard University Press.

Pansters, Wil. 1990. *Politics and Power in Puebla: The Political History of a Mexican State, 1937–1987.* Amsterdam: CEDLA.

Pansters, Wil, and Arij Ouwenell, eds. 1989. *Region, State, and Capitalism in Mexico: Nineteenth and Twentieth Centuries.* Amsterdam: CEDLA.

Paré, Luisa. 1978. "Caciquismo y estructura del poder en la Sierra Norte de Puebla." In Bartra, *Caciquismo y poder político en el México rural.*

Pozos, Manuel. 1991. "Historia sucinta de la población." In Donna Rivera, ed., *Xochiapulco: Una gloria olvidada.*

Raby, D. 1976. *La educación y la revolución social.* Mexico: SepSetentas.

Radding, Cynthia. 1989. "Peasant Resistance on the Yaqui Delta: An Historical Inquiry into the Meaning of Ethnicity." *Journal of the Southwest* 31, no. 2:336–37.
———. 1990. "Gitanos y campesinos: Los pueblos serranos de la Provincia de Sonora, 1740–1800." *XIV Simposio de Historia y Antropología de Sonora* 1:129–56.
———. 1992. "Población, tierra y la persistencia de comunidad en la zona serrana de Sonora, siglo XVIII." *Historia Mexicana* 91, no. 4:551–78.
———, coordinator. 1985. *Historia General de Sonora.* Vol. 4, *Sonora Moderna.* Hermosillo: Gobierno del Estado de Sonora: 254–311.

Ramírez, José Carlos. 1988a. "Una época de crisis económica." In *Historia contemporanea de Sonora.*
———. 1988b. "La estrategia económica de los callistas." In *Historia contemporanea de Sonora.*

Redfield, Robert. 1950. *Chan Kom: The Village That Chose Progress.* Chicago: University of Chicago Press.

Rivera, Diego. 1924. "The Guild Spirit in Mexican Art." *Survey Graphic* 52–53:175–76.

Rivera, Donna, ed. 1991. *Xochiapulco: Una gloria olvidada.* Puebla: Gobierno del Estado.

Rivera Rodríguez, Gustavo. 1975. *Breve historia de la educación en Sonora e historia de la Escuela Normal del Estado.* Hermosillo.

Rockwell, Elsie. 1994. "Schools of the Revolution: Enacting and Contesting State Forms (Tlaxcala 1910–1930)." In Joseph and Nugent, *Everyday Forms.*
———. 1996. "Keys to Appropriation: Rural Schooling in Mexico." In Levinson, Foley, and Holland, eds., *The Cultural Production of the Educated Person.*

Romero Flores, Jesús. 1948. *Historia de la educación en Michoacán.* Mexico: Talleres Gráficos de la Nación.

Ronfeldt, David. 1973. *Atencingo: The Politics of Agrarian Struggle in a Mexican Ejido.* Stanford: Stanford University Press.

Roseberry, William. 1994. "Hegemony and the Language of Contention." In Joseph and Nugent, *Everyday Forms.*

Royce, Anya Peterson. 1982. *Ethnic Identity: Strategies of Diversity.* Bloomington: Indiana University Press.

Ruiz, Ramón Eduardo. 1988. *The People of Sonora and Yankee Capitalists*. Tucson: University of Arizona Press.

Rus, Jan. 1994. "The 'Comunidad Revolucionaria Institucional': The Subversion of Native Government in Highland Chiapas, 1936–1968." In Joseph and Nugent, *Everyday Forms*.

Sáenz, Moisés. 1927. *Escuelas Federales en la Sierra de Puebla: Informe sobre la visita a las escuelas federales en la Sierra de Puebla*. Mexico: s e p, Talleres Gráficos de la Nación.
———. 1928. *La educación rural en México*. Mexico: s e p.
———. 1970. *Antología de Moisés Sáenz: Prólogo y selección de Gonzalo Aguirre Beltrán*. Mexico: Ediciones Oasis, S.A.
———. 1982. *Mexico íntegro*. Mexico: SepOchentas.

Sánchez, Ricardo, Eric Van Young, and Gisela Von Wobeser, eds. 1992. *La ciudad y el campo en la historia de Mexico*. Vol. 2. Mexico: Universidad Nacional Autónoma de México.

Sánchez Flores, Ramón. 1984. *Zacapoaxtla: República de Indios, Villa de Españoles. Relación Histórica*. Zacapoaxtla.

Sánchez López, Rogelio. 1992. "La institucionalización: Una historia de los derrotados: Puebla, 1929–1932." Tesis de licenciatura, Universidad Autónoma de Puebla, Taller de Marco Velázquez del Albo, sobre la Revolución Mexicana en el Estado de Puebla.

Sanderson, Steven E. 1981. *Agrarian Populism and the Mexican State*. Berkeley: University of California Press.

Santiago Sierra, Agusto. 1973. *Las misiones culturales (1923–1973)*. Mexico: SepSetentas.

Scott, James C. 1976. *The Moral Economy of the Peasant: Rebellion and Subsistence in Southeast Asia*. New Haven: Yale University Press.
———. 1985. *Weapons of the Weak: Everyday Forms of Peasant Resistance*. New Haven: Yale University Press.
———. 1990. *Domination and the Arts of Resistance: Hidden Transcripts*. New Haven: Yale University Press.

Secretaría de Agricultura y Fomento. Dirección de Estadística. 1918. *Tercer censo de población de los Estados Unidos Mexicanos, 1910*. Mexico.

Secretaría de la Economía Nacional. Dirección de Estadística. 1930. *Anuarios estadísticos*. Mexico.
———. 1934. *Quinto Censo de Población, 1930*. Mexico.
———. 1937. *Primer Censo Ejidal, 1935*. Mexico.
———. 1938. *Anuarios estadísticos*. Mexico.
———. 1942. *Anuarios estadísticos*. Mexico.
———. 1943. *Sexto Censo de Población, 1940*. Mexico.
———. 1950. *Séptimo Censo General de Población, 1950*. Mexico.

Secretaría de Educación Pública. 1930. *Memoria, 1930.*

———. 1932a. *Memoria, 1932.* Vol. 1. Mexico.

———. 1932b. *Memoria, 1932.* Vol. 2. Mexico.

———. 1933a. *Memoria, 1933.* Vol. 1. Mexico.

———. 1933b. *Memoria, 1933.* Vol. 2. Mexico.

———. 1934a. *Algunos datos y opiniones sobre la educación sexual en México.* Mexico.

———. 1934b. *Memoria, 1934.* Mexico.

———. 1935. *Plan de Acción de la Escuela Primaria Socialista.* Mexico.

———. 1937a. *Memoria, 1937.* Vol. 1. Mexico.

———. 1937b. *Memoria, 1937.* Vol. 2. Mexico.

———. 1938a. *Memoria, 1938.* Vol. 1. Mexico.

———. 1938b. *Memoria, 1938.* Vol. 2. Mexico.

———. 1938c. *Serie SEP, Primer Año, Lectura oral.* Mexico.

———. 1939a. *Memoria, 1939.* Vol. 1. Mexico.

———. 1939b. *Memoria, 1939.* Vol. 2. Mexico.

———. 1940. *Educación Pública en México, 1934–1940.* Mexico.

———. 1956. *Homenaje al Héroe Nacional Gral. Juan Francisco Lucas, Patriarca de la Sierra en ocasión de inaugurarse el monumento erigido a su memoria en el lugar de su nacimiento, Comaltepec, Zacapoaxtla, 12 de octubre de 1956.* Mexico.

———. 1975. *Primer Congreso Nacional de Instrucción, 1889–1890.* Mexico.

Seminario de Historia de la Educación en México de El Colegio de México. 1988. *Historia de la lectura en México.* Mexico: Colegio de México and Ediciones de Ermitano.

Shulgovski, Anatol. 1968. *México en la encrucijada de su historia.* Mexico: Fondo de Cultura Popular.

Sierra, Justo. 1922. *Historia patria.* Mexico: SEP.

———. 1948. *La educación nacional: Artículos, actuaciones y documentos.* Vol. 8, *Obras completas.* Edited by Agustín Yañez. Mexico: Universidad Nacional Autónoma de Mexico.

Silva Valdés, Candelaria. 1990. "La comaraca Lagunera: Educación socialista y reparto agrario." Tesis de maestría, Centro de Investigaciones y de Estudios Avanzados del Instituto Politécnico Nacional, Departamento de Investigaciones Educativas.

Sindicato Nacional de Trabajadores de la Educación. 1969. *Breve historia del movimiento sindical mexicano y comentario histórico del actual Sindicato Nacional de Trabajadores de la Educación.* Mexico: SNTE.

Slade, Doreen L. 1976. "Kinship in the Central Highlands." In Nutini, Carrasco, and Taggart, *Essays on Mexican Kinship.*

Sosa, Manuel Luis. n.d. *Crónica de Zacapoaxtla.* Biblioteca del Palacio Municipal de Zacapoaxtla.

Spicer, Edward. 1954. *A Yaqui Village in Sonora.* American Anthropological Association Memoir No. 77. Menasha, Wis.

————. 1980. *The Yaquis: A Cultural History.* Tucson: University of Arizona Press.

Starr, Frederick. 1895. *In Indian Mexico: A Narrative of Travel and Labor.* Chicago.

Stern, Steve, ed. 1987. *Resistance, Rebellion, and Consciousness in the Andean Peasant World: Eighteenth to Twentieth Centuries.* Madison: University of Wisconsin Press.

Street, Brian. 1984. *Literacy in Theory and Practice.* Cambridge: Cambridge University Press.

Street, Susan. 1992. *Maestros en movimiento: Transformaciones en la burocracia estatal, 1978–1982.* Mexico: SEP.

Taggart, James. 1976. "Action Group Recruitment: A Nahuatl Case." In Nutini, Carrasco, and Taggart, *Essays on Mexican Kinship.*

————. 1983. *Nahuat Myth and Social Structure.* Austin: University of Texas Press.

Taylor, William. 1979. *Drinking, Homicide, and Rebellion in Colonial Mexican Villages.* Stanford: Stanford University Press.

Teja Zabre, Alfonso. 1935. *Breve historia de México.* Mexico: SEP.

Thomson, Guy P. C. 1989a. "Bulwarks of Patriotic Liberalism: The National Guard, Philharmonic Corps, and Patriotic Juntas in Mexico, 1847–1888." *Journal of Latin American Studies* 22:31–68.

————. 1989b. "Montaña y Llanura in the Politics of Central Mexico: The Case of Puebla, 1820–1920." In Pansters and Ouwenell, eds., *Region, State, and Capitalism in Mexico.*

————. 1991a. "Popular Aspects of Liberalism in Mexico, 1848–1888." *Bulletin of Latin American Research* 10, no. 3:279–87.

————. 1991b. "Agrarian Conflict in the Municipality of Cuetzalan (Sierra de Puebla): The Rise and Fall of 'Pala' Agustín Dieguillo, 1861–64." *Hispanic American Historical Review* 71, no. 2:205–58.

Thomson, Guy P. C., and David LaFrance. 1987. "Juan F. Lucas: Patriarch of the Sierra Norte de Puebla." In Beezley and Ewell, *The Human Tradition.*

Thomson, Guy P. C., with David LaFrance. 1996. "Juan Francisco Lucas: Patriarch of the Puebla Sierra, 1854–1917." Manuscript, to be published by Scholarly Resources.

Tinker Salas, Miguel. 1989. "Under the Shadow of the Eagle: Sonora, the Making of a Norteño Culture, 1850–1919." Ph.D. diss., University of California, San Diego.

Torres Quintero, Gregorio. 1923. *Patria Mexicana.* Mexico: Herrero Hermanos.

Torres Trueba, Henry. 1970. "Religious and Economic Implications of Factionalism in Xalacapan: A Study of Some Expressions of Factionalism in a Mestizo-Indian

Community of Zacapoaxtla, Sierra Norte de Puebla, Mexico." Ph.D. diss., University of Pittsburgh.

Tortella, Gabriel, ed. 1990. *Education and Economic Development since the Industrial Revolution.* Valencia: Generalitat.

Tostado Gutiérrez, Marcela. 1991. *El intento de liberar a un pueblo: Educación y magisterio tabasqueño con Garrido Canabal, 1924–1935.* Mexico: Instituto Nacional de Antropología e Historia.

Trueba Lara, José Luis. 1990. *Los chinos en Sonora: Una historia olvidada.* Universidad de Sonora, *Cuadernos del Instituto de Investigaciones Históricas,* no. 2.

Valenzuela Duarte, Martha A. 1992. "Iglesia católica y sociedad en Sonora (1919–1991): Notas para su análisis." In Mora Arellano, *Coloquio sobre las relaciones.*

Vasconcelos, José. 1950. *Discursos.* Mexico: Ediciones Botas.

Vaughan, Mary Kay. 1982. *The State, Education, and Social Class in Mexico, 1880–1928.* DeKalb: Northern Illinois University Press.
———. 1987. "La política comparada del magisterio en Puebla y Sonora en la época cardenista." *Memoria, X Simposio de Historia de Sonora.* Hermosillo (1988). *Crítica, Revista de la Universidad Autónoma de Puebla,* Dec., 90–101.
———. 1990a. "Primary Education and Literacy in Nineteenth-Century Mexico: Research Trends, 1968–1988." *Latin American Research Review* 24, no. 3:42–55.
———. 1990b. "Economic Growth and Literacy in Late-Nineteenth-Century Mexico: The Case of Puebla." In Tortella, ed., *Education and Economic Development.*
———. 1990c. "Women School Teachers in the Mexican Revolution: The Story of Reyna's Braids." *Journal of Women's History* 2, no. 1:143–68.
———. 1992a. "Ideological Change in Mexican Educational Policy, Programs, and Texts, 1920–1940." In Camp, Hale, and Vázquez, *Los intelectuales y el poder en México.*
———. 1992b. "The Implementation of National Policy in the Countryside: Socialist Education in Puebla in the Cárdenas Period." In Sánchez, Van Young, and Von Wobeser, eds., *La ciudad y el campo.*
———. 1994a. "The Construction of Patriotic Festival in Tecamachalco, Puebla, 1900–1946." In Beezley, Martin, and French, *Rituals of Rule.*
———. 1994b. "The Educational Project of the Mexican Revolution: The Response of Local Societies (1934–1940)." In Britton, ed., *Molding the Hearts and Minds.*
———. 1994c. "Rural Women's Literacy in the Mexican Revolution: Subverting a Patriarchal Event?" In Fowler-Salamini and Vaughan, eds., *Women in the Mexican Countryside,* 106–24.

Vázquez, Josefina Zoraida. 1969. "La educación socialista en los años treinta." *Historia Mexicana* 18:408–23.
———. 1970. *Nacionalismo y educación en México.* Mexico: Colegio de México.

Velázquez Andrade, Manuel. [1929] 1986. *Fermín.* Puebla: Premia.

Velázquez del Albo, Marco. 1992. "Los músicos en la Revolución mexicana." Manuscript, Universidad Autónoma de Puebla.

Ventura Rodríguez, María Teresa. 1986. "Una central obrera de vanguardia en la región: La Confederación Sindicalista de Obreros y Campesinos del Estado de Puebla." *Boletín de Investigaciones del Movimiento Obrero* 6, no. 9:117–36.

Voss, Stuart. 1982. *On the Periphery of Nineteenth-Century Mexico: Sonora and Sinaloa, 1810–1877.* Tucson: University of Arizona Press.

Warner, Ruth Giddings. 1983. *Yaqui Myths and Legends.* Tucson: University of Arizona Press.

Wasserstrom, Robert. 1983. *Class and Society in Central Chiapas.* Berkeley: University of California Press.

Weber, Eugen. 1976. *Peasants into Frenchmen: The Modernization of Rural France, 1870– 1914.* Stanford: Stanford University Press.

Wolf, Eric. 1969. *Peasant Wars of the Twentieth Century.* New York: Harper and Row.

Wolfe, Bertram. 1939. *Diego Rivera: His Life and Times.* New York: Knopf.

Yankelevich, Pablo. 1985. *La educación socialista en Jalisco.* Guadalajara: Departamento de Educación Pública, Jalisco.

INDEX

ABOUT THE AUTHOR

Mary Kay Vaughan is an Associate Professor of Latin American Studies and History at the University of Illinois-Chicago. She received her B.A. degree from Cornell University and her M.A. and Ph.D. degrees from the University of Wisconsin-Madison. She is the author of *The State, Education, and Social Class in Mexico, 1880–1930* (1982) and co-editor, with Heather Fowler-Salamini, of *Women of the Mexican Countryside, 1850–1990: Creating Spaces, Shaping Transitions* (University of Arizona Press, 1994). She has written extensively on education, literacy, and women in nineteenth- and twentieth-century Mexico.